THE UNFINISHED BREATH

new poems, elegies and laments

Volume Two

Iván Argüelles

LUNA BISONTE PRODS
2023

THE UNFINISHED BREATH
new poems, elegies and laments
Volume Two

(Written May 2, 2022 – November 20, 2022)

These poems are dedicated to the faithful memory of Max and Joe, whose unfinished breaths remain a part of the Continuum.

"forsan et haec olim meminisse iuvabit"
Virgil, Aeneid, I, 198

© IVÁN ARGÜELLES 2023

Cover and book design by C. Mehrl Bennett
VOL. ONE ISBN 9781938521911
VOL. TWO ISBN 9781938521928
https://www.lulu.com/spotlight/lunabisonteprods

LBP

Luna Bisonte Prods
137 Leland Ave
Columbus OH 43214 USA

LOST IN TRANSLATION

para Armando Rendón

that which must be shattered already is as
we approach the diminishing circle of light
between the first clause of mortal appointment
and its conclusion I read in the eyes of friends
years that have turned to spears of grass wind-swept
or by night bent to the ground and earth's sweet-
rotten smell lifts out of an anterior sleep into
a greater loss of atmospheres and gravity
there is no god Apollo to pick us up when cast
backwards by the insult of some archaic weapon
no Minerva or Harmony to correct the length
of our dreams our sicknesses our nauseas and
shipwreck-failures only the weary and deadening
sense that we just missed the last day possible
or that finally there is a number that cannot
be counted no matter how accurate the machinery
is said to be only the frugal moment of sharing
some crumbs while spilling the goblet's priceless wine
on the moving floors of eternity and what
we desire is already an ineffable memory
the misspent moment with the dying beloved
poetry offers its knees and rudimentary shoulders
to bear the burden of beauty's illusory weight
the passage from a life of letters and glyphs
to one of solitary contemplation unlettered and

sorrowful by the banks of a marginless water
night's shivering panoply of stars and gasses and
immobilities stretches the impossible awning of time
overhead and everything we see is further out of
reach than before flux and embryo of the cosmos
constantly changing positions and it is for us to
puzzle the direction fate has chosen to fly away
leaving us finite husks bereft of animus and hue
in some open-air theater to attend a dumb-play
inaudible voices and invisible masks of tragedy
the script totally lost in translation

05-02-22

TEACHING THE CLASSICS TODAY

world ! charnel house of dissent and misplaced
diacritics quarrels with Juno over hash-tags and
sibylline victories of phonetics and slurred speech
statuesque light ! columns of irreducible dust and virtues
never donned and poorly chosen ministers who profit
from hunger and war the ever-and-anon of greed
is there short-hand for the panoply of weapons
hoarded by Zeus in his gasoline filled garage ?
Hector ! divine idiot scrupulous and dumber than
the beasts of the field why did you risk it all ?
and so this day becomes a re-run of all days smash

and crunch of impulse and gravity the over-all
supremacy of the Olympians in their imploding
spacecraft the poor and disenfranchised marginalized
who dwell in Troys of smoking refuse and illiteracy
how can the epic poem mean anything at all when
sky is being diminished by pollution and hate
the congress of literati and plutocrats count their
daily gains on hacked computer programs exclusive
of the earth's histories and temple-compounds
come running to the fading shorelines the Argives
and rhetors of tumbled Mycenae ruthless Agamemnon
and his cunning Clytemnestra and the saga of Thebes
warp of incest and fratricide ! Sapphic delivery of tones
vowels retreating from their husks and hexameters
wrung out for polish and almost pharaonic scansion
death-beds of sophists and grammarians drunk on hemlock
everything we ever learned scuttled or put to the flame
the chariot's ignition won't start this morning
haze and cities of fog and mire tremble on the cusp
diesel fuel running out of time and dead Greek kids
littering the expressway that destroys the Mountain
peril of language ! insane seas that rush to take
Polyphemus and Circe by their knees to the underworld
wine-dark ! epithets and memories and tombstones
on the Via Appia where pizza is invented and poison
and thrall of Dionysus the great parade from the Orient
truths and the evidence of a greater Mind out there

where noise echoes the infinite message of the Big Bang
Lucretius and Thales going in circles in a movie theater
where the waters part and helium and opium reign
to what end the lists of homophones and Mansions ?
the sun and all the lesser bodies shifting on astral planes
what are they but remnants of an archaic imagination
Persephone ! it's summer again and you must come home
the dark is on us and the late grasses of evening
where words are buried

05-03-22

THE MYSTERY OF EXISTENCE

a day like any other day that never happened
colossal sun rising in the east and trees aching
to reach heaven within the hour freshly washed streets
bowers and lawns from out of nowhere manifest !
the betrayed sky wrinkled in one corner and clouds
that adorn the pupil's eye like a kingdom thronged
with kings of gold and livery – what else but childhood
the merciless joy of make-believe going up and down
the hills of summer imagining one is other than the self
name and belt and pronoun straightened like a tie
the thought of language in its infancy rounding bells
and using vowels taken from a solar eclipse and
time itself a second or two away from the corner store

sweets and pom-poms and the schoolyard full of

dead echoes or cracked plaster-of-Paris gods

where is everybody ? making chalk-colored squares

on the sidewalk as if to deliver a mathematical message

to the UFOs hovering just before noon and the shouts

and glee of someone who has just won some marbles

and chewing gum and scraped knees that express

doubt and perplexity about gravity and motion itself

a thing that characterizes leaves in their early speech

dew and distance the fading resemblance of children

to statues that defy temporality and the houses lined up

for blocks with invisible people inside who cannot decide

and the secret talk inside the hedge-row as if maps

had identities and space travel was the next possibility

but everything ends too soon someone gets dragged

by a Greek diesel breaking bones and littering

the broad-way with new blood and the altars begin

to smoke and the wafting incense fogs the spire

how can anyone tell if it's time to go home ?

05-04-22

THE STORY OF JOE AND HIS DEATH

all along the way home nervously cracking his knuckles

and playing a solitary game of roulette in his head Joe

my brother of so many years loses his way in the gravel

listening to the sound of distance and the enormous ray

of light descending like a hand from a fairy-tale sky

princesses in white chiffon with bee-like faces buzzing

around his level of cognition perhaps the fourth dimension

Joe shakes his hand waving away invisible larva that

populate the air with ideas and circumferences and

the world itself is just that thing a green wavering trance

he will soon enter and educate himself about the future

odd that my brother is so big and yet nothing but dust a mere

epistle of sounds and yearning to be the most other of all

it is almost home when windows realize their artificiality

a poetry almost French in its noise and brassy secrets

it's exciting how he thinks about algebra and suddenly

numbers mean nothing just ciphers that build pyramids

which he can climb without moving out of his eternal sleep

05-04-22

THE MOON OF CANAAN

"And the larpnotes prittle"
               Finnegans Wake

nightingales and Egyptian tears of sand

the world's dark blooms laced by houris

in their paradise of waistbands and slippers

argent silences depth charges in the sleeper's

perfect ear alert to the slightest syllable of grass

noises recondite and fragmented that vanish with a thought

no mind is the best ! ghazals of petrified light !
ambergris and circulation of jeweled pedestals
alarms before three AM in Hyderabad airport
signal that the world's internal writing is gone
nondescript emissaries from the muezzin
whose blind eye is the godhead of electricity
everything is fueled by the secrets of love
the Actor lies dead drained of his elixir
by channels that run backwards into the Tomb
which is the haunted moon of Canaan
birth-note of ecstasy tavern of Unknown friends
riot of a hundred indescribable dialects
choice of Plato over Abraham ! legends and flutes
sinuous enigmas of the alchemical aleph
recorded in the gardens of destroyed wisdom
nothing has ever mattered but the heart's eternity
instantaneous thrill in the profligate afternoon
of the Library when a hush maddens the Reader
with solemnities of the absent Mountain
here is nowhere ! a numeral no greater
than its half which is the noon of the Zohar
statues in love with Sound ! tripartite engines
of knowledge and the mushrooming spaces
that perpetuate the night's infinite hour
until exhausted by the fire the Soul chooses
to fly abandoning bodies of smoke and blood
a harp-note ! all else is a Mystery

05-05-22

SPHINX

numbed by your brazen attitude
petrified gaze of the Harmonies
you tell me there is only one real
literary work The Sanskrit Dictionary
blindness and lunacy I crave in your
depths the monsoons of withering fate
spite and the Vedas in triplicate
lifted by a single paper to the moon !
where is love's intricate monosyllable ?
am I alone in the Realization ? death
and death again is the perpetuity
you repeat something I cannot hear
resonance and bric-a-brac of silence
the first finger to know is lost in grass
the others are in pursuit of fire !
when the twin within is the Enigma
all others are his imaginary doubles
what is there to say in response ?
your fanatic noise of hair and perfume
your opium of craving for nothing
your absence and absolute presence
what are they to me but insouciance ?
a hotel for a mouth and demon eyes
Philosophy ! lipstick and adultery
an edge moves of its own accord
to the center of a parallel universe

taking with it your skirt and soul !

there are no plurals to existence

the single note remains Unheard

time is a register of insecticides

lists and mottoes of the Dialect

will anything ever be the same again ?

woman ! chastisement and luxury

I am held in thrall by your Notion

a phrase in stone and some gravel

a handful of light that resumes only

after you have totally disappeared

05-05-22

I READ IT SOMEWHERE IN A BOOK

here sat the wielder of the thunderbolt

and by his side in flimsy finery goddess of Speech

whose river flows backwards into space without time

and attending either one on cloud nine in full song

the heavenly courtesans and the twenty seven fires

that minister to the immortals as they graze like kine

in sleep the manifold lawns of unseen distances

and as one who has come and gone in trance and reverie

seeking but never finding the right stone or tree

and replicas I counted up to eighty-three but nowhere

the shape and name of brother that was a flame to me

or was all of this just something I read in books
myth and strut of deities in the stratospheres
claim of mortals to some sort of divinity in restaurants
or hiking on nature-trails a brother a constant shadow
a lark laughing into the sleeve of madness stopping
to smoke something illegal but transforming and jazz
and clutter of basement noise as beings come and go
trading suits and skins and masks and pronouns
and brother in his page of absolution and transcendence
dead from the word go but still walking stalking
the underworld of memories reciting adolescent poetry
of eternity and innocence and the stifling existence
of tiny folds and glued to walls of painted seas
the grammar of make-believe the map of the other side
mission of resonance and recall in the library of stolen Myths
books ! in all of them something absent from the truth
science and embroidery of the elements dimensions
more than four and the Mind trapped in its resolution
to be free and traipsing for a moment by Silver Lake
waiting for the fireworks to begin and to summon
immortals one by one from their anvil of treachery
why be born ! why not remain ancient as stone
glyph and consonant of a previous universe
before the gods of false promise came to be
before the leaf with its silent memory

05-06-22

ALEXANDER VISITS THE SAGE PLATO
IN HIS MOUNTAIN CAVE

I have put my matchlock rifle aside and
do obeisance to your lotus feet for far
have I traveled in search of perfect wisdom
and here in the foothills of the Indus valley
at last you I find you in heady Vedic trance
one syllable alone illumining your threadbare mind
and clad in musk and cast-off silks your body
molders in spite of desires and temptations
rebirth ! the cycle of deaths and universes !
the republic of thought and memory you abjure
turning your eyes inward to chasms deep
where the soul struggles to rise and breathe
to fly one day at last and seek deathless skies
where no gods infer or penetrate their daring
and forever the dwelling of bliss and light
that feed on ideas circular or non-existent
in your presence I feel no need for language
the lies of poets and sightless bards is noise
nonsense of living effigies who have boasted
kingship and chronological technologies
yet what are the fables of dust and powders ?
the whims of women barefoot and panting ?
what are the sequences of tongue and lobe ?
nothing ! Greek and Persian in hand-to-hand combat
for the price of gold while winds turn into tempests

and simple rivulets flood the plains of Sumer

like Shah Jehan I have conquered worlds

whole continents and alphabets and spices

all mine ! the bidding of my youth the spire

and pinnacle of religious innovations

Buddhas I have worsted in spelling-bees

and learned to dress my humility in saffron

the way back has been erased ! I am your slave

your honorific pronoun your non-entity

tell me why Socrates drank the hemlock

choosing immortality over window-dressing ?

is it for me to marry twenty brides

and perform the Great Horse Sacrifice ?

fires are lit on plateaus of distance and

gathas sung to a hidden Ahura Mazda

yet today on my knees before your presence

which is the absence of all worldly matter

who am I but Iskander in a Mughal painting

but a shadow flitting on a cave-wall

05-16-22

ADOLESCENT THRENODY

what seemed to be a palace hanging in midair

and birds with the voices of girlfriends

a deathless heat shimmering in the reflection

of endless waters that persisted somewhere below

when angel came rushing down and hit the metal

of the car speeding to the Memorial service

and the others whose names were faceless

wearing suits too thick for summer afternoons

we sat on the terraced slope listening intently

to the noises in the grass and still could not identify

who it was we were mourning and a sudden chill

seized the spine an overture for brass and strings

filled the ear as we watched angel bouncing

from hood to pavement far beneath & whose wings

announced passing of another eon with black suns

rotating in a great symmetry and the plentiful light

was nothing more than a homophone of sound

a change in attitude among those who stood frozen

with a fear of the unknown a theogony of gold

stars pasted to the coffin lid and the god Apollo

disguised as a lowly hermit gave blessings to the few

who malingered in the back rows and what else ?

news from the Beyond of twins wearing sleeves

buttons and combs a mirror held backwards and

the breathing in the leaves the souls of trees

invisible alphabets simply warning us that

memory is the moment when stars collide and

angel was nowhere only the chink of spades

and shovels shifting silence over an earth of

parallel matter and of shadow and gravity

all around the booming of remote thunder

and birds lamenting with voices of girlfriends

and the atmospheres disturbed by the whooshing

of unseen planets houses of mercury and sulfur

the many countless existences interred in sleep

eclipse of the present death of the future universe

when would we wake again ?

05-07-22

GODS WITH TWO NAMES

gods with two names and twenty seven planets

each constructed with a different species of light

the senses abandoned sight and hearing foremost

length and width of space contained in a thumb-nail

mansions created overnight out of grass and water

without columns lacking floors the very reflection

of Mind which knows no alteration of speed or

gravity only the deathless models of glass and time

how to describe the parameters and circumferences

of the place without number or sound the depthless

pool the artificial growths of goddesses whose skin

is their immaculate raiment whiter than asbestos

celestial nymphs whose careers are measured in

wheels and tides and whose flight is mere thought

ideas that the world can exist forever are disproven

is there only one other that rules the spheres of matter ?
voices that belong to entities without birth or origin
vowels littered along the causeway that leaps oceans
only to descend upon cities of carbon paper and dust
when will this ever end ? will the tale be completed ?
recitations of constant repetition the self-same consonant
reiterated totally in the amnesia of a thousand deaths
masks and pronouns discarded as parodies of literature
poetry and speech in absentia and statues learning
to walk and declaim the virtues of the Republic
we have come into being in the shadow and legend
of other times of unrecorded histories of sagas
relating to semi-divine intruders of the cosmos
heroes blinded by lust and pride and seas rolling
back and forth over the plural illusions of beauty
sacrosanct syllables of piety and holy adultery
rock formations which are the threnody of antiquity
have there ever been ushers at the heavenly gates ?
listen and expound on the unutterable exercises !
it is punctuation that remains to be understood
emphasis on the unheard and unbidden word
which of us playing with sun-and-moon corpses
was the defined other ? which of us merely a copy
of what can never be fully represented in mirrors ?

05-08-22

MEMORY

air stained by pools of fuchsia

a paper-boat wending downstream

to bliss of remote weeds dandelions sailing

on the thought of a more verdant India

where Spanish mandolins ply invisible fountains

source and rivulet where elephants step

lost in reveries of cloud formations the length

of one hundred Julys epitome of azure

and cries of kids never before heard

Greek and puerile beside the enormous

shadow of Asia about to leap into Ionian tides

heat in decibels no greater than a lunation

fade and phosphorous of nocturnal music

hair ! cavities where fossil emotions incubate

before becoming tremendous butterflies

with human eyes and a passion for acanthus

atmospheres buzzing with Archaic electricity

larval sparkplugs and ears that can only

hear submarine epilogues to breath

pillaged lawns with loud ant-heaps in turmoil

your shadow shock still waiting for the Moment

mine haunted before its time anticipating

concrete to resume its relentless silence

flow of entities drunk on bottled air !

everyone in the aisles behind curtains on stage

to be born at once and to die before that happens

etched skies of incandescent camp-sites

Urdu ! ghazals memorized by the still-born

and recited by incomplete statues of light

daybreak and the broken promise of noon

subterfuge of evenings spent in illusion of tomorrow

the famous hours when pronouns no longer matter

and bodies are sent to the swimming pool bottom

in search of the City of Dis

how many of us were spent in that homophone ?

how many of us without recall on the Highway ?

sweet vagaries of a song heard only once

but meant to be the last thing one remembers

it goes on and on in a poetry of leaf and ecstasy

bonds of love made in corn-fields

eternity in pearls of sweat embroidering the upper lip

can a radio be totally vacant ?

it is only a direction a blind guess a suture

Puella ! signs and monitors wavering in windows

where the suffix of planet Mars lingers

reddening with the toil of memory

05-09-22

THE ARCHAIC

"Il faut être absolument moderne"

                Arthur Rimbaud

to enter the self through the screen-door

accompanied by fireflies and will o' the wisps

caught by surprise in a mirror of false images

the waters that run backwards & rocks and heights

magnum imperium of last night's celestial distance

you and I are the same in death as in breath

the life of myth and nymphs and glades and oceans

spirits fled from the stone and the six fires

of the sacrifice listening to the rush of grasses

made plaintive by horse-hooves racing

in the gloaming toward some cliff-end of time

and choose among meters the heroic and declaim

that noon has finally come to an end

apostrophes and asterisks masks of deceit

punctuating the demonic text that cannot be read

yet do hands falter and you and I pausing

to pronounce deliberations of a missing vowel

didn't you ? an attack on the Argives from behind !

roulette and bread-crumbs that make a path

to the beyond Ptah ! innocence in the gravel

beside the pastel-colored boundary stones

and hear the crunch of wheels coming home

we will ever remember mom and dad in their car

and the issue of dialect and hue the embroidery

and lace of music crystallizing in the stairway

that leads to the city-of-ghosts the attic

with its dead airplanes still dangling in the gloom

was there ever a more secret bed ?

outside the mystery of crickets and burial mounds

the way grandmother tilted the cup evenings

to drink of the great elixir of Prussia

and without translation speak to the mummers

and denizens of the atlas discovered in the rains

effigies ! portraits of adolescents who died

before their photographs were taken

motors and shouts of dogs fading ever

into the past of discarded school-books

how did we ever get out of that place ?

dandelion wine and eternal Sunday afternoons

waiting for the picture-show to start

and the cavalry and their bright noise and dust

and vacancy signs on all the houses

remember ? one by one the archaic took shape

in plate-glass reflections of the infinite number

you and I walking home confused

as to which one of us was the other

05-10-22

HYMN TO THE UNRULY SUNNE

O great homophone of the descending lamp
to mountains unseen and wastelands wild
to dreary night and starless oblivion you plunge
helpless in your daily career toward sheets of ice
purity of the undefiled moment of absence
threads and knots the eloquence of outer space
shot through the eye like blood-stones and nacre
and we hapless in our granular and fibrous thought
indignant that we cannot be as that blinding spot
that roams the minutes of the ticking day relentless
as a hero who has never found his grave of peace
how many are the sacrificial fires ? seven or more ?
a priest of bitumen and pitch rants in our ear
wanting more than we can ever put on the altar
divinities of Moroccan descent all sand and blaze
surround the city of a hundred gates and fume !
more heat than can ever circle this puny planet
puts to waste the measure of our faulty skills
it must be war ! seventeen consonants that cannot
be pronounced and the image of a cataract falling
off the map into regions of ruined light underneath
the stairs where adolescents teem with their cigarettes
I was of them once ! radiance of inchoate flame
lust and yearning for the unfound home alone
and to sleep and never wake ! suns more than
a billion in the race for definition and fame !

which of us can compete with that angry blare

the soundless noise the roar of deafening silence

myth and aggravation of the solitary Mind !

how restless the desire to be ! and yet quelled

by doubts and skirts of vanishing despairs we pray

to be no more and toss our pronouns to the embers

piloted by uncontrollable horses of holy Helium

sun-spots blindness echoes of the time-before that

no language can extrapolate we long to become

what we never were ampersands and asterisks adrift

meteors of flaming vowels charging through the dark

alas ! a single leaf to cool the brain and nevermore

05-11-22

ANIMULA VAGULA BLANDULA

in a trice poor pale yellowing soul

inches from the finish line falters

holds a hand's shape three fingers up

to the somber gathering sky of Zeus

such legends to have believed and rains

that fall from sutures in the clouds and

Hera angry with her cummerbund

and bare white arms and ire and jealousy

skirts of tempest flare and lightning blitz

the world's house to obliterate

for why go on poor placid trembling soul
the empires have all been lost the dust
red with suffixes of memory and troth
legends of the day but hoarfrost now
that slowly kills the blade of grass
and copies of men's lives tossed in the pyre
junk and plastic that bloat the seas
and myths of innocence that destroy
trees that aspire to divinities and
eras the length of a tomb of leaves
seasons that ripened corn and burned
the detritus of mortal victories and gain
how did the sacred cow come to die ?
when did the plow cease moving soil ?
dance the fatal dance at the mummers' ball
inch closer to the end of space ablaze
like the child's playful bonfire of breath
shaking with ague to the sound of ventilators
poor quivering soul's transitory game
no more windows to look out on fields
where shadows of Mary Lou still play

05-12-22

DITTY

this makes me feel like dancing

like doing a fox-trot

with death's doppelganger

makes me feel like prancing

across the illusory celestial floor

like tripping the light fantastic

with loves dead forevermore

makes me feel like dancing

doing the bunny hop

'til I drop

05-12-22

ELEGY IN THE MERRY MONTH OF MAY

now for the next round voila ! the uncertainties

meager flesh details the poem's cocoon wherein

dwells the soul in its charade of moth and flame

does death begin so early in the misgiving light

of breath and summons love's foregone conclusion

etched in chalk on a vibrating sidewalk just outside

the half-remembered house of feigned innocence

a ball tossed in the gathering air some clouds an eye

tears poured out at the testimonial and shapes of

bodies purloined by heat a forgotten summer noon

come hither little fauns and play your game of France !

dividends of kiss and retort the echolalia of verse
too recondite to be anything but noise the roundelay
and bark of afternoons too soon come to their end
a bone unearthed a script in reverse and distance
greater than the hills where it sleeps and what other
symbol revised by poets who never learned to fly
always questioning who drowned before in the mere
what nymph dragged the remains to its upper shelf
and sings the songs the girl whose Latin is a mistake
afterschool or lodged in a lost library book oaths and
pledges to abide by the heart's empty renaissance when
come rushing rivulets of crystal and memories of blood
endless toil to reconstruct what went before the flood
and rock and stone talking to the nascent laurel leaf
and gods on the chase through parlors of playing cards
chairs and decisions and windows opened to let in all
the atmospheres tempests and gales fortune's debacle
an end to all certainties and what human error sets
on the plane of loss and longing far from the altars
where births were offered and the tiny solstice of hope
rumors ! the continent of the other side of mind
rumors ! the self separated from its pronoun of grief
and left to drift in the vast and unnamed galactic pool

05-13-22

THE BALLAD OF HIGHWAY FIFTY-TWO

truth to tell the end's been here all along

highway fifty-two lies empty and trees languish

in their trespassed soul sky spools in its azure reign

and symbols that used to deck the caravanserai of language

wilt and fade meaningless apothegms to a missing god

remember the time driving through fogs we went astray

the town we meant to arrive was a profound ditch

and the hounds of hell red-eyed and haggard

were at our heels yet we laughed to be such prey

and forgot all our words of prayer and simply

became absolute in adolescent alcohol and

yes that was the time it nearly finished its goal

of breath and lark and angels with harp-string vowels

conveyed us to a place beyond salvation where

flowers with seraphic faces of girlfriends

embraced us with drugs and perfumes from Cathay

charges of clouds and early Sanskrit grammar and

panoply of books strung out like lamps to devour

within time's limit and laid us then to rest

what a simple death in that fosse of mud and asterisks

we slept the smallest sleep and woke prepared

to graduate with photos and emblems and totem beasts

that accompany us to this day when counting backwards

from the star of illegal syntax we ready the number

that has been designed to freight us to oblivion

a song a side-long glance some locks of hair

out of place the ruling solar homophone burns like pitch
and arrays the ancient fields where we played
turning them to crematoria of spark and hallucination
our pronouns rusted from over-use our masks
the detritus of beauty's illusory display and
still longing we thumb a ride on highway fifty-two
filled with longing we thumb a ride on highway fifty-two

05-14-22

ON THE EVE OF STILL ANOTHER MASS SHOOTING

so long ago when Krishna spoke
and mountains had wings for ears
sounding rills in silvery distances gone astray
each warrior spat an oath and dredged
from the bottoms of his being a supremacy
of mind doomed to fail as long as stone
and rock held to immutability and air
alone bore substance unseen with gravity
how can it be the eons of mortal thought
have no circle on which to swing their lapse
no tape-measure no winch or pulley to thread
the errors of existence and we hapless beings
wend our paths between girls and boys
and photos meant to eternalize their charades
a minute ago the party celebrated eternity

and in the next we shroud the lamp with ash

and mourn the ones we let get away

Krishna smiles enigmatically from behind the screen

where fireflies ply their flickering symphony

flashing signals of distress and love none can read

nor does Arjuna stir his steeds to battle

and Yudhisthira toss the dice to lose infinity

unwrapping Draupadi's endless gown

is the fruitless task of weavers in the dark

we learn nothing from falling into the abyss

and bruiting rumor after rumor of heaven's ditch

the promise to never be born again and still

we pull the switch and planets plunge and dialects

lose all eloquence a madness to survive

for what the moon's pull cannot deliver

tides and swarms of relentless honey bees

the image of beauty in a piece of glass and noise

of accidents on the highway down below

still Krishna sends us love and tells us to obey

dharma karma and freedom too all these

slip from our invidious fingertips a wager

to keep breathing though night has long held sway

and the pointless asterisks that dominate the sky

go surrendering their luster to oblivion

and the chasms of each daily noon

and when Krishna spoke and with one finger

upheld the mountain for all to see his strength

who of us was any wiser clinging to a pronoun

which of us gave up the mask to

become as one without distinction

will o' the wisp or countless dust

no image to display ?

05-15-22

WHEN A MAN COULD WALK A KINGDOM IN A DAY

not an afternoon passed that silence of books
was not broken by brazen echo of weaponry
stifling the one ear but convoking the other
to a noise supreme of hendecasyllables and paeans
glorious atavism ! triremes sent spinning against
clashing rocks or drowned by ineffable siren-song
was it there I stumbled upon the small doorway
entrance to Hades and the Cyclades both sun-
spent the drenched hides of illegally slain cattle
the island where word becomes a senseless drone
and the dead begin their enormous enumeration
vocables and epitomes and stones removed
from place litanies to heliotrope and asterism
seasons that last the duration of a window and
drugs secretly distributed to lovesick adolescents
heroes in name only breadth and span of a kiss
unbidden in the brief space between grammar

and math lessons of pyramid and pronunciation

heights of a single syllable shattering sky where

dwell thunder-storming Zeus and his ruthless

mate white-armed Hera and to appease them and

using a red ball-point pen to underline the cause

and the effect of Tragedy and cliffs which are sudden

and the stroll past the clinic to the drug-store for

a tryst with the girl-of-the-day mooning cow-eyed

over a shared straw sipping at the elixir prepared

by Circe a vision that takes in buffet and abyss

yawning memories of the time before birth sailing

on a raft to Ithaca where men in bright overalls

and pitchforks wager for an adulterous game

no one really knows when night falls and the hills

where dialects are spawned and coming home a

bit giddy from a month on the moon with you-

know-who turning on the radio for the theogony

listing the deities who recently plunged like

burning planets into an unwritten poem

05-16-22

EPYLLION

for Jack Foley

nor had I thought so much would proud Sun

have dared daybreak and the ultimatum of dark

besieged the cities multiple and shrouded in mists

the shores pounded rock and wave flaying airs

what little of light the gravid consequence of fate

a hand dealt beneath the shield and to be born for that !

harsh as sounds go the round of interrupted syllables

oracular and devastating to utter the ear only stirs

from depths of sleep primordial and waver before

coming into the spreading raiment of breath like

a wind of lamps a coarse buffet tempests and ire

whatever some dark god a puerperal fever has given

and pronouns and efforts to speak the marble

accents even as distance declares hidden victories

behind hills and the shedding luster will some hero

sally forth and pronounce and learn steeds to tame

highlands of the east where rising the torch of fame

only for a moment and then struggles the human soul

to assay and stretch limits a foot here a fall there

leaves ! the winnowing breezes and listening intent

to mysteries incomprehensible as texts of stone and

grass the ligatures between vowel and consonant

the fierce and only doubting what follows will be

any graver more different in tone as a printed film

running before half-opened eyes the monotone assent

hands ! to recognize and then forget the glimpsed other
shadow effort to understand movement of bodies shifting
in alleys or poring over an atlas of the cosmos in the rain
sudden trading of masks barter of fingers and starting
to count units of thought or weighing precious metals
a cave to discern mountains and the illusion of heights
to reach the air which holds in its cradle the newborn sky
and tumble forth from clouds bright sulfur striking
earth's fragile crusts and trees their souls to yield
and what is terrorism but this thin divide between
consciousness and the brute animal driven by hunger
to rip open dreams and then does someone step out
foot on parapet to perorate blindly to night's wheels
asterisks sent spinning out of control stuttering sparks
the universe to diminish and ends of history in latitudes
of despair and astonishment that you or I could ever
abiding as children the forevermore of lawns lay down
the mind's backside to gaze with bewilderment at the tale
unfurling its loose tide of echoes in nocturnal splendor
testing what is called memory to forgive the losses
a wound at a time and the receding waters the stones
left behind the painted gravel the axle and radius noises
of crickets in the long purposeless copies of language
rolling out to enigmatic seas of gold and magnesium
silencio ! for the dead are driving slowly south

05-17-22

THE CHARIOTEER

years of quality grieving and no end in sight
months curtail their last days and hours swell
with false expectations a dull radiance a refulgence
of twilight despair even as calendars fail to fulfill
their obligation to appear static the gravid impulse
to keep moving despite stellar catastrophes that
often go unseen in the blare and statuary of noon
when least the arrival of the sun's blazing chariot
inters its purpose and mortals prattle on about
career and destiny not sensing the terrific pull
of the gods-who-have-no-birth and shirt and
belt and chrome-plate ornament what a waste
poetry ! we wander the maze of obscure woods in
a finite daze blindly placing a finger to the blade
anticipating somehow blood will have a different color
a scheme of things that seems correct though no right
thinking ever is and the archaic voice that drills
the ear's attempt to echo the even more distant seas
a vague response to the tortured tempests of a lifetime
why ? the idiocy of man's futile obsessions images of
stealth and retribution that simmer below the skin
and prepare their nocturnal explosion when asterisk
and fulminating parenthesis conspire to bring down
the cosmos in a single event both full of sound and
unrequited silence of leaves stuttering oracles
only the dead recognize who the charioteer is

05-18-22

IN MEDIAS RES

for Ali Memarsadeghi

by what flight and with wings of mind
into liquid atmospheres take measures
of light and the redundancies of breath
holding fast for the noon of time eternal
before plunging into sleep's dark shell
to navigate through tempestuous dreams
the imitations of existence and be born
and startled at the extent and depth of light
amid seas and cliffs the possibilities of
language acting as memory and acts
of spontaneous gravity or circumference
the daily sectioning of hours into hues
and shouts corollaries of sun-beams pouring
through a piece of glass the customary child
running witlessly downhill into a schoolyard
filled with the noise of names and strangers
whose hands exchange blades of grass or
fingers that seek impossible futures and
poetry to memorize and recite when dark
surrounds the tiny lamp still flickering
do oil barges teem the Nile ? does a cheek
tainted with rouge await an inevitable kiss ?
furniture marts and traffic-clogged avenues
cities merge with distance to form dialects
the world is an escape valve a short circuit

a sound of mantras the length of centuries
boom-boxes and street corners where
stoned prostitutes do deep-knee bends risking
death by speeding metal or cigarettes and
a philosopher discourses on the ideal use
of thought in society while remarking on letters
that have lost their value the progeny of
archaic vowels the very speed and velocities
of galaxies within reach of the Library !
everything is exposed to danger and radiation
the armies of tumult and reason abrasions
that confound the pistil and stamen of process
antiquities that didn't exist before surface
like Ulysses' raft on vertigo of ebb and tide
Remember Me ! Dido queen of North Africa
immolates the self in a hexameter of burning air
copies of tomorrow are issued like parking
tickets a warning to cease using pronouns
and surrender to the sublime anti-matter
of what comes after thought has exhausted
the imagination of space travel and the child
standing in the middle of his empty lot
listens to the fantastic verbiage of the leaves
before twilight descends to erase him

05-19-22

FATTENING FROGS FOR SNAKES

I never thought it would come to this , Joe

eleven long years unwinding in the galaxies

since I heard your voice cajoling sarcastic

always playful verging on oracular sometimes

wise and always the same voice as mine laughing

like the time you called with schemes for us

to become the Blues Brothers on a television show

what foolhardy luckless games our personae played

who was the aesthetician who embroidered your mind ?

remember the friend on whose porch we invented summer ?

or the evening we played charades and no one

could guess that you were Valum Votan's chair !

we sneaked into liquor cabinets and tested schnapps

falling unconscious in unruly bouts with cognition

the race to become one another was fatal

we listened to songs and fumbled trying to dance

while the screens flooded with fireflies wanting in

to share the great enigma of the soul

we divided the world between us separating cities

accumulating pyramids creating cosmic maps

that in the end were nothing more than x-ray papers

the frayed and yellow conventions of the ordinary

how were we ever able to tell which of us was you or me ?

at birth our identity was one and nothing more

the other was always looming in some poetic background

longing in songs about autumn and staring downstream

from bridges too fragile to last more than an hour
instinct led us to knowledge about clouds and light
and playing dead more than once in the nearby park
we already assumed what we could not predict being dead
it was the lost highway and the nocturnal radio
that took us on journeys with blues singers to the Delta
voodoo lyrics ensnared us Fattening frogs for snakes
though we were inseparable in sleep the waking charge
of careers and pronominal mistakes parted us
but only in illusion for we were ever one bound
by pataphysics and telepathy to the Invisible realm
yet the telephone has never been able to cross the Styx !
what is it about Achilles you didn't understand ?

05-20-22

EL MUNDO ES ANCHO Y AJENO

set forth from the classrooms at 3 PM sharp
for conquest of the world each in a chosen direction
some south some southeast or southwest others still
northwards or west to the forgotten hills each with
a banner of cryptic light and glyphs and endowed
as heroes are with might but short on intelligence
being easily led astray by drugs or perfumes and
the combs that part hair giving to girls that certain
trait that ensnares and some with nothing more than

a book of revelation or poetry and signs from above
couched in a language of indetermination and myth
which of the many would not return by nightfall
fallen prey to mechanics driving wheels across the line
that divides illusion from death and the dying still
with fists raised inclining toward skies of doubt
or buried already in the mountain of words and
fields of ripening summers rich in dark loam and
haunted by memories of Persephone and others who
chanced to linger in Pluto's furrow of deceit the lingering
mysterious by-route where names disappear and pronouns
fragments of the Latin lesson of naufrage and torment
little branches wave scraping white stucco walls and
defiant comrades some by stealth others brazenly
take what they want of the booty and wild cry mixed
with laughter girlfriends with ribbons red and yellow
shaking pom-poms in the secret air of violation and game
great ! hollow victories reticent oratory and trees
fulminated by desires of unborn gods accolades of triumph
cars of bronze and silver rolling silently down Broadway
south toward the motels where Ajax and Diomedes riot
breaking rules flaunting a semi-divinity not theirs
and a voice from out of the glomeration of depths sounds
a noise of reckless ambition tossing aside grammars
and texts of earliest verse of spring and summer and
high above the plenitude of disorder the future evolves
all too brief with tombstones urns roadside inscriptions

wailing of grief and mothers picking through wreckage
and oil slicks and far off sight of river-bluffs nostalgia
and longing the directions confused whichever way
they went the shining skin of faces taut with ego and
resonance of stone set in place and the end of history

05-20-22

APHASIA

still heading south to where languages
      are no longer understood
and standing high on triple-peaks gazing
      through mists to seas of treachery and deceit
there manifest cities of pure dust yellow
      and ancient before day is done
shut the door come on in take your shoes off
the reading is about to begin volumes of nonsense
hair on end bristling with acerbic comments
concerning the archaic who knows better than
and shuffling for chairs and lamps dimmed the heights
crowned by a volatile verse about beauty and hieratic
demands of sleep the woods ablaze with purifying fire
touch each hand with water and sprinkle masks
pronouncing if possible forbidden letters consonants
no one has ever heard of didn't you notice in the back row
how she shines ? all elegance is but a toss of the dice

watching the haruspex in action climbing to the stage

as if it were possible to read the back of the hand

acts of palmistry and Italian literature at best a revival

sopranos in powdered wigs a fierce monosyllable elongated

who is better equipped than the Librarian ?

lifting his Scepter the Zeus-figure shaking with rage

in the face of the assembled gods ! did you ever ?

sent the messenger back to Ilion a disguised dialect

a forensic physician with orders to duplicate the soul

as it emerges from old Priam's open wounds and

so much else to try to understand where no languages

are really spoken and only the sound of the seas

susurrations and surf-tragedy tides taking undertow

the pretty Greek boys who had been trained in the javelin

I know Him ! my brother wending his slow shadowy self

through idioms of despair and glory to get to the top

to perceive and perorate and summon the Hosts !

the movie theater with all its dark magic where we sat

gawking at the ceiling with its painted heavens

revolving and dissolving and cloud-booming elocution

how many gods have never been born ? ask and ask again

the lottery of breath is at stake and the small future

with its midget cars and bridges of death and salvation

tumbling into the unlicensed waters below all churning

black as asphalt and Lo ! above the birds of mystery

circling as guides to the Beyond and we will not be cajoled

no one can tell us what to do once we're dead

all is a wavering wasteland down there rusted automobile parts

hieroglyphic tantrums of writing and disposable logic
an end to all speculation ! the others ! see how many they are !
mantras and deicides ! we have finished the lesson
book-learning and sophistry Aristotle and theogony
dismissed into the night of guttering sparklers and asterisks
the holiday of apostrophes is upon us the great brass horn
noise of longing and sorrow the lawns and grasses
evening when leaves alone remember speech

05-21-22

IN THE ABSENCE OF LOGIC

a house of smoke—who will repair to this place ?
is not thunder enough and the hidden celestial fires ?
born on earth weakling mortals build here a wall
dig there a moat set up altars with secret designs
to become as gods distributing lies and wealth
among the scattered and aggravated nations
histories go in cycles repeating the same illusions
of empire and deceit and lovers still persist dooming
cataracts and pinnacles with undying oaths to be
even so we attend classes learning by rote the sounds
and noise of language principles of tone and accent
disregarding oracular truths of defiance and denial
all existence hangs on a thread easily snapped by
one of the Sisters and students go on memorizing
atavistic mantras tales and hooded myths enigmas

replacing stone with rock treading on holy lawns
defiling temples erected by residents of the Unknown
bells ring ! charades and circle-dances and cars !
everyone is given a ticket and yet no destination
has been planned and no horizon is apparent other
than the great mountain that marks the end of time
somewhere by the seas that instill fear and longing
how does the song go that immortalizes pyramids ?
there is a mysterious math at work beneath the skin
legends of suns that traverse the other side of space
memory has been invented on multiple occasions
to account for the distances between birth and death
pronouns with no fixed designation are handed out
masks and the good-cheer of a night with the other
when the would-be becomes the impossible and clouds
and ether and portents of scientific error and skies
massive incubators of separate universes and stars
by which orators predict fate and salvations by number
the very waters that churn murky and loud in the ear
sleep ! dreams ! midnight trysts ! bottom of oblivion !
where in the world are we ? today is the last ever !
if only everything had happened simultaneously
then we could better explain our derangement
as it is we go on counting leaves and blades of grass
the child within dies of pure yearning for hills
where dialects play with statues of sheer noon--
light the everlasting ! enormous Boom of silence

05-22-22

PROYECTOS LITERARIOS

para mi hermana Laurita

what a fabulous morning a Sunday out of time
and joe up there skimming tree-tops smiling down
trying to explain the puzzle to me how it works
not like when we spread maps out on the sun-porch
nor later when as abstracts in a photograph we
represented not what pyramids are but the numbers
that ascend in a dizzy trigonometry of skies
none level with another and look ! how the lawns teem
with subconscious civilizations molecular hives
of earth and distance and look ! clouds forming
the letter zed for Zeus ! apocalypse will follow apocalypse
this afternoon be forewarned ! lifting his favorite
finger the one he lost in the accident of grass and twilight
much like the Buddha of automobile parts
and trying not to dissolve too quickly in the format
of atmospheres where his voice hovered about to transform
into the ebullience of a missing summer day
and all I could hear were birds absolved of innocence
wild and fluting and flying enigmatically out of the houses
that lined this ideal street canopied with souls of trees
and resemblances of boyhood treks walks down river banks
hiking with a recently baptized friend to some hamlet
in the dusty origins of memory where legendary signs
in red fade into mysteries of thirst and death
time to re-learn Spanish he suggested but with a Vedic brogue

and to forgive Dad those violent outbursts that sent

us hurtling down the stairs into the basement where

strangers with magazine covers for identities lurked

dogs own the sidewalks ! clear as Roland's horn joe's

echo volleyed through the hieroglyphic leaves

I'm not an acrobat I'm a philosopher ! high as ever

balancing on the telephone line over Woolsey Street

joe wavered laughed hiccoughed lingered crooning

one of his favorite ballads "the shore was kissed

by sea and mist Tenderly" it was legendary this moment only

hours ago in the intermittent zone between planet Pluto

and the Stygian swamps and the loud accents of

Poseidon the earth-shaker and the firmament seemed

to shake in a furtive and instantaneous cinema

starring joe as the Prophet who governs planetary travel

and with a gesture only I his twin could perceive

off he went with Toltec-jabbering parrots back down

to the great southland of Yucatan to pen the austerities

of his autobiography as a geminated consonant

in a language comprehensible only to indigenous

elementary school kids in the year 1947 CE

Yo soy indio !

05-22-22

AN ELEGY FOR CLAIRE BIRNBAUM

when it rained light over the steel mills
was memory born from insomnia and the skies
grey and sullen and below the waters defiled
by the onslaught of dead fish belly-up silver
glistening in the sun's hazy realm and did shout
the heroes in their book-clad array of epithet and
dumb as beasts emerging from the antecedents of
history was I among them neither this way looking
nor into the recent past a flower folded in left fist
and psychiatric clues riddling the airwaves was
that the one or was it the other in rebuke and drizzle
sitting in outdoor cafes pride of the alphabet just
born and reckless in my ways amputating thought
from the well of ancient syllables called literature
in the narrowest terms and with pronouns as swords
parried the new future with cat-calls and suburban
sallies by shoreline and mornings half-dead how
was it I survived that violent and early initiation ?
could not understand half of what I had studied
book theft and parody of epic style wave burnt
by some solar curse on raft without oar and prayed
to the Daughter-of-the-Sun for a cure a draught
of pine-resin and ouzo and the far shore always
farther than calculated and the sounds ! mingling
of gods casting lots as to whose wife would be spoiled
and what wars incessant monotony of deaths and

the dying reports of smoke issuing from temples

burnished marble panoply of words without sense

the meaning of the hypotenuse in archaic vowels

always in italics and was it for me to recall an anterior

existence as a peacock or some form of humility

cast ashore by pirates unransomed a daze of hue

and emotion admitted to a bridal chamber and suited

out with a finery too large for my soul and did she

winsome glance at me captivating me for a summer

daedalean structure of dreams and languages

rote and number of consonants the heights only

at a distance of formality and deceit ushered

into the courts stunned by my lack of comprehension

of human motives and she locked away from view

gone as are songs when they are concluded something

beautiful and Aeolian in the mists the ear shot with

mill and repercussion of the stars now turned green

by the alcohol of mortal error and superstition

sail on little Honey Bee ! to reconstruct the shape

of her hair-do like that of empress Messalina

now a photograph lost in the pages of a lexicon

in the dialect of the troubadours sun-spray

on rock and drill of longing for the Unseen Lady

such is the random scope of the universe years

and deathless yearning to be among the leaves

again

05-23-22

WHEN I BECAME A POET

props up his drunken frame with drowsy splendor
jeweled and with portents of a life that will not come
this figure scarce out of classes and beribboned
in sounds too archaic that implore the goddesses
the many that surround the glass and opine otherness
drugs and fumes the hazy orient of his careless brain
did then pronounce the hieratic syllable and upon
the ledge leaps all tense and wire of a puppet pronoun
to be different in climes where elephant and tortoise
on their backs bear the careening world-order and
the skies above resplendent with noise and traffic
are mere symbols of what mortals lack in their daily
fugue between senseless details and the Number that
has no horizon but union with the deathless entity
envisioned in the dream of time's triple declension
absence and presence and beyond either one mind
in its spiraling labyrinth between levels of ether
and the expectation to become real in domains where
verse and meter use hands to fashion ideal forms
circles and pyramids and legends of southland realm
of the Profound Queen whose mysteries encompass
all that can occur when thought and space are no more
and what a relief to walk again on tree-canopied streets
to libraries and drugstores and hear the five o'clock chimes
small minutes of music that transform inconstancy
into the absolute and to imagine this is it the abyss

and its corollary the afterworld the summons to be
outside of the inscribed skin a whirl of love and emotion
the ultimate error of adolescent projections and beside
and in front and behind the ongoing process of the heart
minuscule earths revolving around the object-of-affection
nothing can ever be rightly expressed ! it is a cannon
and its history of centuries and speculation that come
to naught the fevered instant of cosmic inaction
yes ! running chords of unheard music that transmogrify
entelechy and the baths of unreason on Planet Nowhere
summer vacations spent in corn-fields ripening with
perspiration and choice of girlfriend the flitting emerald
of her eyes that involve perpetuity and longing to die
here it is the poem and its inability to conclude anything
farewell it says to all the tender leaves and blades of grass
goodbye to night and the millstone of the stars
fingers gone lost in the intimacy of hair and swooning
poet ! you are naturally dead from the start !

05-24-22

MAYO CLINIC BLUES

(dedicated to the class of '56, RHS)

are these doctors capable of tragedy
dipsomaniac dabblers in the arts while
Stalin goes unguarded on his unholy purges

and we wake daily to headlines about Korea
and the hydrogen bomb and civil unrest in the south
our small world encapsulated in a few small-town blocks
between high school public library and drug store
the grand central meeting place of heart and soul
in the midst of consciousness the great granite
structure of the Mayo Clinic superb with its carillon
unwavering like a mastodon on the analphabetic plains
frozen in time a bestiary of roundelay and denial
words escape meaning the airs resound with dialects
incapable of defining the remotest sense of being
it is all about us -- fugue and interlaced play
of prejudice and hypocrisy the brown-colored vapors
that hover twilights when autumns become mortuaries
a long drive into the sun mid-afternoons when winter
impales the galaxies with a copy of eternity in snow
what hills ! what redundancies of speech and accolade !
hotels and tunnels beneath the x-ray rooms
pool halls and granaries and more beer than necessary
motel on south Broadway ! secret conclave where Romance
philology and adolescent love-madness coincide
Latin hexameters lavishly disposed in corn furrows where
July follows July in extreme weathers of passion and oblivion
where is Persephone in her Senior Prom uniform ?
gone underground with pubescent rockabilly music
conducted by an enigmatically neo-Platonic Psychiatrist
with his panoply of Euler diagrams and Rorschach tests

what has the mind to do with life ! breath and antagonism

there are no virtues only mysterious numbers

gradations that slowly lead to the pyramids of Manicomio

who will be the first and the last to graduate if not dead Achilles ?

pomp and circumstance the unmemorized hymn to Helium !

we are suffocated by an unwarranted future of razed ballrooms

and IBM plants devouring the northwest quarter of town

heaven lasted a few minutes on a phonograph recording

You belong to me ! wear a pink short and ivy-league tie !

come to the dance mobilized for despair and aphasia !

Mayo clinic has been a cosmic joke ! no days remain

that are not fueled by random disease and death

the medics are a plague of reason and intelligence

there are highways guided by the Four Winds that lead

forever out of this sink-hole of memory and sorrow

! give me the Blues of a lost Saturday night !

there are highways guided by the Four Winds that lead

forever out of this sink-hole of memory and sorrow

05-25-22

IT HAPPENED ON A DAY IN MAY

the daily holocaust of American democracy !

shoot-em-up western saga at gun-fight-corral

movies flicker and die and children by the dozens as well

sweep 'em outta here dirty wetbacks and solo artists

with firearms for birthday gift and recipe for denial
Senators ! Rome is no more and the causes are rooted
in Christian catacombs and incendiary speech
Nero ! John Wayne ! the stage coach has been robbed
one time too many and them savages are to blame
Senators and Congressmen to your rifles ! guard
the frontiers don't let them sack the holy Rockies !
our nation right but always wrong ! by the gorgeous Mississippi
bluffs and the skies of high-blue waters and the woods
and ditches and Manitou heavens of the Oregon Trail
by Hiawatha's lost highway and the perpetual motion
of immigrant invasions from beyond the Rio Grande
I'm an old cowhand and line the wagons in a circle
divinities are at stake ! the cotton gin and Plantation
pancakes and prohibition booze the American Way
douse the lamps burn the tee-pees put Christ on the red-skins
learn 'em how to ballroom dance ! how many times ?
I mean the ritual of the kid with an assault weapon !
it's all a bunch of exclamation marks and prayers
wooden faces back-woods ceremonies and burning crosses
furrows up and down left and right where bodies lie
or on the boughs of great oak trees cadavers twitching
and the melancholy sound of Gershwin's Summertime
Judges-of-the-Supreme-Court ! there is no Rome
left to abort only the back-alley cinder box and ash
listen ! that's no song but the ricochet romance of
the bullet and the right to life !

05-25-22

INCONSTANCY OF MEMORY

"in medio scopulis se porrigit Aetna perustis"

       Claudianus, De Raptu Proserpinae

places that have no direction

    and cannot be found

like gods who have never been born

    yet manifest as organs of sleep and death

hail the sun newly risen from the mountain

    that lies before the birth of time

much is the myth of memory the aggravation

and tenuous as ether the flitting imagery

like targets on a shooting range or birds

winging solemnly in a non-existent sky

I was there ! you died in my arms !

I heard the dog barking years after it expired

the echo and rally of unknown voices clouds

rushing into a state of immobility or gravity

impending holding back summer bodies

water and gas ! issues about learning to read

reciting formulas of grammar nonsense of sound

phonetic decay working like a worm in some

recess of thought and the origins of color

the violent shapes that trail after bee-swarms

heat and collision of particles metal becoming

transparent as the atmospheres of Venus

who said what to whom ? lack of clarity

courtroom drama divorce and nuptial theft

I loved her for the way she combed her hair !

after that nothing availed and the nymphs took her back

into the lake of despond and oblivion

Pluto readies his gear and Ceres deceived

cancels one month after another but which ones ?

Julius Caesar ! enemies of the state and

the invention of Italian in the foothills near Arezzo

I lingered by the wire fence waiting for her shadow

to emerge from the chloroformed depths of the pool

radiant for her moment of eternal luster and

as I recall and as I recall stuttering recollections

trees surrendered their souls to the absent light !

what did I know beyond the third declension ?

dimensions and iterations of skin drying

in the abrasive August sun yellowish and hell-like

refusal to accept the various commitments to end

following the side-path through corn fields

furrows where Proserpina trembling stepped

Aha ! her ankle snatched by a bejeweled hand

it's not the way I remember it --

there were others watching a collusion of spirits

the damned and the unwholesome who inhabit

certain dominions of air and rob sleep of its contours

waking up the next day as ever wondering

did that really happen ? windows and adjectives

describing the empyrean of the diminished past

porticos fallen into disuse grass growing everywhere

footprints in the eroding soil of memory

05-26-22

MAX COMING OUT OF A COMA

is this my bed what room is this

where are my toys and spacecraft

are there words for the objects around me

what is this thick heavy bandage around my head

where have I been since the morning when I fell

from the ledge of consciousness into the basement

names are only sounds nothing gets past the window

every night I am more alone than before

it's hard to believe daylight takes months to arrive

or I am something aching somewhere else

like a fog without a past clinging to a cliff

an automobile brought me to this stage of breath

if there is a next time it will be forty years from now

renewed repeatedly I still forget so much

is it how to put shoes on or even to stand holding

on to the railing that surrounds the world

a sea is in my left ear and drowned children

still shouting reaching for a big red ball

as it floats away into the dizzy sky

so much confusion dust clouds secrets I can't remember

a brother teasing me for the sidewalk's distance

or a bicycle that is a bridge in length

there are people with needles and metal trays and plastic tubes

there are people who really don't exist any more

and whatever else the world can be I don't know

glass and light and winds that blow from underneath

there is a wheel elsewhere turning with an irreplaceable flame

and a signal that keeps me from being whole again

sometimes a water and a siren and a park

with a circle in the middle and flowers brighter than anything

bees and ants and hummingbirds keep making noise

but the street is too far away and the mountain

a promise to be different and on a large paper floor

shadows intermittent like the moons I cannot see

and there are books with too many rooms to count

if I can remember what numbers are

and cartoon animals playing with ladders of fever

and hair-lines that have been dismissed by doctors

as too tragic incoherent everything random chaos aflame

mind a series of incomprehensible word shots

flakes of destiny thumbnails and sun-spots

everything is of the moment a conditional life

depending on machines that go whir and night-whistles

long and plangent and the last thing I asked

in my former voice was where is Mom ?

I never heard the answer only a trailing vowel

what's going on someone came in the door

someone else left

the future

05-27-22

APOCALYPSE NOW SUTRA

by what false etymologies do we cling to breath ?

what phonetics gives us comfort in deepening silence ?

why insist on meaning when only noise riddles the cosmos ?

what has childhood got to do with metaphysics and memory ?

we dwell on the inconsequential and devote hours

to a headline about actresses and contraception

the world is in flames ! hunger ! ISOLATION drought

the unmanageable positions of a white collar and tie

stranglehold on munitions five fathoms below the sea

Krishna ! holding the mountain up with a single finger

while watching the guts of a city implode into

beautiful white smoke-circles is that a form of salvation ?

the soul like the hundredfold ringlets of Proserpina's hair

the comb and task of the mirror to devolve and destroy

the advantage of one alphabet over a syllabary in ruins

Egyptian tomb-thieves ! tiny statues of Anubis on the black market

sands and rhetoric of great Hellenistic car crashes

going round and round with a banner saying All you Need is Love

John Lennon died for our sins with impromptu bullet

the list is endless but the oceans are perishable

the shorelines give way to tons of plastic waste

a bible in a motel autodestructs ! moon-signs and solar homophones

the heavens remain a linguistic puzzle with planetary lesions

plunging derricks hit the street in Alexandria ! Osiris !

a Hindustani song raves about the four Vedas each

with a direction and script of its own and death multiplied

each time the unheard Note sounds in the sleeping ear

OM shanti OM ! is America finally on the verge ?

mutilated statues of emperor Domitian surface in Chesapeake Bay

stuttering oaths of allegiance to the Senate-of-latter-day-Saints

I am Orestes ! whining and piercing shrieks of the Furies

Agamemnon Klytemnestra and Kassandra on a burning ghat !

the police are in a trance while children go up in a blaze

holy holy holy ! I will never go to school again

the end has already happened I don't know how many times

myth and slander convey the Truth !

myth and slander convey the Truth !

rifles don't kill only eighteen year old trigger-fingers assassinate

an edge to the firmament is written in the blood of casual shoppers

this is an elegy for everyone who is dead before they know it

grammar and reason ! logic and sensibility ! textbooks

that no kid will ever open again to read in the Home-of-the-Brave

that Thomas Jefferson was a fraud !

Benjamin Franklin was a Whig acting like a Tory on opiates !

the Founding Fathers were analphabetic ruminants

seeking to enslave and make corporate profits

the Civil War was the end of a mendacious experiment

Rock 'n Roll ! Elvis Presley and Aretha Franklin !

let us all join in prayer at the SuperMarket

Sunflowers !

05-28-22

WHAN ZEPHIRUS EEK WITH HIS SWEETE BREETH

how doth Zephyrus today paint the roses ?
long lingered have we this question unanswered
and dews disappear before the appointed hour
as early deaths without warrant too deck the airs
with saffron and violet hues and mourn the trees
the souls departed the violent airs the winds that
carelessly abandon their allotted homes and greater
still atmospheres high above that rush in contest
with the sun's singular and terrible homophone
blacken we in sleep our desires confounded and
no sooner wake then detest the light that burns
unborn inconstant far-reaching which of us will
it see no more into graves darker than oblivion
return the unrequested thought the unwilling mind
to bury in unrefuted pages of destined script
does day break in tears of flashing gems and athwart
the weathers of undiminished rage clouds burst
in a corner unknown to the sky such tempests
and rare angers that define the yearning heart to
move beyond the daily stem and inscriptions too
sad to read and ride in some undirected car toward
horizons and hills where no dialects govern sound
and speak to losses and grief that Zephyrus bears
to this park where gathered in brief circumference
we learn to share longings no hands can ever touch
and scour once more memory's embittered fields

in scent of budding blooms the roar incessant

of bees in swarms of distance and vanishing

05-29-22

THE END OF POETRY

what more could the Latin verb intransitive perform
despite light's transparent weight and the sighs
of omitted vowels the depths increased of consonants
plucking from amidst the briars bright yellow
red and dappled roses a hand of grammar a splayed
finger dactylic in hexameter the air parts with sorrow
to be read aloud recited against the booming wave
as barks depart the resounding shores and tides out
to gain moon's begotten luster do then orate aloud
leaf and faun the verses memorized in sleep an echo
of fragrance a breeze of syllables borne by swarms
that from Hybla paint the rapid airs with saffron hue
the distances of dialect and hills interred by blur and
tone the registers of gods enumerated like letters of
an alphabet or some hierophantic noise that shimmers
reflected in pools of obsidian and jade the draft and
copy of sounds the abacus of orient beyond the water
where mountains elude the fire of time and chasing hinds
and roe the nymphs with invisibility clad the heights
aspire to talk again as in dreams of muffled hyacinth

denounce the rock its rising element of heat and grief
again intrudes where sandy mounts and cliffs sway
against the hour's diminished conjugation how can
so much of a lesson be unlearned and heave the winds
their mighty song rushing from ear to ear the range
of words unfound the error of human thought a mere
episode of color drained from a shell of resonance
and repetition as the afternoon's pale resemblance
shades into twilight's ocher divinity a whispered leaf
and stone the doors of mind disclose their emptiness
and death astride its vaunted dewy steeds proclaims
that silence will gain the vast empyrean of stars and
forever the imitated speech of poets outlast

05-29-22

THE RECOVERED POEM

changed their course the stars and mountains
knocked by Neptune's trident wept to move from base
asleep the breathing target amidst briars and
tangled undergrowth new greenery seemed to sprout
from his inert mind were it better to wake once more
the light of day anew to greet salute the infinity of azure
canopied like a dim memory in his head the fleet
and quandary of time distilled like a corrupt lesson
to be studied by afternoon and Lo excessive airs

and winds a tumult of vowels awoke stirring impulse
and divagation to letters hidden in the trough
of forgotten myth and ascend to where chariots
race their antiquity to the west and praise hills
where dialect and etymology rehearse their tribulation
whatever else a design of circles or buried pyramids
can achieve or number with its enigmatic praxis
and recycled overtures to thought what then is the child ?
a vast and reckless quadrant to the south and east
of fields where mature the romance of simile
and metaphor a body to embrace a haven to escape
the foment and treason of the living word how can it ?
fixities and immobilities the chastened clouds detain
long moments without egress plunge planets to seas
of immemorial accident the writ of heroes and despair
ivy clambers to embrace the secret motive in the sap
and wild allusions to the archaeology of the hive
likened to rock emerging from centuries' long trance
fire to devour and legendary apses and columns
that uphold the heavens for a night before tumbling
once more into their unfinished verse and choir
whatever else the poet requires to complete the journey
of his roving eye or the intellect of his entombed ear
alert ! the seven episodes of the travelling noise
that compose and the future of a simple syllable
meant to emphasize all that ever was or happened
in the single instant of eternity childhood and nymphs

the moistened finger that gambles in the grassy net

to comprehend the moment of oblivion and forget

to rise clad in the musts of archaic beauty

behold ! hands that yearn to become phonetic recitations

long periods of hexameter and magic incantation

the summer of infinite months and heat like a song

reverberating in the leaf's somnolent speech

an evening to explore the lunar cavity and then

to die ! the poem recovered in its ancient sound

extent of universes before time and birth of angels

great winged things with recollection of a lexicon

etymologies of galaxies and divine instructions

to destroy whatever comes in touch with immortality

flowers that last a single day insects less than an hour

our love ! will its labyrinth ever be resolved ?

05-30-22

MEMORIAL DAY ELEGY 2022

some kind of demon infests within me

Revelation ! the sky breaks into multiple halves

it is to imagine that I have written all this already

that memory has been enlarged to incorporate myth

one with the gods of illusive entry and exit

who have never been born and are willing to die

me ! them ! focus of mystery and absolution

passage of time in a matter of minutes windows
and stucco walls and plum trees and a bridge
that crosses over the river of seasons
I was there once and watched the cinema reverse
itself and next to me my other half my devout
and reckless Joe my witness to divinities and hells
how could he have evacuated the body already ?
writing and writing resolves nothing a fantasy
to make words mean something to transpire and
excavate the air and make the winds blow the other way
to sleep ! not just yet and hints of phonetic disease
the noisy decay of sounds that cannot be put together
language and grammar ! Pfah ! Vedic nonsense and
dying and coming to earth again reborn as a tree
or a cow ruminating on roadside accidents and a house
to live in and reconstruct one childhood after another
and say Yes this is it ! a living number with eyes
a walking syllable learning grass and leaf and stone
a portion of time in the hand and leaping into the pool
great waters ! it aches because everything is out of control
I did not ask but receive I did not receive but want !
one day I met a girl and then we graduated and
went separate courses a thing to be only a memory
fields alive with insects bearing the souls of gods !
and heat and tracts of immutable reveries
skin ! the taste of salt and tears and grime
dirt and resolution to be free of time one day

and to keep writing an aggravation with misplaced

vowels with tongues half-acquired afternoons in Italy

near the Apennines and the Adriatic Etruscan mystery tombs

marriages of the dead to the dead in full regalia

secrets of the underworld the elaborate speech of statues

or painted figures using glyphs for words and the meaning

always lost never recovered and the girl who is a phantom !

such as it ever was the expectation of the great Moment

today and today and today always the never of opposites

and Joe feckless wandering among the green stars

he saw the night we tasted alcohol and slept with eyes open

to the eternal revolutions of distance and space

a hill a monument a dialect a lawn and voices

05-30-22

THE TALE OF THESEUS AND ARIADNE

witness to the stars each a house of mystery

a dialect of its own a spear in the hand a wound

the faceless deity of grass beside a sea of trees

recitations in marble and distance the full length

before birth darkness unwinding in unknown quanta

a machine of soundless words thought and provocation

in the same instant of recovery and death the isolation

endless hues the miasma of understanding a fist

beside itself searching for a shape the nuanced

shadow that moves of its own accord and footsteps
only sleepers hear wending a passage across streams
of language and echo a last memory of figures in
the dense stratosphere and waking in an unknown bed
amnesia and foreclosure of mind the variable paths
going south to the unreckoned dead in their autumn
of haunting melody and stucco whatever is undefined
lack and mourning distances never reached a nod
to the heavens a thunderclap the theaters of mind
fallen to ruin of rock and stubble the ear profaned
by the curse of daily mortals pushing or trodden
carried through years collapsed into a thimble
toward some destined finale a curtain-call a flash of
irreverent electric bolts riddling the warp and
trust and the famous et cetera of all human endeavor
chastened and restrained by aphasia and doubt
let us then ! voices in the silently shifting leaves
hills and grief combined in tragedy's fifth act
a performance with mask and faulty pronoun
unable to recall exactly what the plot reveals
sealed agreements with forbidden gods truncated
language non-existent vowels enigmas assumptions
enormous tombs opened wide and Apollo-types driving
miniature automobiles across the acropolis
and always the cry for help and an Ionian poet on
the verge of dementia stammering by the gasoline pump
which is the entrance to Hades and summoned

from recesses of pitch and sulfur demons enticing

and fraught with cosmetics and beauty treatments

braids and combs and allure and the instantaneous

promise of recovery and salvation in a mirror

when was life ever otherwise ? a film in the dark

holding hands guiltless kisses smothered in candy

the love that surpasses understanding and spirits

at the very center of the nocturnal labyrinth

waiting with ropes and Cretan axes whispering

hapless the soul that confides in the light !

05-31-22

RUBESCENT PLANETS

the days that pass and the radio

the heat lying abed half dead with memory

nothing but a buzz nothing to cling to

a breeze rippling through a screen door

neither past nor present--wouldn't it be

better to wake from this insufferable life ?

was it great god Pan whose death cry split the hour ?

and to look for the street's asphalt map

it's all of the moment nothing more or less

worlds in upheaval between sheets and clouds

endless lyric of pyramids with marimba

as the hour diminishes an imitation cosmos

evolves with distances of red omega cliffs
did asunder the heavens weep some distant loss ?
silhouette of a mourning mannequin behind
plate glass gazing into store-bought infinities
bong and drill polished metal in flight
historical lexicons clutter the adolescent mind
Agamemnon the myrmidons phantom police !
antiquity never contested just waiting for night
and the evanescent billions of stars carelessly
flung into the empyrean by a dead Roman Emperor
whose triumphal cart yanked this way and that
jerks its way down Broadway to the court house
is it to herald still another daybreak ?
multiple lesions of the stratosphere in rains of blood !
landscape of automobile parts motor oil and rust
everything fetid and vague yellowing in
a month-long heat-wave of abstract corn-fields
rise ! get dressed ! time to wash dishes
for a meager summer pay with dreams
of Yucatan or the Deccan replete with goddesses
twin-peaked Parnassus with gestations of hexameter !
this is destiny, Man ! reek of booze stale food-scraps
denizens of the bottom rung of hell
sweating in underwear and bottle-eyed
scrubbing pottery in scalding water
no one has awareness ! time is a liquid swamp
oozing toward the Styx without reflection

energy of the heavens ! isotopes and dialects

things to discern and separate in education

upland hierophants crouching in the corridors

copies of all the deities encompassed in one thumbnail !

future is emerging ! it will be sorrowing !

decades will pass in the blow of a conch-shell

one of us will fall prey to a fatal illness

the other will proceed excavating language for

etymologies of summer and grief

rubescent planets

for a moment it all seems Real !

06-02-22

THE SMOKING PASSAGE

shift switching dialects in archaic despair

ionosphere prey to man's violent hallucination

floods with ignition and ruddy ire

to dominate or be dominated in a sea of woes

begging the king for one more chance a toss

of the dice on either hemisphere greening losses

underwater coral bleached beyond infinity

and Boom ! another madman sets his firearm on

"automatic" spraying the foothills with a bloody idiom

by the thousands vertebrates fall and hell

with its chinks and ovaries fills with errant shadows

ghosts of memory and accident ululating
in the gravity of unconsumed mourning the diatribes
and rhetoric of blind augurs whose prescience
has cost many a continent its peace and sleep
advertisements herald in neon light a passage
from this intimidation of success and bravura
into realms where vowels fall silent : a cinema
of hushed landscapes spools its infinite round
numinous warnings in the traffic signals
enigmatic millennia pass in the blink of an eye
lunations measured in the noise of bee-hives
and mountains on the verge of phonetic collapse
the entire ecumene threatened by its own boomerang
history revised in texts of no known script
cosmic origins detailed in the lotus sprouting from
the nascent sound of eternity the famous unheard note
and deaf but living on cigarettes Prophets wander
searching for the immortal stairway //
or certain you are to go running toward unmerited
arms bearing the poem's desultory unfinished verses
weaponry of time ! gods and breath—what's the difference ?
aim for other worlds taint and hesitation of light
extended by the hour into traveling tombs of thought
the great epic ! words and dynasties of sound !
why ask for more ? you are done with this earth
resounding with ricochet and echo of hazard
and retreat with your pages into the wood

puzzled that you are alive at all after so many decades
an echelon of lexical units rephrased sentiments
things that were never meant to be uttered in context
slamming the door on phalanxes of stunned fireflies
the virginity of reason trapped in a bottle
small love-notes passed back and forth in yellow
and rouge and heat rising from the fields
where outlines of your bodies still visible attest
to a moment when love was more
than a smoking passage
06-03-22

ETERNAL ADOLESCENCE

did raise breath to a sequence of skies tumbling
cloud weft the hoarse barking in the left ear
was I a deity dumbfounded waiting to graduate
from high school again and again ? margins tight
with type-font in bold face all hieroglyph and cant
discount and ineligibility set in primordial italics
shooting stars of the brain map and technique
a quadrillion ethers ! why fashion absence in music ?
longing and loss of memory aphasia and height
which is the proper direction to die ? emphasis
on the blackboard where languages design their
fates phonetic disorder oracular length of syllables
lacking a final consonant and girlfriend emerging

from the afternoon's isogloss wearing lipstick and
the emergency coloring of eye-shade hair-pins
force of destiny memorizing names and divisions
uncluttered wavelengths of verse half-sounded and
multiples of zero extended to the nth degree far
to the right of the mountain which marks the end
of time's only horizon and comes the ringing
school's out skirts in profusion gabble of tongues
which could become a book with leaves interspersed
and the bright encomium of the astral body bearing
the signature of an unknown poet fingers that
weave through grass and hands without shadows !
I am there in a mix and medley of noiseless meanings
interpreting sun-slant and the sidewalk's ultimatum
whether to enter the library or drop dead on the spot
cancelling the future hearing the carillon's illicit
hour Bong ! everyone wearing death-masks and
laughing misusing pronouns adolescence of Mind
will it ever settle down ? automobiles rush to
take the Iliad from behind and Achilles pouting
in the drugstore afraid to apply cosmetics to his wound
sudden menace of night watching in the gloaming
a dense hill approach with trees that ache to know
and animals hidden in undergrowth of mourning
it was Persephone who lost her way ! heart-beat
a wild peacock dancing and threat of thunders
tombstones of sleep ! tomorrow the enigma

06-04-22

THE EPIGRAPHY OF DEATH

stuttering stammering ink blocks of air

what does the wind in it infinite resonance

have to declare in the cloud-mists of heaven ?

a-shine with being the sea texts its raging waves

to worlds beyond the sun's feeble limit to shades

where mountains topple in apocalyptic phonology

it's a finger pointing south where ghosts of grass

cling in vain to promises of dew to radiance

of lunatic dialects uttered below earth's surface

soil and ingrained ears of hearing blossomed

through eons of buried sounds dictionaries

of things that have no meaning in the scores of light

galactic mourning in the plundered cosmos

of before-time and situations of childhood and

aphasia of stroke and cancerous deviation

the world and its multiple others afloat cut off

from the moorings of depth and despair left behind

small hands the color of puce and cuprous ire

what gods ! metallic photographs of death

coveting the thousands of girls who own the streets

and masks of puppets without a pronoun of dolls

and cadavers of isotope and vermillion thoughts

how little is the much that fills the cup !

there must be countries where nothing happens

mosques and hundred-tiered hindu temples

cattle brought to the brink and the midnight noise

of sacrifice in letters that are nothing but sounds

alleviation of vowels in cathedrals of broken consonants

intonations of afternoons when five o'clock

is the terminus of being a man and a wailing

of sulfur and iodine lifts the roofs of grammar

into atmospheres where death's epigraphy

becomes loud and white and deafened deities

tumble from their triangles into a dumb estate

like mortals dazed in the labyrinth of breath

06-05-22

THANATOPSIS

the pennons and strife that often define life
weather reports down-sized kingdoms dust
the paraphernalia of the skies noiseless bric-a-brac
what's to us the uncommon denominator of death ?
planning the daily route through hazard and angst
talking to old acquaintances who are no longer there
reading in the etymologies of thought an archaic oversight
why didn't we know sooner there was to be no tomorrow ?
capsized boats devalued punctuation hues without size
who and where was the charioteer and his mountain ?
surfeit gifts of ivory and tiger-skins yak-tail fans
three thousand serving girls per guest and all the ruckus
and steam of an epic poem half libation half portent

and augury of doom in cycles no one can comprehend

so today palms are read a flute drones in the ear's hive

sessions counting beads and guessing how far china is

from its historical denomination of silk and bone

a bridge is cast over a hundred waters and loud

diesel-driven wheels reduce distance to its inch

overwhelmed by a passion to ignore what's ahead

the faulty mind breaks with its past and is about to faint

each word in the recitation loses meaning only

a blur and buzz of voices from a Berlitz lesson

in a small Italian city lost to the analphabetic centuries

what is darkness ? what are cloud formations ? summer ?

we have existed this long—is it enough ? a herald

on an invisible solar steed shining and swart hails

the outgoing hour and submits to an incremental destiny

everything slowly going under an unforeseen hill

suddenly risen in an undeclared west of black sunspots

transfiguration ! surrender the old body to its text

of languishing and doubt lay the head on its stone

what was it all about this flash and technique ?

one minute is sufficient to remember everything !

06-06-22

THE LIMITS OF THE DREAM

take it away ! take it all away !
what finished there is of little breath
the aching heart the crown that slips away
no red pen no Chinese lithograph no print
capacity of ink to spoil the early skies
no dawn in chalk and aluminum to braise
the clouds scurrying from sleep's imperfect dome
script and writ glyph and pictogram the mind
allure with thoughts of immortality simply
because words can say the dreamer's must and
require no more than to be read and uttered
the archaic tome the unfound volume the musty
dust-laden scrolls of enigmatic meaninglessness
the heavens iterated in their fourfold inch the azure
a simplex in the poet's cursive thought to convey
what never can be understood the furious unfolding
diaphragm of the seas and raging cliff-events of time
it took but an afternoon to unlearn unraveling
atmospheres and distances all yearning longs
to own and yet no deity is there no stubborn
principle to navigate the shoals of pure unreason
we wake to trumpets blare the agonies of battle
wounds and triptychs of the soul in puzzled bliss
a wager that a following day may not occur
nor the earth's tenuous girdle break forever more
fishes and electricity ! whatever kens the bottoms
an illustrated book of verse a loss of diadems

children forgotten at the rifle's door and shouts
what brings us full circle to ends that do not meet
parallel universes sketched by a broken thumb-nail
a glass and its reflection in the ampersand of space
all alone ! texts and more texts of unfinished sound
syllable and lore of the underworld to graze
among lists of noise and chronologies of grass
and never once reach the limits of the dream

06-07-22

TOO EARLY TO START DYING

coherent everything random chaos aflame
flicker tape black and white unfinished dreams un-
ending silence followed by the primordial Shout!
said all before waking sparking to the other
half in jest half in noosphere and betrayal by sleep
of time's unutterable law unfolding ten times
the size of the bed slept and tranced a floral joke
in language of the troubadours daisy may this
daisy may that in the sun's spawning black eye
learning to spell is no easier in the grimoire
of lacked desires as if to wake pondering
the dark relics of the brain behind the hedge-rows
that define the uncertainty of space and bright
the heliotrope in its incandescent rush of morn
Hello says I to me brother and we both know

right then and there how little remains of the light
let alone the swift agony of breath down under
which year and hour are you going to pick ?
a game a lark a rollick down the grassy slope
toward the mere where the little deer flock
to gaze at their eternal reflections and already
the fierce and imminent day is hard upon us
with its unlawful literature of truancy and heat
to have lived so swiftly in the remains of that hour !
sunset and its dialect of spark-plug and hostel
hills reverberate with tiny Greek myths
gods disguised as beggars for a rind of bread
and the flood of stones a cascade of cliffs
all the seas turn into mirrors of atomic ash
! nothing can be explained away so easily !
celestial maidens associated with trees or eons
spent on a single stone augment called heaven
just yesterday we were on that river-bank
watching our lives eddy downstream a great riot
sounds and noises without circumference each
of us betting the other would go first and Lo !
consonant clusters detonating speech acts of
statues turning blind on their knees pleading
for Juno to lessen her ire and the constant bickering
between the twins in their diminutive episode
of leaf and grass as if the possibility of an extended
minute were all that was needed to live forever

06-08-22

THE HYMN TO CHARON

garlands worn between fields and night the dense

suspicion of unending and the tremor of voices

torn from leaves dark blood oozing between vowels

to have plucked and chosen from this bitter growth

to make one's way to knock against the surface

knees imploring a second chance wafting fragrances

of opium and death the hands that make a brief appearance

before exiting from the stage of memory and allusions

to an anterior world to a form or species of light that

transcends whatever and mind incapacitated a flow

of disconnected thoughts a minor repair at the corner

an elbow or a shoulder torn from grace the motion

to remain still impatient gravity planetary plunge

hair on end the whistling comets of error and rumor

aggravated by man's unprincipled notion of victory

nevertheless the formidable distance between now

and the wharf where the ferry-man ponders weight

and the soul's penchant for flight cannot be overcome

lessons of grammar and teratology the reason for anything

to have being and sense and the curriculum of noises

circulating in the ear's labyrinthine demesne if only

which is always the clause of hope and darker yet

the following passage is a reading of the bone-text

about animal circumference and the possibilities

of literature in an era of political unreason and chaos

the very collapse of a cosmic system and others jostling

a crowd of simulations and resonance mask and pronoun
ghosts phantoms legless entities swarms of blind midges
stinging nettles and adders the reproach of failed love
all of this and poor Proserpina in her stained wedding
gown and the slats and mourning and the sound of water
rushing underfoot small sequences of consonants like
rains of gravel tempests naufrage peninsulas of gas
where is never anywhere the pointless compass of dots
leading nowhere and the arroyo of infinity leaking !

06-08-22

AVE VERUM CORPUS

destined the page darkening cities innumerable
on the margins of a great feminine water
and slept through the first hour of eternity
and aroused by a pinprick of solitary light
the body weighted with enormous vowels half-sounded
the other ligaments consonants overtures to space travel
slight modifications to the syllable that controls death
a salient version of light shifts like a splinter
through the grieving smokes and fires that have no return
a depth-charge of clouds ascending from the earth-crevice
and chariots of seemingly endless rutilations passing
through the sun's swart homophone and memory itself
embroidered in the eyelid of the Cyclops in his apiary

of dreams slopes and descending rills crystalline
and minute in the diminutive second hour of eternity
were all not lost in the crumbling phonology of time
wasted avenues circular as oracles seeming to defy
gravity the hospices and motels the casinos and dolmens
islands ! unthinkable woods and copses thick with noise
commingled speech-acts aborted in the middle by statues
envious of the unapproachable theogony of space
thousands nay millions of deities tumbling like hues
and pastels and fading paint dollops on the moving mural
that divides this life from the unremembered previous one
the body ! an apse a transept a hole in the ceiling a fosse
unbidden words coming out willy-nilly in a copy of daylight
fusion and fugue to define the corporeal essence
the thinking mortal the doomed entity the blinded seer
in his apostrophe of existence a fatal error to breathe
and assume that breath is the key to immortality
rumors ! objects that lack names long afternoons
in alleyways or one-way streets barricaded by longing
everyone thinks I have been here before but when or why
and no one exists at the same time outside of the skin
that defines the illusory birthright of the flesh
agonies of the pronoun ! dancing deep into the night
embraced to the eternal and ever unknown other

06-09-22

DOES POETRY ?

the morning's roses have failed their hue and

the dappled deer lie dead in their reflections like

Narcissus in his small pool – to what avail the hour's

brief circumference or the memory of a night in May ?

does poetry ? is there a winsome face at game's end

a solemn vow a line of verse intractable for its lack

of meaning and why this roundelay of doubts and

sorrows this string of sounds blown to the zephyrs

what ear will ever capture the severed noise of clouds

looming at the center of gravity about to rain such

greenery and longing and the world's tilted theater

some lightning on its stage and masks that pass from

hand to hand despite the forgotten script and love's

enigmatic vowels that pale in the darkening signal

it's just us ! we cry to one another though no more

visible as pronouns of walking fate and alarmed

that the earth's voluble tale of heat and circularity

is coming to its close and vain figures on a projected

screen our resemblances start and faint and sleep's

deep sister death begins her game of picking shadows

does poetry ? one by one the eyes go out and sky's

inaudible twin the burning atmosphere begins its flight

nothing that ever was maintains a hold and we pass

into eternity our bodies the freight of leaf and grass

06-10-22

IN A DAYLONG HIKE WE CIRCUMFERENCED THE WORLD

the time Joe and I met the Friend and wended our way

eastward in dirt dust and tumult to where the sun

has its signals to start and his horses neighing and pawing

the sultry skein of air far above our slight brains a frame

and woof of destiny it seemed in the cloudless azure

a book without pages words without sounds and hands

in search of fingers as we walked slowly in opposite

scheme to the direction of the world and high a laugh

a noise of grass and the tickle of fields sprawling to

north and south the gainsay and fold of mythography

sheets of wind the isolation of soul and bliss the fueled

re-entry into breath we tired we sank we rose again to

keep up hiking to its dissolute end a ramshackle store

where ice cold coke was sold and revival of the senses

and day itself wore out its Greek syllable by syllable

to create a western hill the lapse of light and time buried

in hush and muffle of being as it circles round the final

route and Friend and Joe and I at last the unknown goal

attained the single most emotion of after-death the haze

and torment only sleep succors and collapsed in sweat

and consonants sore and numb the wager to reach the River

we never won but in mind's map eternity was secured

and for a brief instant the world's other side revealed

06-10-22

THE MAYPOLE

for Ali Memarsadeghi

Discord pressed with her right hand the brow
a dolorous echo a threat of water and its
feminine substitute steam the sectioned and
quartered inch of sky hanging above daybreak
intuition to return sleep to its inadmissible vowels
sound-track to a memory that has yet to take place
organdy and chiffon and lavender and roses all
lined up in a poem written so long ago no one
can recall why nor how to translate its arcane symbols
motives for flight from breath resonance and repercussion
allusions to the beauty of stone and shadow grasses
aching to modify their own future a fiction of leaves
intertwined with consonants borrowed from Dravidian
haunted Buddha-types hanging around the used car lot
it will be hours before the street finishes or the monkey
attached to the organ-grinder absolves its own infinity
reaching back toward the origins of thought a sound
a mixture of noise and hive the mountain begins to loom
with its charity of wings and densely wooded slopes
a human might imagine but it is not so the ending
has possibilities of renewal and a philosophy of gravel
and wheels and windows darkened by fear of oblivion
the headlights turn veering toward planet Pluto
the undergrowth teems with fossil midges and fireflies
cataracts of pre-geological history in the small book

offered as a reward by Ire and her sister Harmony
how is it ? geminated letters and the park of evolution
castles in Mexican dialect the inner fires that burn
mind's intent to be superior with exhausted ideas
listening to the tick-tick of the first bird of the day
hark and Lo ! we will wake again and exchange
pronouns and identities for the brief flickering light
promised by the Dream-Master in a previous life
when Thou and I and whoever else were but kids
swinging on the maypole in the middle of the dark

06-11-22

FALLING THROUGH THE CRACKS

you can see it in their faces red and yellow streaks
in their eyes modernist post-modernist anthropophage !
the dichotomies ! dredged out of a millennial sleep
thrust into the fluorescent lamplight of schizophrenia
bargain hunters of thought with mental chisels and
degrees in higher cloud-physics and teratology
will it ever learn ? exclamation marks and prongs
to delve into the cognitive factory and make a mess
of it the streets that careen out of order off the map
devaluation of the peso and rupee vedic under-current
doors swinging wide off their hinges and apoplexy of
history in its last unsung chapter writ and habeas corpus

everyone is guilty ! stop eating meat off the sidewalks
burn the tents massacre the innocent ! temptation to
suicide and nirvana teachings of Mahavira don't step
on the ants a poet dwells among them and cease !
listen to the air to divide in multiples of a trillion
outer space the remnants of memory swinging on a
gallows ! yes and erase all punctuation including italics
it is forbidden to speak to statues and preach and
take oaths to sanctify rock stone and gravel and deny
the wheel its invention build pyramids underground
worship the vast and black homophone of the sun before
it fades away forever in a night of unheard decibels
make it forbidden to read ! I once saw a man playing
with hieroglyphs in the attic of time it was bedlam
and he looked up into the blinding radiance and
got up to dance with the other who was not there !
I am that man and I live on the follicles of madness
eat and eat nothing ! watch out for the corners and
stop walking on solid pavements ! you are sure to fall
through the cracks into the bottomless hell of concrete
and sleep ! there are four rivers you must beware of
and the menace of occidental medicine and waiting
rooms of mendacity and glossy magazines and finally
the Nymphs ! encounter with any one of them is Death

06-12-22

HOW JOE AND I SEPARATED

how could we keep it all straight ?

to memorize the laws of breath and light

by rote the letters and hours playing kick-ball

with kids probably twice dead already

and us unconsciously preparing for the great flight

transcendence of leaf and air to master pyramids

how many eyes we needed just to pass the gate

where fallacious Juno in her ire kept at bay

the demons of memory and talent and us buoyed

by maps of thought and entelechy the burgeoning

buds of reckless storm and sweep of mind

the dance ! the illustrious step of floor and screen

from what parapets we gazed solemn and giddy both

the future like an avalanche of midnight gravel

that betrayed the wheels coming home late of destiny

and us back and forth with playthings swinging

on a metal bar between the various heavens of

oblivion and grammar speaking languages

half-way between nonsense and the Absolute

how swift ! a diadem of syllables a pearl of noise

so recondite no ear unless one of archaic stone

could ever hear and hills that came and went

friends without name and streets of brief circularity

behind which mansions mysterious and forbidding stood

alert to the heat of enigma and creation

paint daubed winds hands invisible with cosmologies

sounds and interpolations of secret planets
noon-time whistles and bells that cause tears
drugstore paraphernalia softening the end of time
what wild ! what ripping sutures wide open !
the ride through impervious metal shining bright red
through fields of summer loss and sweet anticipation
to go and keep on going through plastic sheets of fear
cities ! one by one with their lakes and parks and lies
to sleep one night in the suburbs and wake transformed
a vision of radiance and despair the depths ! a wrong
turn a sacred emblem misinterpreted a teaching
meant to be misunderstood the crossroads !
only distance stands in the way of memory and
shock-still on a street corner called July we
reversed the angles of space and traded divinity
for the amorphous corpse of childhood in cement
echoes ! all that remains of sky's remote resonance
and that was all it ever was a last goodbye
the unknown grass where together we used to lie

06-13-22

OF A SUDDEN WE WAKE LOST IN SPACE

what is gold and the tripartite thread of thought
the foaming waters of Aphrodite ! two lines of poetry
the essence of why we are ruminating on the tangled

skein of stars and nights that last less than a minute
and grass folded over to hide the body ! a wonder
to live and walk the thin crust and fall in love not
once but twice and more falling into the maze where
metaphor and paradise collide ! songs and ears that
puzzle with memory and the ancient that becomes
the first in everything swooning into the abyss where
sun's bleak homophone can scarcely reach afternoons
when lessons of sound reveries and recitations of the
beginnings and nothing else ! a ship a man a fate some
water the feminine gender of so many nouns ! how ?
we read and forget what was on the page and ascend !
where did we leave off in the last life ? and to resume
lost in summer's heat a circularity of madness and
yet sky above divided into multiples of a million shines
we watch the drug take effect and destroy language
with the parallels of another existence and sudden
as the riot of vowels at the conclusion of a sonnet
in old Italian what a thing to explore ! who can
understand anything at all ? fingers search for words
in the teeming yards of weeds and hives and the buzz
of eternity is everywhere ! it is called the approach
to death the imminent piece of sculpted marble
so much to admire without knowing why the head
fills with rock and sagacity and the hour has no way
of starting its clock and we stop and pose in the glass
waiting for the figure to become whole ! who and why

someone always comes along with an accident and

sorrow becomes paramount the grieving sororities

of noise and reckoning and to put to rest the small

deer who have died for no reason at all by the house

which is the reunion of symbols and dark ! how many

times do the moons pass from view ? pyramids and

archaic longing the wish to remain forever

06-14-22

A SONNET BASED ON LINES BY GIACOMO LENTINI

"Quand'eo li parlo moroli davanti,

e paremi chi vada in paradiso,

e tegnomi sovrano d'ogni'amanti"

Giacomo da Lentini

I am sovereign of all that love return to paradise

before I stand and die it seems to me if I speak

and none remain who cast en eye to other worlds

below or above the finish line of time this spark

divine this otherness of flesh this twin of light

that abides before I go and lets me enter paradise

I go and among the sentient grasses turn to shade

the last of all summers a spent lamp of intensity

in paradise its glow is a splendor glorious to behold

and should I speak and before her my turn to die

a wish to lessen night's eternal stroke and to some

I am sovereign still who love and abide by rock

and stone the wheel that turns I learn to die and

summers gone and madness before I stand to die

06-14-22

WHITE-ARMED HERA : A SOLILOQUY

what is wrath and to rage against the light ?

cities are wrath with their turbid boiling waters

to be colloquial is wrath and to be in love is darkness

the self is ire against breath and the multiple vowel

water is feminine anger the volley of steam that

obliterates the sky in denial and futility

beauty ! gorgeous and sumptuous melancholy

to rave against brick and marble the venues of night

sentries posted at every hour armed against the eye

starlight and flickering firefly the sameness of death

eventuality of betrayal at every turn of the drama

in their knee-high boots and deer-pelts the Nymphs

who conduct subtle stratagems of envy and deceit

love again ! beautiful languages taut as bow-strings

that inveigle and disarm the heart and divide its consequences

in a teratology of absence and mourning the deceased

left to wash ashore like Adonis in his 17th century poem

the thousands in an equal state corpses of desire

what is news from the Orient ? the black sun is rising

to take in its obscure flame the endless mountains
the dialects and passions of sound made to imitate
the species of mind and its desperation to know
what lies outside the borders of thought—Folly !
daughters of Harmony ! illusions are wrath and sunlight
what is the news from the Orient ? today is nowhere
clinics and libraries and burning open pits that spread
miasma as far as hilltop Mycenae of the lion-Gates
noise and bickering ! swarms of unintelligent ideas
that poison an afternoon's idyll by the rivers of Longing
resonance of doubt and suspicion that govern sleep
intuition to flee ! crime spawns crime in the stage-play
where puppets with human pronouns plot to seize
control of the cities ! in absentia Zeus the Iron-monger
is greater than in his presence and motels turn to smoke
living altars dot the shorelines boats cannot sail !
there must be someone writing in the clouds this epic
fragment these delusional syllables this oracular
presumption of emotions and intelligence
who am I Queen-of-the-Heavens ? paper and tinsel
children perform the park and become in turn
the small deer they are meant to represent and drown
in sadness indistinct memories of leaf and grass
the waning of all principle and horizon
Grief !

06-15-22

MANITOU WINNEBAGO DEATH HOUSE

for Slade Schuster, Bob Ness, James Balfour & Tom Davis

turn left on the road to Bamber Valley
where the broken bridge where the signals
mutate and sky's indeterminate inch fades
into a bleached stark moment
inescapable from the ruin of the school hour

is the spirit world the continuation of something else?
is there something we have forgotten to see?

when you get to the top of the hill
which hill you may well ask
where the haunted house stands surrounded
by an orchestra of whispering pines
take your skin off before going in

not sure who is talking who is thinking these thoughts
where the individual goes falling asleep
are you?

the afternoon coming home from a random place
called nowhere deep in the silver woods
by a lake without summer 'neath a moon
without gravity a system of suffering a notion
to die without anyone knowing

like the time we were driving in dense fog
white-hell of eternity and drinking to a song
about distance and flight Angel hit the hood
and Whang! went flying into a ditch
what did we know ?
all rust and feathers remnants of a god ?

far to the north of anywhere the sibilant torment
of winds without compass nor compassion
through all possible cracks of the universe
freezing temperatures and flayed hides
snapping in the ultimate degree cold
nothing visible but sleep

the norm of identity is plural in pronoun and thumb
exegesis of sounds heard before birth
the long epilogue to immortality cloudy and
with predicted rains and higher heat
levels of sanity in question walking
that long lonesome route to bedlam

when you get there the long-house still stands
as identified in the logjam and river-wend

pioneers of death ! they are making a map
of total rectilinearity wiping out the hills
and their totem dialects and

on pond surface with green scum

the reflections of the small deer

worshipped in the once-before

we will not stay long the ears are tolling

enormous afternoon memories of cuprous

noise of jangling sleighs tossed aside

of deities wearing make-up and tight jeans

prepared to whoop it up Saturday night

in the cavernous ball room

of the after-world

the highways ! diesel traffic heading east

promises of a new life of unending dawns

nothing curtailed of breath the illusory

dominance of a single word salvation

and fluorescence of an alternate sky

far to the beyond of longing

(Minnesota 1956)

06-16-22

COMING FULL CIRCLE

at the point where sky ceases being interminable
there will we meet again a summer of instants
multiples of zero in the green integer of memory
when everything is conditional in the fixity of loss
a hand presumed its shape would endure forever
and fingers in the sepulcher of grass and waning
perpetually in search of the shadow-knowledge
of circularity the twin events of birth and death
simultaneous as the flick of a switch and walls
that burn in the spatial remote of the origins
and come to terms with speech and its confusion
which is me which is you ? never answer the question
proceed through the maze of consenting air posed
by a primitive sonnet in its heat and cold of desire
the sensations ! the myriad seconds we confounded
identity with the shirts we wore or the incomplete
Latin of a day in the sun each the mirror of the other
river-bank and collision of particles trees amazed at
their own spirituality reaching for unspoken heavens
leaf and bower nests and birds with human eyes in
flight with sleep the hovering inconstancy of infinity
where did it all happen ? by the knee in the garden
soil of the ancestors tilling dirt and worm upheaval
the nature of the cosmos in the bead of sweat clinging
to the nape or brow and teasing specters of dead kids
on a gala highway romp and the dance ! sections

of wind and song haunting the ear with immortality

a pyramid to climb ! a motel to hide with drugs !

the so many that never materialized and small

animals feeding from the palm of the hand and

paintings of the never-before-seen in your mind !

come home ! the circle has been redesigned to include

the half of the moon we never visited and there

between you and me and the road that goes nowhere

fast with its speed and viscera enigmatic invisibilities

and lay the old head down on this rock and listen

for the moment to begin again spectra and noise

leafage of the archaic and the pool where we dived

to discover the famous underworld of Teotihuacán

axolotls of divinity ! now it is time to fold the map

climb the ancient stairs and back to bed waiting

for Mother-of-Paradise to put us to sleep again

06-17-22

DRIVING A STOLEN CAR WITH
A GODDESS IN THE BACK SEAT

must learn to leave the persons behind

in the back seat alone and shining a goddess

or merely a rag-picker from the abandoned hotel ?

involved with beauty the selves need to multiply

looking in all directions for the Tomb !

who has not cast aside the shadow in remembrance ?
in which of the previous lives did this mask apply ?
look I am a tree ! and you a precious bird of loss !
whatever distinctions remain of breath and height
whatever the eye revolves in its insatiable sleep
whoever are the masters of the Wheel
can any of this matter even as the driven world
falls off course its axle broken and the dark sun !
tell me Brother which is the way to Oblivion
spending hours in the grammar of wound and grief
listening for the leaves to wake and talk again
and summers come and go and the fractions divide
into great seasons of resonance and longing
how did we learn to swim ? where was the chasm ?
and by now the years are reduced to gravel
and the ear fills with the testimony of a single grain
where once were fields overflowing with heat
and the cursory lessons of love and infinity
why are we here watching ourselves dwindle ?
this spine and shoulder these loosened petals rose
and ocher like the strange histories of Etruria
what do they symbolize ? life is an aggravation
doubt and miscarriage and alimony the forfeits
of a day in Court ! which of us can open the door ?
is there a mirror ? and in the back seat mysterious
and radiant yes a goddess with a hundred veils
and essences and fragrances of the far southland

where elephant and tortoise conspire to control earth
how can we ever know the cause of everything
when we ourselves are but halves of the Greater Half ?
delusion and fancy the riddles of the dance !
a day like no other this is the only Day repetition
and romance and the inconstancy of certainty !
there ! a book has disclosed its missing pages
footnotes and the memory of having been !
the road ! it has no conclusion only by the side
enormous ditches where the fallen abide
selfless in search of hands to open the skies

06-18-22

MEDITATING ON A PHOTOGRAPH OF THE TWINS ON THE VERGE OF ADULTHOOD

can it be out of the shadows we emerged
other of the other brooding in symmetry
of darkness shunning light and solar homophone
the days of anguish and solicitude statecraft
of waning innocence on the edge of grammar
dynamism in fourth dimension rapt in silence
and noise of the remote and heavy tread of wheels
on lugubrious asphalt speeding to undesigned cities
to master and abandon in an hour's notice
how we shivered in the warmth of escape

and riot to become incomplete in this photograph
where we both conspire to excel in depth and
intransigence faces hooded with eternity's
brief mask the warrant to die ahead of time the
everyday perspiration to outdo the normal living
each as intent as the other to rival infinity's post-
poned high school graduation and itself
the miasma of chiaroscuro division of identities
who came first and what do ten minutes matter ?
kicking and bawling into the snow tempest
of a January riddled with geminated consonants
vowel and virtue of a Latin dialect in progress
lakes underground ! floating gardens reversed !
sky unloads its negative exposures before our eyes
let's go Man ! blues shouting evangelistic bebop!
that's what the light says scrawled over the oracle
of our faces divergent and encompassing distances
we could never again recover until sleep us parts
wearing suits too great for our knowledge and
dimensions and tripartite sonatas baroque and
intricate as the alcohol that defined us that day
the funeral of whom ! we sat pensive nonchalant
significant with an intelligence of grass and insects
clairvoyant for a moment only the collapsed
civilization we inherited in our lapels and ties
smart sharp menacing as gangsters at a wedding
who did we think we were ? Adonis ? James Dean ?

King Creole ? movies rock n roll loud and
intransigent summer cloudbursts finite as Death
around the corner and ever more inaccessible
our lapsed childhoods terraced and roofed
dizzy with cigarettes and idealized girlfriends
the end was always there the tombstone and
the Mexican sepia-tint mountain looming larger
than the diminished sky of burning celluloid
Trotskyite visions ! you 'n me, Bro' on the verge
somewhere between mojo and space-flight

06-18-22

HOMAGE TO JAMES JOYCE

what is a piece of literature ?
a scrap of paper a half-effaced parchment
a bone-text or an illegible stone inscription ?
an epitaph a tomb-marker or a roadside death !
is it ever an act of humility ?
or is it merely patterns of sound uttered
in the winds of night some far away time ?
remembrances of a blade of grass a childish scrawl
on life's forgotten blackboard a syllable !
nothing ever comes to be as it should just
events in a train of noise and shibboleth
babble and erasures in the compromising air

an echo and nothing more of a recording
made when electricity was in its infancy
the forced betrayal of lovers' vows in summer
silent invocations to deities of language and heat
what is missing from the text ? is the mirror worn
backwards in the sleeve of memory ? how is it ?
many have elucidated on the gravel that
casts a magic spell while the wheel ceases turning
yet everything else is in motion trying to express !
it was yesterday when it happened
gravity and the flux of emotions and shouts
the riot and paraphernalia of a creative thought
paragraphs that have to be filled in by squiggles
and dots of a leaking pen and the inks
and sabotage of remembrances on the pale
leaves ! the very transcription of their speech
whispers preserved in a discarded conch-shell
translations from one unknown tongue to another
guidebooks to idiomatic lunacy
anthologies culled from the weeds and marrow
of an archaic oracle that disposes of vowels
fictions in the hem of a burning dress !
designs and conjectures of mind ! histories of sand !
to teach theories of alphabetic nonsense !
attributes of red and circularity and atmospheres
where myth and legend originate
arguments between thumb and index finger

as to where the apostrophe should be placed

as if to make the world whole again !

life ! abandoned in a footnote by the raging sea

what can Poseidon do ? allure of Venus

in verse after verse of narcoleptic meter

the thigh and the shoulder and metaphors

that ring with grief and sorrow

in the end just a scrap of paper a puzzle

of letters in the ensuing darkness

silencio !

06-19-22

THE ONLY POEM WORTH WRITING

but the great desire fills me with even greater doubt

that light and all it surveys the pinnacle with its five o'clock

and the noise of sidewalks chattering airs the flames within

ardent to break bounds the lush and plangent alike a

mere glance and swept away by love's first chance a folly

the world's subtle errors the rumors of distance and azure

flights of mind into nascent tongues idioms too complex

to speak only to languish at the portals of longing so why

is night before afternoon will out and chasing reveries

and drugged by nonchalance and passion the fumes and

resonance of the heart like an abandoned railway line

how ! to remember what it was that signaled the blaze

that tore through the veins like riptide and splash !
omicron and omega on either wrist the plumes of winds
zephyrs of platonic hesitation and abloom with madness
the laced greenery of a sudden season wrestling like ivy
on ancient brick the reddened indifference that day-stars
dispel and relentless thought to overcome and create
anew the description of the eye's continent of love
stay ! yet do pass in a trice the vanishing years the sweet
hives the melancholy and distress the forgetting ! when
is a dialect more like a hill than death ? we plunge again
and again our memories trying to retrieve that eternity
which is nothing but instantaneous reconditioning a poem
the first and last ever to be written and recited and repeated
and strike the changes on its chords replacing vowels for
obscure noises and to sleep inconstant to what we promised
to be forever ! leaf and dark the evanescent day gone
the long and fading sound that empties the ear of its past

06-20-22

HOW LONG IS AN AFTERNOON IN ETERNITY ?

it's this box we live in this scenario
painted on a moving screen somewhere
because we are born still-life and of our own
cannot shift from planet to planet and aware
of sigma and tau and deposit slots for airmail

messages to the outer limits we polish the crown

reddening the intense inch between then and now

how is it ever possible to reach the hill

to rest and delve into by-chance memories

of the day when and the lawns that spill over

the markers and roads of inconstant detours

we linger longing to hear the swarms in hazy azure

to return ! and to forget as never before

innocence lapsed in the several myths

laid in stone engraved epistolary of sound

relegated to some icon of silence in a past of

pure hazard to ask if you are still with me this long

afternoon of windows and storms the tremendous

rain that lasts infinite seconds with a paperback

full of ghazals and chansons to be memorized

phonetic decay consonant clusters and night

a hand is a digression five fingers and grass

the weaving and embroidery of fiction

to be read aloud and Daphne and her hair

turned to marble and still speaking Italian

as she enters the black honey of her death

leaf and bark the twisted branches darkening

a god is to touch and lose consciousness

06-20-22

GRIMOIRE : SUMMER SOLSTICE

what are we to make of this great volume ?

no amount of page-turning reveals its contents

the sun is a black index ! what are right angles ?

the world is enveloped in a parenthesis of flame

a mere cinder in the terrific rush of the cosmos

hurtling between deafening sound and deafening silence

etymologies of mineral deposit and fish-scales

written in a language only leaves can hear

chapter headings in archaic stone and sleep

densities of ink derived from a secret Latin lexicon

what are afternoons on Saturn ? which is the hand

and which is the finger that guides through ruin ?

what is weight compared to memory ? between

the front cover and the back a host of insects

that fly and buzz and hum of illiterate phonics

if only we could remember what direction to take

passed around by word of mouth the text begins to burn

long passages describing the downfall of angels

subscriptions to demonology and the fierce echo

of sounds that render meaning useless and illustrations

depicting flight and amnesia and melancholy

children who have been denied ! acrostics and ivy

the greenery of a false season known as summer

mountains ! the secret is in them and their wings

that flutter between the penultimate word of each page

and the useless diacritics of a day on trial

who can account for aphasia ? swart solar horses !

everything is about to take place if only one

had a knowledge of letters and signs and noise

situationism and an inability to read from right to left

prophets without number ! sacred script in free fall !

here and here are the wounds and the gauze and petroleum jelly

the radio is on fire ! voices detonated by a single wire

I am Orestes ! soon it will be Thursday afternoon

in the morgue and the gyres and triangles of air

backwards and front up and down the brow

listening for the corrected Delphic syllable

Apollo ! Hermes Trismegistus ! Thoth !

earth is an enigma of unutterable scribbling a nuance

of breath and longing and whoever can recall the birth

before the Birth and the essence and the being afterwards

whoever is King ! nature's immense library of birds

and the lore of wind and chasm the very Volcano !

tomorrow has been postponed and the lecture

salvation is at the whim of the Goddess-of-day's-end

drugs and potions and revival ceremonies and the wit

to forget everything and to lay the head on its stone

disremembering the word-order and the hexameter

things are not as they are ! Light at a stand-still !

catalog of the Eye ! absence of the All !

06-21-22

WEDNESDAY ELEGY

is it the compassionate Buddha or Narcissus

who stares back at me from the pool of memories ?

mirror image of a stranger in the garb of the other !

what was I once in the far off a butterfly an ornament

worn on the brow of a semi-divine entity a mere cave-echo ?

market day a cart with two white oxen bearing wares

fine stuff silks from Cathay a brocaded chemise

in whose sleeves opium is smuggled as a perfume

for the mistress of a piece of fiction in the courtyard

of the Japanese emperor ! rules and regulations of air

symbols of water and the eternal feminine in hues

that match both speed and gravity in the sleeping ear

leaves that talk to poets in the middle of an oracle

the nature of the cosmos summed up in a thumbnail

and the rose that grows in defiance of windows and

the sun with its enormous noise of darkening glass

who can account for this day ? death is in the most

minute dew-drop in the way grass yields to winds

in the fixed glance of the spotted deer moistened

by remembrance of a different birth and sky itself

the transparent membrane of a forgotten summer

afternoon when we returned from the liquid depths

to become ourselves for a transient moment each

the face of the other untranslatable pronouns of sound

registry of a memorized poetry thousands of hexameters

in length and the seas that rhyme ! exhausted by

waking prepared for another Wednesday to whittle away

the excursion of time through the unperceived brow

a flash of light the breath of a brief energy and grief

at every turn of the road and to wait listening for

but never hearing the ignition that starts the engine

of Mind ! all I survey in this trance called life is

but the simultaneous repetition of images syllables

names with no attachment to thought enigma and

precipice of the universe on the edge of the Hour

a starving Gautama a drowning Narcissus flowers

culled by an invisible hand whose vanishing fingers

go diminished in the plural shadow of oblivion

06-22-22

LIFE THE LYRICAL WAGER

birds fled in terror of the half-moon and armed

the woods with men strangers in glistening mail

whispered leaves and lay down the grasses to shadows

mighty before refulgent the sun's broad entry made

way for expanses of land ready to burn earth's apex

a corollary to sound the immense booming of craters

no greater than the ear of human folly and then did

error roam amid sleeping trenches and their swords

twitching for blood the thirst in epic vowels the lines

arrayed in mysterious contest syllabic densities and could

hear chatter of spirits the mingled dead still alert
to memory and the abiding soliloquy of oblivion and
who and when the thrust of language the noise above
the din of archaic seas ribboned with gold and ships
that ply mind's neglected austerities the virgin voice
risen from the oracle's pondering stone how could
be this event a flame from waters drawn to trace
like letters in the fleeting clouds and then drums did
resound and repetitions of ceremony and scrutiny
the lessening quarter of the invisible realms a hue
and bluster the forms emerging from a single hand
and divinities in disarray goddesses with pleats of
ivory and gravel in their dishevelment crying for
a comb a tie to bind wild locks their eyes savage with
red vengeance still echoing words half-understood
aulic distances of pure marble quarried from childhoods
in the thoughtless paradise of bees and hummingbirds
enormous and beautiful the Buzz ! sawing uneven
hemispheres of air with a melody none can recall
except in deepest sleep and then again clangor and
mourning distilled references to death the almighty
and swart horses plunging like planets out of a Lamp
the gauzy filaments of fate torn this way and that
that mortals can never understand why the marching
relentless of consonants out of formation and decibels
of ambulance-driven tragedies played out on a paper
that can barely sustain its ink ! life the lyrical wager !

forensic interludes of pyramids upended and the sands
that blow from nowhere to erase the corrugated brow
is this what once was ? kings claiming ancestry of ivy
cymbals and clashing rocks and destinies of mud
insect larva pupae blindly searching for a pronoun
the burdened masks of tyranny and isolation aflame
to you and me the Poem ! recitations of silence
night with its unencumbered vertigo of stars
blowing out one by one in time's witless dance

06-23-22

DECONSTRUCTING MEMORY

hundreds of years in a single lightning flash
what part of the alphabet is that ?
whether we follow Rama in his jungle retreat or
Aeneas in his flight from Troy to an unbidden west
where stubble unhewn rock and gravel reveal
the first Italian poem ever memorized
we still remain outside the pool of reveries listening
for the one voice among the many shouting
the summons from the statue of sleep
to wake and seize the heat of unseen corn fields
in some part of the brain the summer of 1956 is unending
a woman who represents all mothers embodies
this unique July of constant thunder-bursts

abiding by our longing for antiquity

to her we lean and whisper pages of assonance and ivy

the secret of immortality is buried in her ear

is Nahuatl the original language ?

what is an epiphany ? what is hem-stitching ?

which is the first place in the next world to visit ?

what is the double imperative which gave us birth ?

isolated and geminated we circle the same month

trading pronouns affixing vowels to the enigma

playing dead in the small rapture of grass

evening ! the foundation of loss !

the sun is a darkening glass destroying grammar

everything is an accident on highway 52 heading east

we have drowned in that tiny mere outside Mayowood

in search of the deer our souls inhabit

counting backwards in Catalan we arrive somehow

at the wharf where Columbus docked his three thoughts

we own the New World ! we are finally Aztecs !

the cigarette at the apex of Intelligence can never be finished

you and me los cuates dandled on our grandfather's knees

the right knee is yours and mine is the inflected point

in a photograph taken in the prehistoric moment of Heaven

necessary and indispensible consonants clustered

in the back of the garage on First Street

with its mysterious whetstone wheel and empty whiskey

the neighbors are always watching ! they Know !

what is a diamond needle ? where do afternoons go ?

we keep going back to the spot where sound was invented

hearing and sleeping and dreaming and waking

absolutely Nowhere ! it is a mountain ready to fly !

it is because I cannot be in mind without you

and windows are forgeries of light

the Platonic symposium is where we got drunk

and learned that riding in the back seat is best

a total of more than eleven years separates

the still-point when dust and miasma consumed you

from the cosmic instant when you folded up your map

declaring life is an apostrophe a burning asterisk

and memory is the immense noise we cannot still

06-24-22

THE UNSPOKEN MOMENT ENDLESSLY EVOLVING

making way through dense rock defiles and darkness

the seas a distance from the eye and sleeping sees

never to be turned back the rout of noise and bodies

assailed the tormented dream a sail snapped in twisted

winds rains the thunder-struck a mast of hope deleted

so forth went with poem in hand the unopened book

an afternoon spent and gone to the ragged shores once

arrived set foot and sandy mapless terrain misunderstood

a flinty speck of light in the roiling angry cloud-mass

undertook to think and stand-still the instance of sound

that separates this life from the next a script unraveling
in the turbid air to read if possible like Chinese signs the
stone-lanterns unlit and beckon a goddess suddenly as
a wraith appears in garments unspoiled wavering feet
inches from the turf to command with eerie voice beyond
meaning syllables uttered to grapple enigmas the altars
to set fire and tar and pitch to burn night's awning
away ere day come forth unwarranted and cursed who
did this spell indict this text unfurl shaping diphthongs
the goddess her raiment rent into the sky returned
a last and longing sigh of warm breath and caverns of hours
the signals like asterisks now disappearing in the zodiac
houses misspelled windows and dormers and memory
of the Hive and the mountain-side in bloom all hues
of antiquity stone and gravel underfoot did circle to
no end the fuse and with hands useless in their pivot
attempt to shape destiny fingers and pulse the vivid
moment when not one but several words nascent in
their husks of oracular ciphers how far ! to learn
to read to second the scope with intuition to move the
pennant and its meaning at last to fix if only for this
brief lifetime a portion of immortality aside and Lo !
brother and friends the lawns traverse in dawn's ire
to illumine the pages of the evolving tongue and shout
as if from a statue born the confused childhood of
recollections and plastic playthings and space-travel
however distance can allow the massive ornaments that

revolve in the advancing atmosphere Planets ! each with
a number and significance and turning fast to the small
pool of air growing in fractions of mind returning as it
were to its bedrock of archaic augury to know if nothing
else to realize the seconds of time that cannot be seized
alas the edges worn the maimed thought the cursive
script illegible in its wreck of homophones how did
this come to be asked again and repeated an echo
traveling from ear to ear and rests no more anywhere
the knitted syncopation of language in its labyrinth

06-25-22

SOME MEDITATIONS ON THE UNSPEAKABLE

Oh ! sun comes in rollicking his swart black horses
homophones of time the restless moments gone
endlessly bright for just a few hours then does
death his chance toss the dice of fame and loss

What ! grass fades its sheen of verdant luster
drowned in phases of untimely play its orient a
sudden shape gone wrong the day's barricaded
sounds but faint echoes in evening's distant swoon

But ! for leaf and sparrow the cloven skies amassed
distinctly thundered in some deity's sovereign ear and

came crashing night-planets hell-sent burning rains
what was to know of their small reflections ?

This ! call it life name it breath summon the lamp
to shine its exegetical splendor and wane away unseen
did they not seek to pretend with others and numbed by
grammar and pronouns to unknown depths returned

Evermore ! they say unspoken eternities in a single blow
the instant fire invents itself and smoke of ladders builds
the famous regard for shadows the vanished letters that
form the alphabet but can never conclude its scripts

How ! this otherness to divide hemispheres into remote
metaphors the likenesses of what went before memory
held its sway and to conjectures of noise and cloudy spheres
to nights of green burning asterisks in oblivion's infinity

Why ! so much to name and so little to comprehend
unpronounced diacritics the small deer staring startled
into the camera's eye and to dwell forever in negatives like
dreams in some child's dying wish to come to life again

Who! has made this error great this rumor of undying ?

06-26-22

ON THE BANKS OF THE ZUMBRO RIVER

the sun rains without number its embroidered rays

the infinite is a small digit beside the ire of his lamp

and yet finds us mere sacks of breath alight wandering

between rock and mire the world to measure in thumb's

span and the index aimed at eternity's invisible arc

beside and before or behind you walk brother with me

among the countless ghosts who have already forgotten

their own names and toward this pasture of memory

this secluded river bank come to discourse on the source

of madness we each harbor in the filaments of our soul

even as the willow bends to weave its slender-leafed

branches with shadows the vanishing tegument of mask

and pronoun persons who once yielded to your arguments

to disdain the material life for one of superior intent

the unheard music that governs the immortal spheres

but and always but this day curtails and summons from

the great unconscious of some other life a longing that

is never realized a summer lake a contained grove where

gather small animals who have shed their being in exchange

for a moment without recollection in the undying heat and

shine of an immemorial recognition and then to expire

unmourned leaving grief to the residents of the city

built upon the edge of oblivion and between the many

you are the least dear brother hanging on like smoke

to a ruined altar and flickering like fireflies your words

pass through the screen of distance and to capture just one

of them to bring you back beside me lying beneath the stellar

shower we once observed together sharing the nocturnal

song the airs the mountains of wind that none perceive

how far you have gone now along a trace I cannot see

and to count with numbed fingertips the quota of years

before all dissolves in the frail magma of the Unknown

06-27-22

"MORE THAN THE SUN IN OUR EYE"
E. Pound

things we have never seen yet strike the winds

like drums in the sleeping ear and stone hoods

that gleam with ancient rains do we step out

from boyhood into the vast unknown athwart

boats that cannot float and sails that snap loud

in the intermittent silences that brood on memory

what village and plains sloping down from heavens

obscured by a cinematic tempest do we approach

as kings anointed for a day and assail with noise

of gleeful discovery yet by hour's end fail to grow

beyond that first note of archaic solemnity and

what ! the louder sun his horses cannot restrain

and fills the void with cities too enormous to

comprehend and towers that crumble with a thumb

and streets and avenues racing toward evening's

swart curtains and whatever way we choose

it always leads south to where the ornamental dead

await with their scepters and augurs' garlands

gold is sonant and the moon's unseen other side

seems to glow and fireflies that mass against

the plaintive screen can we be firm moving forth

from the gift of breath and assert another life ?

to be had been the most we could expect and to

shift as shadows among spirit-types and pronouns

and the paraphernalia of a day in time without

divisions of the minutes remaining of the light

how ! must we then return each more alone than

when we emerged from the moist dark cave to

be fulminant in the graveyard of the world

given over to play and speculation of otherness

we momentarily ascended the pyramids to their

peaks that carved from the sky whole dominions

of oblivion and disarray and called that Triumph

the exclamation marks and asterisks of a language

that passed from mind to mind recklessly lacking

sense merely an assembly of broken consonants

and vowels that vanish being uttered in dismay

can we then today apart from one another confirm

the whetstone and the mill that grind out stars

in the awesome but absent firmament of time ?

06-28-22

"WHY ARE YOUR HEARTS MAD WITHIN YOUR BREASTS?"

Iliad, VIII, 413

marveling at the great work the soul kindles

the self for the unknown trek like lightning before

the assembled gods awestruck or blinded

by Zeus omnipotent hurtling still another fiery

missile into the protracted earth below the fury

of rain-showers of pitch and asbestos bringing

forth cities mortal-occupied doom-planned how is

the birthling to know any direction ! summers

elapsed in the curve of a thumb and grass grown

overnight to the size of distance and yearning

everything rushes to a point of darkening madness

the urge to increase and become all-knowing

consuming chapters in the Book-of-Lost-Knowledge

taking on stances and allegros of nonchalance

and standing wide between the insect planet and

the vanishing noosphere bedeviled by doubt

at every traffic-light wondering that machinery

has come this far and the talking instruments

that plague the air and the divisions of thought

into unequal hemispheres of radiance and destruction

a Greek epic ! heroes destined to plunge headfirst

on painted postcards into Hades fates and auguries

that will be repeated in every generation that

owns to breath and from afar the enormous green

foliage the leaves that have learned to speak and

just as quickly fallen into aphasia over-hearing
that man's lot is nothing more than a spear of light
spent the minute it is cast into the atmospheres
so goes the soul into other worlds of chaos and grief
the last thing it will ever experience is the Echo
of the ancient birth-pang in rock and gravel
in an earth long relegated to the passage of time
tossed asunder between the trillions of galaxies
that remain forever unnamed without a pronoun

06-29-22

THE PAINTED BARGE

the painted barge the skull that governs history
afloat somewhere near miasma and the porticos
of hewn marble that have stood centuries without
blemish and the skies lower than yesterday glowering
cloud-stuff anti-matter aphasia and literature
voices barely discerned through the din of devils
in their fancy suits and ties and strutting like poetry
in a recital chamber the music tuned up to Dorian
pitch and the rhetors and sophists declaiming one
another the benefits of liberal education and alcohol
the canals give up to dry lots weed cluttered and
distant with torn billboards and diesel roar
in the dusky background the world's a septic tank

an avalanche of dust and cinders dimly sparkling
skyscrapers operated by remote control in the emirates
the world's gone ashes the painted barge hauled
to the mudflats for repair smell of motor-oil
and bracken rot the pollution is of the gods !
who has ever seen them ? evidence is in stone and
inscriptions so illegible as to be useless sounds
and noises that assail the ear and seas roiling madly
just below the hair-line of Aphrodite—can it be ?
hands in search of their others and gloves discarded
and archaic in their convolutions tossed into the ditch
beside the entrance to hell between two gasoline pumps
abandoned since the last war and the occasional
appearance of girls naiads wearing Venetian cast-offs
glitter of illusion and tarnished jewelry in bad light
who can account for the end of the world ?
listing in the shoals the painted barge—
let's name a few of those gone from days of yore
Etruscan hosts gravediggers Livius Andronicus
shop owners who have lost the way making lists
of items no longer available the plaintive sirens
of medical wheels charging through the unlit night
children ! what fault is it of theirs that disease
and death are still with us and long siege-works
walls and masonry totally in disrepair and orators
and teachers of forgotten tongues and at last the sight
of a mountain in grief for loss of its wings
flights canceled airborne spores in free-fall waters

and the feminine gender of the nouns they employ

as a means to salvation paraphernalia without patents

and on and on the futile books and recorded music

on disks spinning uselessly south of the equator

where the dead are warehoused in Quonset huts

alas ! will I never see my brother again ?

06-30-22

PALAEONTOLOGY

had we but known what it said in the first language

they pondered over sound and leaf the mystery

green once then marveled that breath no more

issued and the stain was on the winds the unseen

trembling at the root shivering the grass who

they were if a path were laid out to trace the way

the soul was delivered on its wing and the spray

and stir of an animal in the brush a leopard

with symbols for eyes and could hear the drum

of the heart and called that life-force however

diminished and named the trees great spirits

listening whether night went beyond the dream

to wake ! always a miracle searching among the

flowers for the goddess who had approached

coming forth from the surf feet inches from earth

and instructions given and plans for dwellings

the city ! there we were unfolding and folding

the yellow scraps designations and directions
could we but understand north from west and
the hills where the sun slept and birds in flight
twelve at a time and what to do with the patterns
in the air and the associations with words if any
the depths ! to paint by ear the recalled accident
the boys learning to spear distance and hands
of recoil calling the shadows by ancestral names
and huddled in the winter of the eye always intent
on some message from the clouds gathering in
the collective memory colliding with stone and
water which they claimed was woman ! today
keeps being a repetition and formations of noise
adjectives and metaphors which are nothing but
a literature of sorts the enormous colored arc in
the mind that is the sky ! summers ! now there
are roads and structures four and six floors from
the ground and elevators and x-rays and tubes
that move under the surface and yet death for
which the word is fixed in rock and passed around
by hand as if it were a tattoo in the palms something
to read and resound the echo ! watching as we do
how one by one the pronouns assigned at birth
worn from use pass through the atmospheres
and fade away nothing but detritus in the ear
and we sleep we sleep in the claim of infinity
souls leaves blades of grass unborn birds

07-01-22

ANESTHESIA

comes a time when sun quells his unruly steeds

night as it must the tempestuous adjectives of the stars

where is the glass that reflects back the autumn of time ?

sitting as we do in the despair of the ages counting

ciphers and asterisks as they wane and drop from view

the library with its enormous Saturday portals !

when moon trailing behind a sulfurous distance

and the din and roar of planets plunging senselessly

into the inner ear and Venus or Pluto in disregard

with the gravel of memory in small gardens

tagged for illusion and aphasia in the backdrop

of language the ever inconstant confusion of vowel

consonant and accent the triple digit hills and grief

how does one dialect become so separate from another ?

grammar ! rules to still the conscience and mourning

as noon approaches with its convoys of resonance and

echo defining heat and the incremental switch to darkness

does the knee ever cease weeping ? cathedrals and

statuary positioned for speech always abating and the clinic

and its monumental spire of amnesia and what's more

the carillon and the effusion of sound at five o'clock

when the matador gives up the ghost in his labyrinth

of Spanish poetry and the girls in tow of the centaur

who grazes on the effaced lawns of history how they laugh

at troubadours or mendicant devotees of the Buddha

lost in the dusty paths leading in and out of the same Hour !

no one arrives ! centuries are curtailed in a thumbprint
literature is assailed for mendacity and the scourge
of rhetoric and augury ! comes a time when the cosmos
with its infinities of vanishing lights turns off its noise
silence recovers its undefined body of sleep and death
mortals all we stare in amaze at the burning walls of air
flammantia moenia mundi ! yellow gauze and tapers
flickering as the head turns to stone and the eye
loses its center in a dizzying swirl of ether
dot dot dot

07-02-22

THE BREVITY OF IT ALL

para mi hermana Laurita

what makes this light these few bright rays
fingers like blades of grass the lamp that strays
a legend of hills that cannot lift to skies remote
why am I ? the streets devolve their straight ways
into terraces of sleep whitening deeper as dreams
their measure lose and cries from afar like balloons
drifting into the clouds does a church bell ring do
mourners file into the grey divide ? what afternoon
is this so dim a dusky moor or edifice provides and
sections of air and the sudden flute that burns the ear
meadows rise and streams that purl and eddy in

a memory that plies and intertwines the palaces
of magic that don't exist a storybook tale of flames
and ice the princess whose eyes are worlds divine
do I then know why ? we walk side by side on surfaces
beneath which our older selves lie buried a thought
we have that maps are true and everything else a trance
doors appear and shut their faceless glass hemispheres
entering is not the same as going forth into a night of
mountains and abysses the chalks and streamers of
play and dying which are all the same and children
who require no names and combs and prattling
on about the movies we'll never see and lengths
of time briefer than the blinking of an eye the camera
brooding on indistinct forms and motels of south
which the great highway knows and who this other
with voice just like mine can be his shirt and pants
his shoes exactly as I used to wear ! it's Joe
of course the way he stares into the fourth dimension
devising pyramids and songs of jungles wet with rain
the prime number is up ! space has a single boundary
the day's hours are like the minds of bees ! all hum
and devotion to the deathless gods whose fingers snap
and create ciphers no one can ever count ! but and
alas ! the one hour allotted us has come and gone
what did we know ? alive what does that mean ?
here was Second street and here the yellow unfolding
maps of cities we'll never visit and here's the movies

and the tales of dying and sadness of a sunny afternoon

bang ! bang ! you shot my horse ! bang ! bang !

why won't you get up again ?

07-02-22

MUSA PUERILIS

flower-collecting through the ages leaves and ivy

swarms of honey-bees from Hymettus and love-letters

inscribed on tree trunks in the archaic archipelagos

what is that winged thing that flies from the heart ?

she-loves-me-she-loves-me-not a butterfly a blind fire-fly

that maps the dark of all recensions Ezra Pound and Longinus

painting by ear all the sounds that red imagines staining

a thigh of wind the purple crocus that dies with sunset

the path to Narcissus and the nativity of sorrow

in waters feminine in gender and other nouns that flit

in the gravid air of love's tumult a song if only it could hear

and the length of a thumb in tribulation a pair of knees

the sockets where music unwinds its threnody

brief fields of distance and heat the panoply of clouds

named after vestal virgins and Romulus ! a god swooped

up by the pen of history kingdoms of the illiterate

where was first the lion-gate erected ? and the fleet ?

set to sail through maelstrom and plots of fiction

a deity for every hour of the day and evening with its

terrible assembly of consonants meant to glitter

forever and a day until Venus and her thronging nymphs

the lands retake and set asunder palaces and quarries

where to go with girlfriend ? to amaze with plaits of words

left to books and their artificial realities what else ?

among the blooms a symphony of hues a chaconne

variants of crimson and amaryllis the flowing breeze

that takes rapt Helen from her divorce to southern climes

where Hawk and Crocodile conspire with grammar

to set new rules hieroglyphs depicting unfought battles

and signs that alter the sky in a moment's notice even

as distraught pairs of lovers wander from the schoolyard

in search of the ship that will contest the seas of Love-and-

Death and set sail by hour's end to worlds of spice and

travail a poetry and desperation of undiscovered words

to heighten amorous detail and flattened specters omicron

and deceptive tau flutter like banners in the cloudy murk

what now ! whose hand is the token of shape and desire

whose small fingers wrap around the dice of bone

the halcyon moment when heart-break and reunion

seem as a promise from gods of language and resonance

yes and no the filaments that drill the late day's foil

and head to stone the eyes go out and all ends as in a

tale from ancient Thessaly enchantments and roses

and thus the errant spool of thought the dividing

line between fields of grief and fanciful daydreams

with their clinics and ringing carillons the unrevised

stroll back and forth from the stream of imagination

to the second page of a Latin textbook with pictures

of spear-heads and gaping crevices through which

fall painted heroes to their hell-doom and the boys

reciting irregular verbs or parsing hexameters

that seem to have no end and distance and longing

the heart fetter with chances of no-return the dying

vowels that cling to girls and combs and ribbons

the braids tied into knots only Persephone can untie

lands below earth and earths that have been burnt

on altars with the famous anthologies of yore

poems epic fragments hymns to goddesses small

lyrics tear-filled expressions that lie by the roadside

as cumbersome ox-carts wend their way to sunset

somewhere in the dusky hills west of knowledge

leaf and burrow the evanescent burden of night

07-03-22

MY FIRST AND ONLY POEM

"The woods of Arcady are dead"
       Yeats

here I sit 'pon thy gilded tomb dumbfounded

these last few centuries and still in ignorance

linger beside waning poplars and skies

of cloudy speculation whole afternoons in rout

of desire and longing the spent passion of

words too few to orient and symbolize

the heart's great event unspoken soundless

as the death that follows Orion through

the glittering spheres this moment of audition

before invisible gods whose language is a

brevity of noise and cavernous echo a paint

staining Zephyrus who blows in mourning

over sere meadows and ivy that once spanned

walls of moldering brick and rampant guile

a wonder to have started from the middle

spinning to either end a beginning of cropped

roses and daffodils the winds to their bosoms

hold for an eternity of instants and in the air

a memory disintegrates of love's languor and

opium while shepherds of distance wander

dazed of mind lost and unslept nights though

planets and day-stars set in motion a statuary

of light and mottled remnants of ancient speech

that echo in the repeated ear of mute stone

in ethereal silence I once wrote in disappearing

ink emotion and instability when everything

is discovered for the first time and pale queen

the moon shows her fading horns how thrilled

the eye to watch and count the greening stars

envy and resonance of brassy shields the hue

of trembling atmospheres the first and last

noon of time before the rusted cannon that

guards the poet in his mocked reveries

I wrote I write and keep writing these stanzas

lines that abruptly disappear and reappear

when all maps have been folded and the empyrean

shifts its thumb of inches to the Etruscan west

hills and dialects and dusky woods where

an augur marks the entrance to Inferno with

an Ypsilon of cold flame and Lo ! a voice scarce

from the leaves is heard a lament of tragedies

births and deaths on their whetstone wheel

small inscriptions bone-texts sonant gold

that riddles the script of Being before the vast

unnumbered silence erases all I ever wrote

since first I sat 'pon they gilded tomb

07-03-22

THE COMING AND THE GOING

pathological intent of the lyrical in surprise

the coming and going through the revolving instant

! flash and anatomy of air because speaking and

began to recite without knowing why the labyrinthine

verses of the Rg Veda altars and sacrificial flares and

priests beholden to stone and wind and the densities
of corporeal desires the deathless inanity of breath
it is hard to believe I am still here the so many
parts of me who have died the mind's personae
fractured and scattered like pieces of Osiris
bloody remnants of words unpronounceable shaking
in winds drawn from the hip and blowsy memories
of love-soaked sheets the irony of nightfall at 3 PM
was I ever other than who I am today a representative
of skin and mask a forged litany of rescue efforts
in dialect and at the root a kind of aphasia
to be able to relocate all the right sounds that added
up form meaningful integers a cosmic thought !
is it heat ? or the contest of wit ? cognition !
to feel everything again for the first time and
butterflies like children among the leafage
and blooms and the grass intrepid wonderful dark
the maze of an element no one understands and
to put your finger on it and call it language
the famous error of noise and rhyme the rumor
of history just coming and going and the head grown
heavy as stone and to sleep it off in Greek !
the absurdities are what's real the coming of age
in a trice in love with the first stranger who makes
eyes at you and the Friday night chase to bedlam
amorous contingencies ! the State Hospital !
is it Anatolia ? or the hybrid corn grown in fields

where Scheherazade and I used to play at kissing

fondling adjectives that transpire at the touch

gone ! metal and winter have taken over

threats of disease and the rout of dying

once and for all and the stammering routines

of denial and owning to madness for salvation

OK ! I did it writing the self-same edgy verse

in iterations of fifty or even seventy thousand times

howling at the moon lonesome coyote of Olmstead County

and the Cocytus and Acheron below my feet burning

nowhere to turn but the graveyard to lure the shades

who I once was ! am I here today ? the fireworks

are still scheduled for tonight and the celebration

at which I have always been a foreigner an other

coming and going relentlessly phantomatic

07-04-22

THE HALF-LOST POEM

decked the right bank with all manner of flowers

like a garland for one recently dead and prepared

for the journey out and on the opposite bank

fixed a wheel and rock and stone to grind

and voices on the alert causing winds to pause

and let down the branches and the suffixes to nouns

of no little value and the reading from a bone-text

and the memories of the departed soulful and
like so many other Tuesdays no sooner come then
gone into the atmospheres and the drone and buzz
of bees nonchalant in the afternoon's hyacinth-
drenched ear and what else is to make the knees
stammer and the shoulders to weep with human
weight and the loss of balance on the tight-rope
and the smaller conflagrations just outside the copse
and suddenly the poet in his tatterdemalion robe
and astrolabe steps forth reciting backwards his
once prophetic auguries and the stare in his
eye gone to the right where unseen planets plunge
into the hour of need and rescue workers whose
intent is to salvage the soul's precipitous remains
appear with a stretcher and a Berlitz grammar
of ancient early fossil Italian to communicate
with the now half-dead poet listing leeward and
whom they lay on the canvas even as his speech
transforms into a hill-dialect a rumination on
the many suns that have disappeared there and
soon his night of fireflies and shimmering asterisks
is upon the land and the busy insect hemisphere
vivid for a moment returns to its epic stillness
a gravity of distance and missing rhymes reigns
the half-lost poem descends to its postcard Hades
unheard forgotten and wrapped in leafy silence

07-05-22

ELEGY : JULY 2022

forsaken by the margins porphyry and eglantine

small rewards for a lifetime drilling the Muse

beatific delusions afterschool on the promontory

that reaches indecisively for the stellar moors

ready to falter fail and fall at any moment

the rope frequently snapped the tag-ends of verse

broken off for lack of suture the words themselves

inadequate for the skin's response to time and

dwelling even deeper within the small cameos

of girlfriend in her role as nymph bringer-of-death

bittersweet seasons encompassed in a single hour

of yearning and the scent of hives and honeysuckle

roads unmapped and houses unfit for habitation

symbols of the mind and its longing for distances

lunar and solar and swift and cutting winds that

bring down the tree-of-life in the midst of sleep

how to wake in the diapason ? looking around

confusion of splintered marble unfinished statuary

temple mounds artifacts of sound miniscule

reverberations from the insect world shaking

with an error of intellect and to shift moving

the gaze from the soul's wasteland upwards to

the ladder of illusions where a final cigarette

waits to be smoked in a drama of metaphor and

pronoun in which each mask is an enigma without

identity a fiction in aphasia and memory-loss

where are we ? rumor of buzz-saws and flying

things looking for human remnants faces and

punctuations of thought elevators and bathyspheres

a cinema of interjections and alcoholism weary

of the feet that maintain the shadow's balance

even as earth tilts off axis and blood rushes

to inform the iconography of noise that history

was concluded yesterday in series of phonetic

disasters that no hexameter can repair and

leaf and grass shadows of silence all that remain

of

07-06-22

THE LABYRINTH OF JOE'S VOICE

I am Joe, so I say looking to the black heavens

for the other hemisphere of my voice the swart

resounding through atmospheres archaic and new

me, Joe, the telephonic reverberation of what is

and that period is over with the incubus the radius

between thumb and index by which all time is measured

the nightmare albescent shining in fake moonlight

to dance with her that scheme is finished I am all

that remains of the sundered zygote in the winter

of birth and gather months like fallen heads of flowers

the fields once ripe now the fallow autumn of song

so cherished the skies above we scoured, I scoured,

on our backs how many thousands of nights ago

foretelling which green stellar combustion was mine

alone and the fractions of a number too great to conceive

why do I fall dead so swiftly ? here on the sidewalk

in Culver city 1945 from a wooden wagon fallen

skull-bone chipped enough to turn the brain's maze

into an array of constellations and cosmic seas

the ships to sail and mast and keen rudder the tiller

and wake parting the enormous feminine waters

and off we go, I go, how can this be death in sunlight

and reveries and gossamer fissures between loves

the evidence is there in the ashes I have become

no echo no shadow no finger missing in the grass

just me, Joe, yes I still am writing this epode

and follow the jasmine scent of after-life not the long

eerie Tibetan tunnel with blue dimness at the end

of nothing but the brother in his sleeves that last

a whole summer and back to school with compass

and network of maps geographical interpositions

that separate us, me, Joe, from the hoi polloi and

did I grow proud overweening Narcissistic with

calibrations of Mayan space travel and pyramids

yes that must have been and more, but I am still Joe

not Iván not the hermetic scribe who dawns daily

with cycles of verse and verbiage lengthy vowels and

unpronounceable consonants references to deities

shaking with the years and eons, me, the Joe of myth
and memory the kid on the outskirts of sound not
the paper boy but the real boy spent in evenings
of bewilderment called life and trying to establish
harmonic convergences and Mayan factors and
guides to the noosphere, not dead but still living in
this voice which is me, Joe, who is writing this verse
Valum Votan in my white Gandhi-garb and prepared
like the phoenix to rise from the ashes looking
and sounding just like my brother !

07-07-22

TWO MEDITATIONS ON DEATH

i

when smoke no longer clings and night yields
to the open mouths of light beckoning the dead
from their postures of ossuary and broken marble
then is waking less of grief than of hesitation
and suspect error to move forward shifting as
a color lost among the stars long since faded
and assume a sense of body however infirm
nerve and eye may appear and step as if alive
still after so many decades behind ramparts
and fosses facing a cardboard army of intellects
and rogues each with prattle and hearsay about

world dominion and the mind's enormous possibility
then do words cave in and gestures amount to
circus antics and the foils and ribbons that cast
about the airs how melancholy this reduction
this absurdity of plate-glass and tinfoil reflection
you moor the self to a small hook dangling from
a cloud-work and escape for hours mooning
in the verger where love first struck its strange
note a bell of sand a distance measured in vowels
borrowed from the Aeolian dance and who
is to say you are no better for memory's rumored
truths and assaying step by step the walkway
across some invisible divide join your shadow
to realms unseen and stunned in noontime reverie
pose for the sun to strike you down with its black
bolts sending you as an inference to the bottomlands
how often has this occurred ? wretched soul
the tiger recognizes not itself in the mirror's land
nor can hands that grapple with blades of grass
a garden make and still you listen for the foreign
pier to snap at water's edge waiting for the Nymph
to proceed in her liquid luster to embrace you
one last time when evanescent earth tilts off
course into a senseless and parenthetical swoon

ii

this big guy comes up to us with a poem in his hand
a lot of words mumbo-jumbo or be-bop in his hand
maybe not so big his face on close inspection unshaven

a derelict a hobo someone else's town drunk perchance

could be a saga or an epic fragment or some pertinent

verses from the Greek Anthology in his hand shaking

a bit now maybe from Parkinson's or a recent stroke

too young for that and a cigarette unlit at the proverbial

corner of his mouth do we know him from somewhere

left him alone last night in a bar talking to the self

that belongs to somebody else a stranger who goes

around taking souls unbidden a foreigner recently

arrived on a trawler from Costa Rica and mumbling

in dialect about the hills he left behind and something

about love the moon the isosceles triangle in the heart

versions of mountains and archaic stone residue of light

his eyes like symbols of lamps flaring in the void

what does he want ? poem in hand a crumpled piece

of paper yellowing from use and transpiration the air

suddenly darkens and a thunderbolt out of the blue

and this grizzled navvy takes on the looks of Zeus

our-father-in-heaven and starts reciting syllables

nobody understands the glass is great with his reflection

bits of grass and soil clinging to his cast-off clothes

Zephyrus whips up a small tempest about his brow

withering us with a stare from Beyond what can we do

but step back and wait for the ditch to open taking

the whole lot us into the Netherworld still hearing

his booming voice resonating with the unread poem

07-08-22

AT THE MARRIAGE OF CADMUS AND HARMONY

ask again what poetry is or is not

the red lining in the copy of breath that

emanates from the hovering cloud of summer

the dactyl left submerged in the unfinished

verse the quatrain or the ghazal lingering

in unspent ink and ask again what reason

it is to keep talking to statue and mummy alike

the unearthed consonants filled with sand

the dry river-bed of insomnia the question marks

at the end of every unuttered thought or the syllabic

equations that fetter speech and sleep above all

the ominous pitch that filters the mind

with unsubstantiated footnotes to unremembered

moments in the sun everything in a fusion

of light and verdure and the constant anxiety

to forget and only to forget the ones who passed

into other realms the ash and subordination

to fire and ether the elixirs and drugs

that compose poetry while the hand slumbers

beside its own shape and skies arise out of

a simple stone by roadside and oracles

of impending grass and the vast and numinous

sound that infers every meter with new unmeaning

a wonder we sit down with nothing in mind

and yet pour out entire Mondays of untrammeled

and pure homophones that rival the sun's great noise

spontaneous as the waters of a feminine Logos !
unconscious without cognition yet like leaves
talking in our waking-trance to mythic beings
invisible to the intellect beings that inform
the air with quantities of unseen matter
and births and false indentations of daylight
when a thunder of tremendous histories evolves
at the tip of a stylus with waxen signatures of the gods
bright crimson and like primitive Chinese allomorphs
how and what ! a poem is only a raveled skein
of hermetic conjunctions small vowels that
pass through an insect's myriad eye taking in
the cosmos of a wheat field a hundred-fold
and to burn ! to seize the electricity of a glance
from a Nymph who is not there ! adjectives and
similes and distances that yearn to die
a poem is a suffix to the innate solitude being born
and experiencing otherness without being able to define it
a death a multiple death an orient of deaths
that cannot be left alone amidst the swarming buzz
and hum of the analphabetic intuition to love

07-09-22

THE HERACLITEAN FIX

fire said I am in the body of all beings

and lay the head down as of stone below

the myriad skies governed by Kronos

and wind and ether replied and in the breath

and soul of all beings we reside restless waves

the seas beneath and rock and chasm the mighty

planet divided and myth came to be with

its hundred-headed lies and sworn to secrecy

in their elaborate unseen mansion newborn

gods and goddesses fitted and trussed in skin

of immortal nacre at once began in strife

to war with elements and language alike

and plunged between some thirty three suns

and vagrant vapors causing great illusions

and death above all in all its sweet manifestations

****

mortals learn to envy and prevaricate

and to make films and radio talk-shows

interviewing would-be deities about the origins

and the shortcomings of the cosmos and filtered

light and the waters of evanescent grammar

gender-quarrels and women determined as granite

to stand between the hemispheres of darkness

ride panther and leopard through the portals

where poetry invents enigmatic dialects

the downfall of man ! concupiscent alpha males

destroyed in failed punctuations and phonetic decay

nation states carved from illusory borders
the globe whittled down to size by poverty and famine
wars kindled here and there and cities full of rage
apocalyptic parking lots filled with burning metal
and tires spinning out of control and expressways
without direction swerving into mephitic clouds
 a wonder to see the morrow ! tottering Kronos
all spit and out of control urine flow wants
to speak but aphasia holds his tongue and his eyes
rolled into the red perceive only his puny brain
at one with the end of time ! where are we ?
fire and wind and ether and the roiling feminine seas
all conspire to form consonant clusters black
as the unique solar homophone and to reign
for an instant only before disappearing forever

07-10-22

THE YEARS WITHOUT MAX

"Tudo, que todo o mundo fazia, era errado"
                João Guimarães Rosa, Campo geral

sorrow for the breath cut short
      that was four years ago and the hand
puzzling over its missing shape and the wind
that bears invisible cities and histories of water
long forgotten though only four years back

cut short the aniline solution and the chemistry
of sound and reveries and the noise of literature
    or is it merely linguistic structure put
to song and the Muses errant barefoot in the hills
above San Francisco Bay of mourning and
the colossal solar homophone holding back
from heaven the steep ravine on the other side
who can guess why the years have no borders
time is the fluid intent of leaves to die
as well as the grass underfoot and the chirring
of secret insects with the bodies of gods
    sent hurtling from their planets
almost half a decade now and the positions
of asterisks in daytime that none can really see
the shine and luster of memory now a thin patina
a pastel fade and distance in the dialect of echoes
somewhere beyond the vast Pacific that rolls somber
beyond the fabled Golden Gate into a miasma of loss
do we ever understand ? to grieve the way gravel
pivots beneath the wheels and soon it is night
and more than that what is there to pronounce
a name a sequence of letters blurred
    after four brief years no calendar
can mark what the heart endures the passage of
hours the synthesis of days without number and
the relentless silence that destroys all four directions
tomorrow !

07-11-22

LAMENT FOR CHILDREN OF THE HESPERIDES

covered the whole page ancient gold flaking
nails cut too short the goddess of trim and inks
herself displays as a threat to air and cloud alike
no less the lives she abbreviates with a whim of her thumb
horses ! wild without order or direction hurtle with
the sun's terrible shout an agony of noise in ruins
the rubble that swirls for thousands of light years
between number eighty-nine and number ninety !
holes the extent of space itself and the little almanacs
consulted by astrologer and medicine-man alike
and sporting the antlers of a great dead animal
and dancing in the circle attributed to Pythagoras
copies of the goddess and her dwarfs and minions
make glee with literature reciting nonsense rhymes
in the manner of the tragedians whose memories
have been sabotaged and what of the children ?
they say enough and return to stone their little eyes
sleeping dimmed by cosmic fractures invisible to
the waking thought a process of wheels and spokes
hills that deny their own dialects histories of spools
and dimensions that last an hour what is one to declare
at the borderline where either you lose your mind
or proceed to the next traffic-signal which is hell
++++++++++++++++++++++++++++++++++
the depths the winter cesspools the septic tanks
the gutters that never empty and the forty-week rains

what good are promises of the gods if the days cannot
be distinguished and statuary resembling the judgment
of the youngest year slowly fade on the court-house lawn
there are cries and hollers and reunions with chapters
of lost books and pensions and trials by error and rumor
flags and masts of unpiloted ships deranged drowning
in the maelstrom of earthly desires and so much else
that cannot be published divine serpents whispering
mechanically in the evening grass and lorn and futile
gestures that betrayed lovers make in restaurants
governed by Greeks and Persians still at war and fiercely
resonant the mountains that appear overnight and
sacrificial fires that consume cities in a trice atom Bomb !
what is it we are trying to recover in our short passage
between the apostrophe and the exclamation mark ?
to die sundered the knee from its focus and cathedrals
of sound revolving on the tenant's grieving shoulder
houses for maniacs and gunfire that murders glass
are there indeed no windows left ? the reverberation
of stars between gamma and iota is but a pallid sign
a reckoning that the speech acts of the immortals
have exhausted their definitions and pronouns and masks
the paraphernalia that makes us human have no value
the child and the river of his inconstantly brief existence
the tray and the meter and the mistaken diagnosis
walls ! the past ! leaves torn by a missing hand

07-12-22

UPON BEING INFORMED OF MY MORTALITY

the leaves have had their say

in love's brief roundelay

what are thirty Trillion galaxies to this puny

mortal chasm the waking day with its surfeit

of obligation and debt threats of disease and

virtue's constant struggle to remain steady

in the face of massive sun-storms and comets

capable of erasing earth's fragile surface

and television shows of political rant and

movies that are reruns of a former life

was I alive when ? listen to the solar horses

as they round the western bend their hooves

striking stellar dirt and the immense lengths

of ink spent on the ever unfinished epic poem

Ulysses and the Flying Saucers ! the tragedy

of a Rose and the fornicating deities duplicitous

with their motels of graded envy and treason

give me no more years and let the span of air

between thumb and index finger be what remains

of the gift of oxygen for I am undergone a season

that can return no more and lost first loves

and friends whose speech has turned to stone

what is an error compared to the eternal inch

a blade of grass in my sophomore year and

the cannons of reveries exploding silently

in my adolescent head like ampersands and

intervals of consciousness gone astray and
to say I have loved and have no memory !
one by one the human integers fail and fade
passions of illusion and despond overwhelm
moon's arbitrary silhouettes that make for song
with lyrics unabashed of deaths gone wrong
what room is this ? in what quarter of the skies
am I afloat anonymous victim of amnesia mere
figure of speech an intaglio of absurd vowels and
noises stemming from primeval yearnings to be
what are flowers for ? burial and nostalgia for
the long summers spent in fields of ignorance
sweat and perfume and eyes of jade staring
into the abbreviated revolution of the heavens
a spark of flame a lighted wick a torch of fireflies
the dance that happens only once then darkness
the leaves have had their say
in love's brief roundelay

07-13-22

THE ERROR OF IDENTITY

I look for myself everywhere
but never find myself only the parallel abyss
of blood and thought & the acrimony of light
on trial sentenced to instantaneity by statues

that yearn to become shadows again

what shall we do with the holy corpse of memory ?

inch by inch the thumb grows distant

mountains take the place of mind

fingers of grass in an ovation of leaves

the simple eye that registers nothing of the sun

but the immense black vacuum of sound

myself is the small opening at the back of time

letting out all the excess verbiage of the years

hissing and humming and buzzing of lawns

where the body of night becomes weightless

millions of invisible insects becoming prey

to the greater and more terrible plant-world

myself is the puzzling integer of ether

or the implosion of water within an ear of stone

the draining of pronouns in a deep well

the resurrection of the Delphic oracle

what shall we do with the holy corpse of memory ?

I have visited places on the moon's other side

with my brother the hieratic cadaver's other

in rooms the size of sand or ink

we lounged reveling in the remoteness of noise

issuing from a text of disyllabic verses

it was always five in the afternoon

when the Mayo Clinic dominated the Hour

hemispheres of perpetuity ! everyone was seen

going home alone down endless avenues

mask and tomb and faulty pronunciation
myself the digit of erased cognition
it will always be a future digression of rumors
an insoluble enigma of parting and sorrow
a preparation for the removal of sleep
the enormous phonetic disorder of the brain
because it clings to the error of identity
myself myself myself the wound that does not heal
airs and atmospheres and weeping
grief is at the core and dolorous imitations
of persons who loved overmuch and lost
what shall we do with the holy corpse of memory ?

07-14-22

PLAY IT AGAIN SAM

Enough ! the undulating wound of sleep !
yes anachronisms of Latin word order
sleeves of infinity put on backwards
at break of day bone and hollow of memory
the futile disregard for lawns going down slope
the cities ! each of them at the tip of an ant-hill
process of space to identify itself in a thumbprint
registry of oracles ! smattering and jibberish
the jazz at the end of the brain replicated
by a small strobe light and the cameras

rolling full speed to capture the digression

of thought as it snaps in half in mid-air

I was there ! I saw it disintegrate a million black suns

the deserts of Arizona are nothing in comparison

speaking in oblong syllables the god Apollo

massive erection of light and eternity

standing at the school door with his grammar

and munitions of sound nothing but equivocations

a moment to salute the dead who are many

and minute in their terrific glass insectary

and revolve as we do through numbers that

cannot be quantified we ascend ! wings !

poetry is the unnatural error of language

the adolescent mission of unborn angels and flight

air is nothing ! a few meters of invisibility

and the immense body of gravity descending

to the dance where firefly and hummingbird

play charades with the unheard music of time

Enough ! simulation and copies of the gods

nattering with cocktails on the second floor

where philosophy is lobotomized and tiny incisions

are made in the defused cadaver of Osiris

cloud physics of etymology and myth

how can we ever replace what we cannot remember

in the slow evacuation of mind ?

07-14-22

THE DISCARDED MOMENT

those born from myth and who calmly walk

the forest path nights of starless depths who

train their minds to an orient behind the stuff

that makes mountains and who shadow in circularity

the other world where mortals rise and perform

and pass away into the realm below where sound

the muffled waves and shores of those gone and

whose direction is far to the south of space

it is time to understand ! but fail to gather all

the strands and threads and sit purposeless

on the margins of the pool in expectation of

insight or at least a goddess to extract from

the corporeal husk the soul or so they write

in archaic letter-head and texts chipped in bone

hieroglyph and pictogram without noise or

rule as to what to read and what it all means

the furlongs of dusty west and the tangled

groves where animals surrender and the dawn

so late in coming to meet just once the brother

who disappeared so mysteriously in the unknown

where words address their silence in opaque

syllables a vowel lengthened a consonant doubled

the whole indescribable tumult of language

still-born trammeled with hiatus and nexus

where are the unprintable names ? the legendary

solar horses unbridled charging through echo

and the enormous seas beneath seething in
heat-waves tempests of darkness and resonance
be what may the end has already happened not
just once but in multiple phases and places
dereliction of identity and sorrow hands removed
from promises of shape and shadows of blood
skeletons of air and fans and windmills and cities
that exist only in the minds of insects as they scour
the planet for greenery and seasons of rope
and despair and what else ! from afar the telescope
fixes its magnified lens to discover that beginning
and finale are one and the same immense and
brilliant spark of light and instantaneous sleep
histories of repetition and color ! birds of mercury
the fading parchment and design of mind a dot !
and lamenting ! atomic fission and oblivion
triple the skies and by noon the awning flapping
wildly in the monsoon turns red like the messenger
of death and the beautiful verses that follow
that no one will ever hear again

07-15-22

CHIAROSCURO

do we speak of the intelligence of the skies

and quarter our selves half-shade half-light

in the photograph that captures our seventeenth

and final year being together in the intellect

of heavenly clouds and summer's heated ascent

do we then consider futures divided between

northern and southern hemispheres animals

with sight set on heights and splendid gravities

consumed by desires to become more than total

entities fireflies ! screens and hieroglyphics

step by painful step to the summit of mind and

the corollaries of doubt and superstition the way

each in the symbiotic life of twins plunges like

planets veering off course in a sun-storm and

the capsized thoughts and conjectures of math

subdivision and suburb of the city beneath the city

rho and kappa and the other disordered letters

literature itself a footnote on the margins of

the great Water shifting in its dialysis of sound

when ? chiaroscuro emphasis of color beyond

the spectra of possible hues and echoes and

resonance of painted hyacinth and geranium

gardens ! ancestral plots of nostalgia and noise

the remote droning in the atmospheres buzz

and entelechy of the archaic Hive if only

that moment captured by the camera in some

unnamed epoch of time when adolescence reigns

supreme and everything else starts moving backwards

nothing has ever occurred outside of this dazzle !

metal is what makes angels die and speed and

the incontrovertible evidence of a cigarette burning

as a signal for the dark to begin and the poetry

barely memorized in order to be forgotten AOI

07-16-22

THE FOURTH DIMENSION

whereby the arcane is apt shaking hands

the heroes from their globes descended

one the other will always be a smirk a smile

a descant in the key of delta the rivers flow

sideways down through glen and glade

the hawk supreme its eye involves another

sky and maps its origins in diverse sands

that blacken the sun's great hollow homophone

we retrench our forces we divide the cities

we enter into pacts and agreements with gods

unseen who whittle away at twigs or rearrange

the driveway's painted gravel and return

the wheel to its myth of alcohol and resonance

the gyres and plumb-lines of death and sweet

hollyhocks that line the distances of lawn

and atmosphere what of the disparities and
nostalgia the fusion of azure to its glass and
the sum of all thoughts the fourth dimension
parallel lives foresight and blindness apertures
to a space beyond the one that surrounds us
intelligence in humus and detritus naufrage
of desires the loneliness of all eventualities
which of us would go first ? a designated
partner window of the unknown hemisphere
you and me Bro' witless novices of language
junction and separation of the Greek unities
tragedy and accolade of statues bidden to
live half a day only before the celestial
plunge from pedestals of uncountable number
and the pyramids of song and jungle refract
whole but only once and splitting asunder in
atomic fission the one was me the other was you
the two was ever the same and the light of
a thousand fireflies ignited momentarily
the eternity of our birth in stone and air
south of everywhere the fourth dimension
dazzled the spark and tinder of our possibility
gone ! you were the first but I am close as
always to being second

the one borderline is all in capitals and other
in italics a soulful discontinuity of sight

illusions multiplied in the mirror of cognition

only to be shattered on the top rung of a smoking

ladder from which survey that everything burns

in its narrow scope and dialect and what !

the distances between the first letter and the second

are infinity and its counterpart the non-existent

switch off the light ! pretend we never happened

birth and the tombstone promised on the third

turn from the left and smile for the photographer

already dead these many millennia

that everything burns the loopholes and knots

the rope the winch the trolley-car bell the ear !

remember the first time we spread the map out

it covered the entire living room floor

and from her attic of unknowing Mother

though watching simply disappeared

for you and I were wild puzzles charting

the fourth and most enigmatic dimension

grass ! fingers ! the ever darkening leaves

Atque in perpetuum, frāter, avē atque valē

07-17-22

the novelty of grace and to be born
among hierarchies of angels and demons
winged mountains and skies double the size
of ink or sand and the rising register of sounds
planets named after counterfeit deities and
gravity and the weight of distance and flame
pursuing its own origins in order to self-destruct
the entire cosmos turning on a pin-wheel
illusory species of light and darkness the vale
and grief of breath the tears and anguish
coming to be and restless to walk or navigate
and to take flight with the

REWRITING MY AUTOBIOGRAPHY

i

begin at end of old supposed to be , waters running
through thought and thread, a section , hyphenated,
gives us the collusion between flesh and blank
so much trying to sleep, so little left to wake,
so I , nevertheless in old bookstore rummaging,
is that mine? lists of rhyme and throw them
into the bay , what is it I am doing if not
reading writing taking walks and thinking , no,
reflecting, when I am not getting dizzy, or when
love's illusions everywhere, to get in touch with the

various, women, let's call them, teleportation of

the tender and vivid , viscous ? portions of a

mind doing itself in again, and again, cornerstone

of the cosmos simply put is grief, beyond that

the day's shadowy cathedrals embryos of dust,

glorious and former lamps! to be ending suppose

a reading, stop by the broken traffic signal, hail

a grammar-book in hand, the wildest speculation

painted, the disregard which is the Buddha's smile,

encounters in the supermarket, labels and bar-codes,

the smattering of Dravidian required to enter,

hiatus and blank when staring into the void,

azure chains of dharma! vertigo and nausea and

cigarette-memory of the burning, at the tip of

a city half-destroyed by the malevolent jungle it

was supposed to rule, now moldering stone edifices

and dried water-tanks insect paradise,

ii

Listen, dog-ear! that was thunder down and no inkling

of the, a future in re- , annihilate the (your) self

all those attempts, nostalgia of a kind, the errant

latter day, a light, some light, married like that

all crumpled in mid-afternoon heat wave, drenched the

saga about, and Talmudic references to a book of

origins, instead of today counting backwards, the

years remaining probably 5 or 10, to the right

below the smudged print, a hoof ? a fiction rather
than the definitive study of, ash pleat dividends
from a reading of Pliny, Lucretius to follow, then some,
eastern skies trembling, down the stairs a baleful , less
than hopeful, we are in the ruins, basement of classical
antiquity, anguish, dash-entries and liquidated frissons
d'amour in an unlit sky, dawn cracks the envelope,
booze barbiturates hoodoo downers and peyotl jargon,
as if the world seen from a rooftop were real!
jazz omicron motor-tilt dancing cheek to cheek with
death's swarming girlfriend(s), darling you send me,
darkened theater-thoughts before psychiatric swirl,
forward which really means back, nights softening
Italian lessons, dismissing the future what's to know,
gathering around the darker skirts the Persephone-types,
how much more writing there is, French abacus
with a secret omega, delved into the Cretan back-file
to compose perfect response to all that has been read,
grammatical interludes between episodes of pseudo-
fantastic, silver masks leading to and from planetary houses
and the greater mysteries, the rains the tropical siestas the,
hives and subterranean intersections of syntax and
depthless water, how would it work out, I mean
the women, the obsessions, MOM, walking on
some soft night-earth head in dream sleep in glove,
the fades and reveries and carefully, references to the
mountain, Now, the past has come to eat its own vomit,

darker, overdrive headache, concussion snare-drum,

with conga and mambo-jive, jungle rot intertwined,

a few inches to the left and the entire Sanskrit dictionary

caving in an army of trumpeting elephants, innocent,

all days become the One Day over and over again,

iii

forty floors below the backwards winding river disgorges

the prairie's penultimate syllable, a wash of cyclone grass

and dead cement, opium the perfume, exclamation marks

that justify nothing, head dreaming ineffable longing,

islands cut off from the, void, stolen books, staring into the,

we ought to encounter death every day, should be a way

of understanding, who we, are, levels of detail, minimal

comprehending No-Mind in that phase, the Dharma,

sadness but not regret, to realize each day contains

the fullness of death, where were we? scatter-shot memories

leading to first epic, drawing black boats to the shore,

igniting flares to the unknown god who delivered us,

can we go on without glancing back, advantage of existing

in the imagination, first wine-dark sea culmination,

metric density, darkened thumb filmed agony, ours, finally,

red kimono desperation against the wall, hyphenated reality

07-18-22

NO SAILING TODAY

no sailing today at summer's zenith
memories stand still in the upper spheres
nor rains nor heat stay the planet's wayward plunge
through towering cloud-columns and galactic dust
star-flecked far flung geomancy of the gods !
when we are born what a surprise the light
the agony and dichotomy of what we see within
or out of reach the hand a mobility fused to air
and what comes next years ! decades in the event
of trust and imitation though few ken the instability
of navigation and flight and look to the skies
for a signal in the passing houses of the zodiac
does the lion or the bear keep to the heights ?
when did the soul learn the body's fragility
was no place to be caged ? child ! as often
as we tried the prescriptions the x-rays the incisions
the months collapsed into a single hour the roaming
quantity of calendars the aggravation of sound
and the suffixes to noise before nightfall
whichever way the vehicle was speeding meant
nothing a wire of directions all pointing south
where the dead display their bodiless shadows
reciting by rote names of cities and paper toys
one and the same as are all things in the end
leaning over from the sun's inevitable balcony
blackening resonance of an unheard language

the ear ! gathering the crepuscular murmur of leaves

or waves in the distance of a painting of sunset

to lay the head on its stone releasing the count

of ciphers from zero to zed and sleep

the immense unnumbered void before birth

no sailing today the horizon's been erased

collecting all the winds into an invisible knot

and the depths ! where echoes go to die

07-19-22

ONE POEM AMONG MANY LOSSES

the gods have no regard for grammar

their speech is of sonant gold a flux

of stellar error a mendacity of light and dust

down below in olive groves and in grape clusters

they huddle and cheat and swindle lives

of men puny mortals disrespectful of right thinking

by oak and elm the dryads multiple and shining

like leaves in a spring shower and the world

becomes new again for a day the stones that

give luster to fresh cut paths marking the way south

where the dead await a signal or direction

the gods contaminate sound and the origins

and create images of themselves in the winds

and flight is a riddle and the elements that compose

and in pools deep and splendid arise nymphs
whose skin is a glistening torment like glass
that cannot be removed from the eye and sun
becomes great in its black resonance making
of noon the eternal pivot beyond which men
cannot move shaking with fear and ague and
the destinies and designs of privilege are as rust
things that have lost their sheen and night
that lurks in the mulberry bush or in the ditch
where broken cars lie the faded promise of metal
and wheels and pyramids miracles of mind
the geometry and shibboleth of progress
as cities come and go mighty and well fortified
but nothing in the spear-point of avenging deities
whose wrath is a beauty to behold like a dream
that radiance is all and the bright polar stars
but in the end recrimination and judgment
hold sway and the pedestals of the goddess
whose helmet and buckler bring grief and duplicity
to the small kingdoms and there is heard a mewing
a shrill cry in the ear and shifting noises
a debacle of echo and literature the learning
that is an ether of idiom and dialect
the mountain is greater still the heights
where thought yearns to reach and the possibilities
we are given scope and plaudits and row upon row
of wives women sandal-wearing plaintive
sorrowing in their capacity to know

the world and the children they brought into it
a memorandum of burning paper that defines
without consoling the human condition and
feminine waters rushing sleep to its death
such as it is the present tense gives way
to the darkness that is inevitable and hills
and distances of longing and memory
that wavers like fireflies against a screen
before being extinguished in the plural silence
that ends before it can begin

07-20-22

SAN FRANCISCO BAY EPIPHANY

what is the branch of science that disallows any reality ?
love is the capacity to know and just as soon forget
the world we inhabit so erroneously and rumor
and flight and the digitization of mind today of
all days ! swift is the vengeance of the gods
limitless space is an illusion even as the thumb
proceeds to measure the debacles of distance
and cognition yet we do proceed step by dogged step
into the abyss and recite poems about the nature of
Things and the sounds that are meant to represent
have we not graduated from high school yet ?
struggle as we do to exit from this dream and
listen intently to the sky where a grammar of silence

unfurls its clouds and thundering vowels emerge
violent consonants of flashing light and sorrowing
the lesser rains the portents of what is to come
bringing breath to life and the jagged contours
of growth disease and dying the fixed is never sure
the infirm and the incomplete are all that exists
statuary half-shaped and blindness which is a gift
to those who cannot bear the visible outline of time
come ! to wend the way through hills and fogs
to enter the sylvan distraction of an afternoon forged
from heat and passion and to commence the learning
a Buddha in mechanic's overalls a grease-monkey
speaking a Himalayan dialect approaches
offering nothing but an empty begging bowl
and his slurred speech conveys a drugged perfection
the infinite brevity of everything
can it be he is Jack Kerouac on the road ?
dissolves into a preternatural state of levitation
five inches from the ground and the odor of pine resin
great stone ears and the loose wind rising from the salts
and marshes of San Francisco Bay and Lo !
night with its small cabins and lamps and
the sound of diesels climbing the Chinese landscape
and the irrelevant dot dot dot of the stars
we are come to the still-point the endlessness
of the unheard Note we are no more
than the burning in a firefly's memory

07-20-22

ADOLESCENCE

tears like rain at the milestone where dumped

the old body lacking soul now sent to the winds

fluttering some shade or spirit into the phantom world

so we opined restless on our backs drinking beer

warm by now in the hill dialects above the birthright

hospitals of time ! whatever is learned is just as soon

confused and the verbiage of history the chronologies

the faked dates the assumed battles drawn up

on stiff paper outlined with green and red the brown

for mountains and higher elevations reaching

toward heaven the angelic postures the brain takes

falling asleep in the wild each a hand or a knee

counting the unnumbered night whole eons in an instant

passed into a volley of dying planets barely glimpsed

on the ridge below the shower of still budding stars

sleep the puny interval between eternities the section

of an hour the minutes and conflagrations of metal

and misfortune the wheels upside down still spinning

who was he ? growing up posthaste with a new Latin

and the birds and their carols behind mirrors the inky

streams of legend and recitations of noise the rites

of language and myth gods and woods too dense

to remember the flames that spelled destiny in the air

wind and torment perplexed at the rock standing

in the way the fourth and last hour before dawn still

awake trying to figure the heart out what irregularity

of pulse the demon hidden deep within and the leaves

darker than ever whispering in the unseen greenery

text and spell the mysterious attitudes in a glance

of the girls walking in feigned haste to the drugstore

cosmetics and opium and diluted drinks combs and

hair-ribbons loose as the gait of Aphrodite in glass

too fast to understand what it all means the rapid

alcohol and the rash conjectures about space and

the end of time the false recall of a former existence

come on ! soon daybreak and the knotted breezes

that ply the mind with unspoken poetry rounds of

broken verse hexameters distilled from the archaic

and the pretense to fame the exulting statuary of noon

horizons ! exclamation and asterisk the rumor that

tomorrow is infinite bejeweled full of smoke and ladders

the keen edge of an atmosphere replete with voices

imagined or otherwise denying mortality !

07-21-22

SONG OF THE SILENCED LEAVES

we invoke the ancient languages if anything

of their power remains and the sun high

in his idiom of magnificent blackness

who drives forth the day and the multiples

of light assonant and deafening and scatters

with a mere resounding vowel armies of cloud
and suspicion and the written texts of oath
and curse the cities that waver on their edge
and seas confounded with tempests and despair
a single moment to triumph before the lamps
withdraw their luminous echoes and the
horses so vain in their restless fugue riot
in the atmospheres that are the mansions of
the thirty thousand deities and then does sun
bolt across the mind and suffers his eternity
to diminish in the withering plot of time
so do we then this venerable moment offer
shadow and plight to the almighty puzzle
riddling the soul with catastrophe and enigma
the bewilderment of breath short-lived and
the pieces of glass that cannot reunite to form
the whole of abandoned space and what !
noise of sundered axles and wheels sent spinning
from their job and the voice of one who claims
to be the Moon proclaiming to none avails
the vast extent of memory and its dwindling
disaccord and statuary its noon of justice
and denial the fomented accents and strophes
of dialogue with the invisible and far-gone
is there room in the smoldering air for those
who gave fire and letters to wandering mortals
and set the mountain on its side and plied

the plural winds with poetry and illusion ?
gravity of sleep ! endless tumult of the brain
surprised by scheming chapters of biology and
the ascent of thought from its primordial cell
bathed in the first sunlight to present-day chaos
asterisks ! nothing but hiatus and nausea beneath
the now ashen solar divinity a Buddha truant
and derelict in the assumption of Absence
where in the universe ? flight and nirvana
the long evening of the silenced leaves

07-22-22

SAINT VENUS DAY

Venus in her low-cut armor and
wielding a sword of pampas grass
astride her peacock chariot raids
the mortal heart with infusions of
cupid and disaster a flowering
of great disorder and beauty a
very poetry of nothingness the bliss
of surrender and torment the night
of total loss of control the hiatus
and junction of air and wind the
fuse that blows the sun up into
violent hemispheres of longing and smoke

lights her cigarette ! proud and smug
drool and envy of the lesser deities
of Mars strutting like a dog
on the hot Phoenix pavement and
Babylon and Chaos the cities where
she hides her skin before bathing
puffs on her elegant cheroot and
fixes Brazil in its infernal cavity
prepares for a dance-night with
stricken paramours of wax and hair
a comb ! a nail-file ! lipstick !
the dross of human eventuality
she can become triple in water
or a painting from the cinquecento
she can be everyone's heart's-desire
concussion and elevation of mind
myth and transformation of sound
buzz and hum of oriental swarms
upending mountains and dialects
the spore of antiquity in her eye
the vast narrows of Greek philosophy
a naked nymph on her jutting rock
a wave a spear of sand a Thought !
nothing more than gossamer and
entelechy the furious dividend
she shares with undated calendars
it is always the day after Yesterday

and in all her flounce and yellowed lace

she has nothing left to conquer

but the wasteland of immortality

07-22-22

WHISPERS AND VERTIGO

twelve tones counting from rock and gravel up

where love lies hidden the punctuation of

radiance but for the shape of Aphrodite is not

recognized nor mind have greater value in its

memory than air winnowing in ascent to the skies

each an attribute of some god or other and do hands

reckon their own future in archaic lands of epos

the color of burnt sienna that riddles the winds

even as the grasses bend down in obeisance

and leaves also alert to the turns and curves

of human speech do imitate the sound of verse

the hexameter rattled out by schoolboys in

a distance of chalk and smoke the very hills

where dialects are born for discourse and mystery

the plangent rumor of music resounding like

a spell in the dormant ear of Dionysus as

do relics of noise the shuttling whispers and

vertigo in the lush undergrowth by the entrance

to Hades and make way for schemes and arrogance

in the thriving fern and fungus below where
webs of communication resembling dreams offer
warning to the generations to come about
the great Unknown and vague incoherent plans
for growth and extinction which become Loud
in the resonance of the enormous solar vowel
that destroys the noon of statues and courtiers
who will be the first and the last ? a brief finger
curtailed in its destiny of lawns and twilight
a signal the shape of the dying moon or ink
in the crescent of the brain where thought vies
with aphasia for articulation and repetition
to be understood ! loss and longing the variants
of the mortal lot hearing murmurs in concrete
or the moist places where trees root their anima
and soils teeming with the error of worms
struggling with amnesia and the question remains
the soul ? planets and long-dead stars and asterisks
plunging out of the light into eternal darkness
where are the pools of reflection ! night a copse
where sleep takes on the disguises of memory
you and I you and I – remember ?

07-23-22

THE REPETITION OF ERROR

from the heights of this mountain a dream to espy
crowned the various goddesses wraiths shining
interminable the radiance of the sky behind the sky
called paradise yet available to none who wander
in bodily raiment unable to shed the skin and who
sing lauds to the ones who gather as a single being
yet multiple like the plural waters of feminine gender
grammar and back-pack the hastening day adjourns
three o'clock time for drugs and cosmetics the panoply
that brings to illusion the reality in glass darkening
a sun higher than the mobile shafts of cognition
and the prattling and debate about the soul that
minds devour to know yet escapes like air hissing
from a child's fist to be born it was like a gift
unasked and query and puzzle the variable landscape
the hills risen overnight and meadows and groves
where hide nymph and dryad and unspeakable centaur
who will assay the length of a mortal hour ? listen !
blown by orient winds a secret god unformed and
bearing license to kill and revive stands before the
civil war cannon and distributes shares in oil-stock
to the unwitting who equate wealth with glory and
from even further up on the ladder that goes nowhere
other deities tussle with human frailties and denounce
birthright and advantage and scour the crevices
of cosmic demolition for a remnant of beauty

for the sorrowing of mothers and the grief born

in stone and gravel the enormous painted delusions

that revolve like wheels of promise summer afternoons

when longing is most intense and the grasses spawn

shadows in the noises of feigned grandeur and jazz

how brief ! one two three and out go the lamps

like swarms of fireflies yearning to get in the screen door

the dance ! the roundelay of passion and deceit

all of this happens in a trice the faces become worn

and death occurs even to the already dead down the hall

waiting for the signal that changes directions and

the descent from gravity is an error and the mountains

tilted on their side facing south and the circle

of goddesses dissolving as one in the mirror of dreams

leaf and wave-surge and sandy tumult of silence

07-24-22

BODY AND SOUL

when the soul has fled there's

no repairing the body nor can there

be discerned in the winnowing airs some

shape some form winging outward from the lees

and boulders stained with crimson envy

and mountains the height of sleep looming

and the Mother-of-the-Seas resounding

in the ear's small shell a little comfort

and shines in an alternate basin reflection

of the wayward attitude the entranced

and errant sun bearing with it the heavy sounds

the vowels eclipsed in a former life a theater

of misrepresentation and error and then

do wounded mortals in some refuge seek

oils tools winches and pulleys in vain

and sally forth again some in battle armor

others with spite and ire in governance

the world to defy or deny and build overnight

great cities fortresses from sand and dung

and recite from damaged memory the Hymns

all to no avail as news accounts of destructions

and demolitions arrive by couriers blind with haste

and chariots spin around and crash !

what is there to really understand ?

scraping the bone filing the tooth scouring

the wastes for a trace a sign some direction

fourfold and erroneous that may lead

to the quarries where new souls are designed

language employed to justify rumors

depth-charges and knee-replacements wind-velocities

nothing stays the mind from its scheming projections

tomorrow is a promise and adolescent libraries

consulted for new truths and pyramids

the volley of consonants back and forth

ricocheting and riddling thought with compromise

and debt and how much more sorrow !

in the end the ping-ping ! of narcissism

that characterizes the body cauterized but not healed

salvation is an import from Thailand and the scripts

that detail the birth and death of Gautama

and the narrow defiles of Nirvana the loud-Silence

we are but pronouns scatter-shot in the void

reminiscences of play in backyards filled

with noise of insect tyrannies and death

one by one the windows implode in brilliant flares

hands removed from meaning yearn

to return to the Archaic moment

cast into an arroyo the discarded husk of being

slowly deliberately consumed by Night

while the soul invisible aloft resumes its

place in the enormous vacuum of time

07-25-22

THE GREATER RECKONING

the mysterious languages that seep into the ear

asleep and then waking what a triple error !

sun at its heaviest forgets to climb the heights

shines a rocket of rays across the Himalayas

that reach as far as Sri Lanka where demons

hold sway and the nuisance of here and now
the fretwork of a noise rising from the seas
waters of instant recognition and denial
a message for humans in the illiterate skies
portents forged in dismissive scripts chaotic
and threatening as clouds and thunder-heads
put to flight chastened deities from their lairs
it's summer ! the greater reckoning of heat
and autocratic mountains drought and famine
the scattered minions for whom philosophy
has no appeal and the freighted missiles
fired carelessly at the moon in the hopes of
reaching new understanding ! radios and digital
devices entangle the airs with crossfire and death
the furious invocation to Mars ! little by little
dross and enervation consume adamant cities
the narrow passageway intuited by the Egyptians
is come to naught and the hieroglyphs of intellect
illustrating the sandy catastrophes of learning
are erased by a single thumb or hoof – History!
drizzle and opaque mists and green distances
of yearning and Arctic slopes crashing silently
in the evidence of eternity and whatever else
is encompassed by the greater reckoning and
ellipse and the numbered quanta of inactivity
in the yawning face of total annihilation what !

I am a beggar of lice a panhandler shifting
shoeless across the hot pavements of Sumer
I am a mendicant a chiseler of cuneiform
a messenger blinded by Thoth an element of
quicksilver a decrepit apostle of Advaita
a bard with two missing vowels I am a dot
an excrescence carried by the winds over
the Fertile Crescent towards the native lands
of the Arya and the Dravids I am less than
thought a sliver of mind a cavity of letters
holding a broken stylus in search of wax and
mostly I am carrion still moving among dung
beetles and carpenter ants a footprint is my bed
a rumor in the comb a loss of memory a sound
stuttering across the page an unfixed planet
sighted thousands of light-years ago that
bears my unknown name I am a pariah who
once built cities I am my own brother
who is the greater reckoning

I am the I am the I am the

systematic withdrawal symptoms from breath
the ancient and final book after book disclosed
the void between sounds the shattered letters
mutual discord and velocity that combined
destroy the archaic heavens sonant and echoing

in stone and water the pleasures once by shore
and bank rippling small tides a finger parts
and therein a face appears forlorn and beckoning
a brother to reckon ashes and dialects of distance
the first and the last built like a tomb hovering
in the air midway between the chronology of space
and the distinctions that divide time from time
faltering speech of statues left to crumble
on lawns of justice and penance and constant
sorrow the canonized grief of living without
redress and then does the greater reckoning
deal its hand one soul does not recognize the other
size of shoe material wants circular numbers
empty automats frozen dinners and despair
writ big on the wasting solar homophone

we are at the same time presence and absence
error of thought and rumor of memory

07-26-22

TANTA MUERTE!

and as for the rumor a Buddha is among us
no understanding but what mind yearns
and grass underfoot and the insect world a whirl
we have lived decades now and in poverty of

intellect and error the upper hand a position
to defend ? red lacquers the western half and
face down in mulch and interpret what goes on
down there tunnels and drafts of labyrinths where
does the soul hide ? a fission of music a template
of wax in the noon sun engraved with signatures
of Arhats the forty thousand who involve a single
drop of water or a scheme of air a poetry of
sounds mallets of teakwood a rough sketch
of the Indian sub-continent indicating places
where the Buddha suffered or starved the self
how much to unlearn ! fuse and belt comb and
hair-ribbons bright fluttering a wind will take
it all away one day our footprints dust and thick
mud the forty-day rains and the pharmacist
whose signals go misunderstood a sadness to
remark how the swift and unerring arrows in
the hundreds sent by Arjuna fly all directions
to slay the unseen Foe in this tomb of light
no one will come out of this alive ! footnotes
in italics the rudimentary suns of havoc and
ire spinning in the spatial balconies and higher
still the nameless gods who wear the planets
like jewels at play with fortune-tellers and ghosts
blood and monsoons ! panoply of doom-spells
and the mindless histories of a summer afternoon
news arrives from multiple distances that deaths are

mounting piling up like the Four Mountains
not one but many not many but thousands like
the countless galaxies that glitter pointlessly
in the firmament that decorates time's infancy
look to the west ! I know them I know those beings
struggling with new store-bought wings to fly !
mouths filled with grass eyes glazed and opaque
fingers pointing in error to the paths of Mercury
who tarries back and forth bearing souls to
their allotted spot in the pharaonic sands
++++++++++++++++++++++++++++++++++
it is all et cetera woof and weave and ashes
incinerators and ignition bricks and clay-pits
quarries where new pronouns are fashioned and
copies of Sicily in hermetic glass the veins and
partitions of the roman empire gossamer and
stolen silks waters of tumult and degradation
thrones capsized and diamond and tufa markers
grave-sites and roads that lead straight to Inferno
soon it is never ! the Etruscans had it right
mirrors engraved with secret identities
and everything moving backwards into isolation-
wards and drugstores the cosmetics industry
of the dead alarms and fuselage and home-town
a ruin of hours and smoke finalized oratory
the valedictorian's aimless speech in cribbed Latin
sent to our separate destinies with confused masks

already dead and potent with ambition Ignorance
the discarded laws of statues and seers burning
in small baskets once carried by market-Buddhas
bearing fruit and the shapes of old deities
husks of atmosphere the end-all of et cetera
look to the west ! I know them I know those beings

07-27-22

THE UNFINISHED BREATH

what is the unfinished breath called ?
when is the last wave of the seas unfurled ?
what is higher than the sun when no shadows appear ?
why are statues ? the unending present tense
and cares more numerous than grass and the heights
of a thumb in its protracted inch to measure
all-space and the balconies packed with mothers
in the solitary grief of birth-giving and name-taking
the losses and the depths ! what is more human than that ?
death and its winsome girls all frills and chariot-rides
and the groves and meandering streams and summers
that last less than an hour and the countless sounds
that pass for language and the oxidized cities !
how could all this pass in the instant of recognition ?
is light not forever ? and the skies ripped open
by an imaginary Zeus hurtling one cinematic bolt

after another into the small ruin of the mind

the battle plans and the schemes to grab loot

to unearth buried gold consonants and to speak

as if endowed with divine inspiration ! each of us

is culpable and who dares to admit to pride ?

a finger gone and the absence of Hylas in the rocks

and moors and gravel underfoot and the tiny voices

of the leaves in the great labyrinth of memory

which of us will go first ? what a question !

you were the one, Joe ! mimic and sage you made

a brief appearance on the stage of existence

we played at harmony and skittles ! you leaped

I watched wondering when we'll meet again

there are cafes that never close and midnights

that have stayed the revolution and glassware

and the antics and foibles of mayors and undertakers

none who can answer any of the questions

that school-kids ask as they go on playing with masks

and tousled hair and striped t-shirts and the dust

that involves the origins of the cosmos and pronouns

that have no place in the furious orient of the planets

come on, Joe ! give it another chance at immortality !

that's what the unfinished breath is called

07-28-22

ELEGY AT SUMMER'S END

so comes to end this wine of elegies

these unfinished verses scattered in dawn's

remote hair the blemish of lives unspoken

memories painted on a cloth to remind

that breath has passed from some while

to others it is but a chance of fate to breathe

tomorrow's illusion rides a solar horse through

clouds one remove from the end of space

and time's drum-roll fades from the stone

of ears and truth forever lies in its cave

what is to become of us pallid wraiths

waking from a dream of mobile statues

and noise and redundancies of years

what is it to speak to mirrors and yearn

to touch impalpable figures like numbers

flashed on a screen that vanish when

added to the sum of zero and childhood phantoms

on the prowl are evidence of mysteries

buried in the hills that give birth to dialects

and histories that cannot be told

do we lay siege to books and music as if

to own the universe and yet in sandy reaches

thought dissolves and mind's priceless

jewel turns to burning paper in the eye

come down from torments of sky deities

whose shimmering is but a brief water

nymphs of vertigo and distance undress

the hours of their vain schemes to endure

we are left in a maze of doubt and insecurity

disease and envy clad in cinematic raiment

only deceive the glass that they reflect

to sleep in gravel and moist grasses

lingering in the moment of extra depth

we enter the realm of dark and disappearing
                              leaves

07-29-22

ALTERTUMSWISSENSCHAFT DENIED

more dear to me these loves of lives past

flowers garlanded around a throbbing pulse

nomenclature of the gods ! circle-dance

of the sun at his zenith gamboling and down

below among the reeds and wattle huts

my loves in their puzzling libraries of yore

antiquities of paper and marble ruin and

destruction ten cities at a time all Troy

the vagabond Argives who gave fate a blow

on hills redundant with puzzling dialects

how little did I ever know and how much

wasted on books futile with error and ire

the envy of the seas the rocks crashing

of their own accord the will of the dead

hiding behind vast painted shields and light

burnished failing a rumor of unforgiven lies

poetry a phalanx of verse and tone dense

with punctuation of heights and vertigo

slander of the wise opprobrium of bards

and birds far-seeing that circle the skies of

paradise and dowries of Venus and Aphrodite

never knowing which name will win the day

furious endeavors in ant-hills and sand-lots

automobile graveyards rusting hard by

the fanes and pits holy to Saint Apollo !

so many my loves buried in etymologies

lexicons of water and nymphs wearing

nothing but skins of dazzle and orient

which way to turn ? it's all burning loud

disease and gravel torment blind byways

truant deities ! lurking in cellars drinking

cheap Sicilian wine and the burrows and

caves where truth becomes a mutilated beast

and the stone which philosophers claim

is the soul of an invisible universe and what !

my true love comes sidling to the window

as I count the missing planets and whispers

in some insane Etruscan tongue a motto

a sun-spot a hieroglyph or asterisk that

divides the air in two disunited harmonies

one is infinity and the other immortality

and returns to the shadow where leaves

are born to mourn life's vanished page

07-30-22

THE LITERARY ERROR

so much for life today a shadow

pressed between two burning leaves

a section of sky cut out from memory

to replace the lawn where kids played dead

among the thousand bushes of the dark

and yet the light comes out to flash again

and toys and figure-eights made of ice

and hikes out to the river-bend where

illusion couples with the clouds above

how great a moment the last summer was !

concrete of distant cities mapped out

one dim afternoon and x-rays and wafers

that contained whole continents of air

floating like some futile evidence of breath

tracks and signs and hidden mansions

with unsolved mysteries about gods

and windows that need blackening

to hell with the Greeks and Trojans

in their puerile fits for high-school

textbooks amo amas amat discord and
lies amateur conjugations trefoil and ire
the world as such and life the trance
and yew and cypress by the roadside
tombs of dreams the morning after
sounds of grief echoing in palaces
of black crystal and jade the semblance
of ornaments and envy in such poetry
as resonates in stone ears the panoply
and plenty of grass and climbing hills
dialects and foul-play in the plaza's tents
associated vowels and clinging consonants
the earthly toil of ash and cinderblock
brick by brick the street evolves into
distances of clinic and mausoleum
seas dive from their own cliffs and die !
it is coming today to recite in Old French
gests and rumors of brass atmospheres
horn signals and hazardous waste
of eighteenth century illuminati
a hand ! three fingers left ! weeds !
the mirror turns its back to pronouns
wearing masks of soiled contrition
life is ennui ! life is forged memory !
kids playing dead in their yearbooks
drive their crazy cars into the Wall
someday this too you will remember

the Latin adages and suicide attempts

Dido ! fulfilled promises to the gods

who dress hair and arouse tempests

from the depths careless of water and

its multiple genders the drowning

that takes the soul from its parapet

and feeds it to the fishes of eternity

07-31-22

THE UNREMEMBERED DAY

not one or its copy but many duplicates of

mirror images ecstasies and devotions

libel suits divorces divisions of three into nine

fission and fusion of a single atomic particle

and the soul indivisible as rock stubble and

mired in husk after husk of mortal disunion

isn't one image enough ? given the news that

the fatal day is nigh or that the ambulance's

siren has ceased working or that multiples

of zero really amount to trillions of light years

twins opposites and lunar consonants

all unreal as consciousness of birth or death

it's all finite a whole life-long the hills and

devastations of dialect and sewing scraps on end

nothing but a battery worn out a filament snapped

routines of electricity and dial telephones
who ever thought it would come to this ? grief
and distilled water in manufactured glass
turnaround of noise in midnight gravel when
wheels and insects teem with secret industry
why am I still here ? so many others have fled
the hotel is to be razed and the avenue turned
into a lot for recycled waste and the homestead
where we sang songs of cattle-drives and mysteries
of the orient is but a thumb-print on the map
unreal the chapbooks of smuggled verse
the stolen syllables of an archaic hymn
sunspots and asterisks that denote immortality
unreal the planets that flare at noon with their
statues ant-heaps and dining cars winging
through mountain tunnels with tourists stoned
on ether and opiates as unreal as the promises
to forever love and hold the partner of the dance
dead now as ever was in her frame of calico
and lilac and the fireflies and pyramids of song
and screens that divide language from mere sound
all the unreal fictions they write about in books
illustrated paper and cuneiform prayer-wheels
handles of intuition and the dragon that smokes
a final cigarette after years of swearing off
and the stairs that only go half way
and skies of pure immobility shifting carelessly

through a hummingbird's emerald eye
unreality adds to unreality the curse of breath and time
no one ever counts past the highest number
no one ever understands the words of the Buddha
on his death bed of moss and stone
just the echo of scissors cutting through an envelope
filled with letters that were never sent
and the murmur of leaves shutting down
the unremembered day

08-01-22

NOTHING TO DO WITH POETRY

this poem has nothing to do with poetry
nor the things that matter in jingled rhyme
school-boy stuff in opened geography books
desks scratched with ink engravings of someone's
heart's desire or the backside of the moon
how many days have passed since the 5th century BC ?
can we ever go back to that distant misty China
of Confucius and his analects or to the India
of Shakyamuni sneaking out one night forsaking
family duties once and for all to question
the meaning of life and the death that comes
with birth can we ever interrogate Socrates again
or filter the sun's rays through some pharaonic gaze

nothing to do with poetry and its frilly lace

declaiming in false voices love's eternity

to do with poetry the ruins of rock and time

long afternoons of silence in the grass and darkness

that comes with every day despite the solar promise

to rerun the same old show of imperfections and

Etruscan riddles scribbled backwards in letters

stolen from ancient Phoenecian shores

who can say which sound came first or what

intellect devised the ordering of noise

into phonetic integers and proclaimed the victory

of all mirrored speech into meter and creation myth ?

nothing at all to do with poetry these littered

fuses of depth and light these asterisks and

exclamation marks that damage the page's edge

whatever it is this has nothing to do with

the sacred intimations of decibels uttered

in the Delphic fane or the ricocheting echo

that shatters Dionysus' ear ! there are seas

awash with the golden assonance of sunsets

behind Iberian hills and dialects and aspersions

of idiom and grammar the greatest error of all

and significance of graduation day and empires

that toppled because one god was better than another

what has this to do with poetry ? at a loss

to define the limits of mind's confused topographies

or the theogonies of restless thought and heights

and western enigmas and the debacle of gravel

scattered like magic bones across a drying cow-hide

to read in every space a text that never was and

interpret the archaic Vedic OM as the navel

of the universe to do with poetry nothing

but the compromising histories of the chisel

and its reckless incisions in baked clay

what is the hand and its futile yearning ?

fingers that number sleep up to mystic Five

and islands that are rotundities of obsession

circling the inane waters where the cosmos drowns

what is there to remember and recount ?

I had a brother once and we played with accents

that invented maps and cities beyond the pale

the dots and squiggles of the brain and

fierce hours spent drilling the sky with poems

strange unlearned reckonings that had

nothing to do with poetry

I had a brother once

is all I have to say

08-01-22

CHICANO MANIFESTO 2022

    para Armando Rendón

chained to sunspots and black homophones
solar destiny of prisoners violated in troth
misuse of language parking meter fines detritus
in the back seat offal of the gods ransom notes
beware the badge and its shiny ! level with glass
the micrometer shows distance fleeing on foot
mountains conveyed by polluted breath of demons
wearing bowtie cravats and silk nooses all named
microsoft the penchant for virtual realities in
this dumb soap-bubble dream who can know ?
illegal and alien both the migrant worker soiled
in his levi-strauss overalls hitches a ride in a diesel
sedan pickup truck packed with other grape-pickers
heading as always south to pray with the dead
in their cathedral of sand and mud the labels
all in half-erased Toltec and waving bottles of
cheap dago red the filtered lamp of afternoon
smothers the city of Fresno in a dim hill of smog
how can they get to Los Angeles in a day and survive ?
freeways bussed over patches of dead Quonset huts
military evacuation plans drought and homicidal
adolescents roaming Pachucos with fists of noise
like radios animated by a visceral memory of
the pyramids far beyond human ken and upside-down
skies and bleached kinships to the Maya whose

obsidian razors cut through the thin surreal film
called Los Olvidados it's all irrelevant unholy
twenty first century skyscraper domes filled
with greedy dot.com yuppies and a whistle
blown as always too late as night's transmogrified
judgments once more condemn Paco y sus hermanos
to fifty more years hard labor in the Golden State
even as the coastline slurps into the messy oceanic
depths where drowned dope fiends eyes wide open
resurface to testify to the dying archaic sun in
dialects of unspoken nightmares the enormity
of an eternal jail-sentence and the deserts rolling
like futile seas toward Las Vegas and points east
gamblers manifest destiny second amendment rights
Bang ! Bang ! la vida la pinche vida, hombre !

08-02-22

THIS IS DEDICATED TO THE ONE I LOVE

on earth to say there are couples that don't match
and flames of equidistant breath their smoke release
the sign is higher than summer and the cipher
cannot be discerned all sites and directions weathered
and grasses of twilight lift weary shadows to a god
whose nature is as unknown as death and what's
to sacrifice if not the soul's plagiarized copy afloat

in clouds where sleep is buried and poetry too
descant and folio of vast unremembered lines
recited among statues when noon is least in sight
courts of law and Bibles at the bottom of the stairs
wedding kits and bows like nooses that don't fit
yet memory persists in stop-watches and glances
from girls whose eternity is the single month of July
planets of envy revolving in a plate-glass window
reflections of a pool too deep to merge with light
ascension and defeat the parallel life of Adonis
dying not twice but infinitely in Aphrodite's lap
like us these myths incorporate so much of loss
and longing the matters we cherish most like
air and the winds that torment mountains in the west
grammar and meditation for the already dead in
their symposium of ash and the weight of language !
so long ago the school-yard's empire of dust and
personae hidden in leaves that ache to speak
despite the sun's reckless lunge across the meridian
alone am I ! the mummer's confessed holiday
distance and dialect held to the ear's secret seas
confusion is order ! wave after wave of assonance
and the gold that divulges man's narrow capacity
which is the most of every day that never comes back
yearning and triangles of sound reverberating
in compositions written by a hand that lacks shape
prefaces to books in irate cuneiform and legends

that occupy the moon's solitary backside and Love

that awful moment when unmatched doubles

reunite in the mystic One and blind with infatuation

forget to lock the door and thus prepare to die

08-03-22

THE BATTLE OF THE GRAMMARS

by magic entered the king's fresh corpse

and got the twenty million pieces of gold

thus procuring the divine grammar promised

by the god of the Thundering-Voice at the end

of the Age-of-the-Universe when earth was just

a drop of water followed by the shattering Noise

and the syllables of all possible speech

turned to fiery brands of seething metal

routing from their cloistered pens the cattle

and the birthright of lesser beings and swart

and dignified the sun's blazing homophone

first took possession of the sky maiden

and thousands of eons passed at the whim

of a thought before entry to the next world

was made manifest in a poem no one remembers

the fierce and eloquent moment when statues

acquire memory and the dream of language

how are humans possible ? roaming the green

satellite the ancestors dressed in consonants
of bark and husk like mendicants sought
salvation from One who was yet to come
princes and elephants carved on teakwood
and walls of sound enormous as cataracts
rushing from the Himalayas assailed the Ear
back and forth the prattle of lesser divinities
arguing in restaurants that knowledge
can only be gotten in cemeteries at midnight
who else but the dead understand order ?
when glass reflected vowels to be memorized
and slate and clay or waxen tablets
and chalk with fingers of grass and clouds
imminent with history lowering and rumbling
like mountains to the west of time
and so the famous et cetera that ends any tale
the constant beginning again of each day
because everything that has been learned
by rote is forgotten upon waking
and the disciples sent out to preach and pray
and the subjugated kingdoms and petty wars
the battle chariots filled with lust and syntax
the authors themselves of endless treatises
explicating punctuation silence and rhetoric
dead from the ankle up still orating and
augurs and alphabets of bird-flight
predicting flood drought and famine

just who will understand ? pitting one rule
against another claiming the first is only second best
and strictures and litigation and divorce
loves ! what are passions in the rule of law !
case gender and number again and again
water is supremely feminine ! the rest
is prey to phonetic decay infinite and lost
sitting in rows like zombies students
keep imitating pronunciation of the dead
copies of antiquities ! when the school-bell rings
oblivion has already possessed the books
sunlight is brief and lengthening shadows
whence comes your delight in the graveyard
and skull, My Lord ?

08-04-22

THE VALEDICTORIAN'S SPEECH

still-life and a crown of light
the painting of human endeavor
in slashes of bright and white like
flowers yearning to be more than presence
a letter from a book a copy of a copy
imitations and shadows reworking
the alphabet in segments of fire and ash
canyons and pitfalls the step of mistakes

a hand coveting its own shape

aggravations of sound and echo

each in pursuit of the other

life and breath and the mysterious wood

one enters but never exits

a voice from a far reach of hills

dominions of noise in a single leaf

what else can explain this enigma ?

I am you and you are me

the pronominal fix the situation

without resolve the puzzle of glass

and reflection and the mirror of walls

sleep ! secret envies the braid of ire

come with me ! how is it possible ?

mind separates itself from thought

evocations of distance in the skies

summers brought to an end by a small crystal

of water the jagged edge of time

lessened by a degree of heat

the ancestral force dissolves

death is in the repetition of error

the rumor of fields spreading south

where language gathers its skirts

and the voice on the phone

asking for something

without resonance

08-04-22

BLUES WITH A FEELING

on the way to paradise what did Brother see ?

new worlds that became suddenly old

places ruled by talking beasts and folded

nightly into leaf-beds of palm and fig

the nether palaces he swore never to visit again

revealed themselves opened their burning gates

to let him in saying this is it a jazz-man's paradise

horns blew and drums charged the clouds with

azure pelts of noise radios blared nothing could

be turned off and the blues masters whose

faces twisted with agony of joy wrapped

their guitars of pure sound around his intellect

no Dante no Bodhisattva no Michelangelo

stood in raiment clear as waters of the skies

no angel of mercy no fifth wife speaking

in all three tongues at once no thermometer

nor x-ray nor mother in her faded twilight dress

accompanied him none to carry his weary shadow

no other just like him becoming back and forth

in a mirror no one else could see only some supernal

echo some pebbles painted and thrown away

as he stepped from car to car on the confusing

boulevards that seemed to move sideways

into groves where dryads and nymphs with towels

waited to dry him off all in a lather from the Process

and lengths of distance like hills where dialects

are born and die and broken marble fragments

of speech and gods of sudden intuition flashing

gold-tooth smiles offered him a plenitude of vowels

Sanskrit and Tibetan translations to heaven

opened and shut their volumes of illegibility

his lost finger reappeared in grasses darker

than the sublime graduation oath he had taken

in the summer of 1956 to become as pure memory

to the ones he left behind a shining of the instant

a satellite of the wayward and lurching Sun

and still he proceeded in delusion of syntax

and cacophony toward some fixed dot in space

a curvature a loss of linearity a darkness that

erased the fourth and last dimension a sigma

or omicron wavering like planets without course

but paradise he never reached nor the shoals

where shipwrecked souls mistake the maps

of childhood's intricate deltas for the greater end

and alas his likeness in this poem still mourns

the inexplicable disappearance from this realm

leaves and footfalls and autumn serenades

the moment of no return we shared simply

not knowing when

08-05-22

LISTENING TO THE NIGHT 1956

"I'm gonna leave here running
because walking is most too slow"
Key to the Highway, Jazz Gillum

graduation ceremonies in the endless grass
tribes rivers and hills threatening the horizon
cars newly minted with motors of instant death
rolling pavement distances measured by the thumb
farewell forever in the circling heat of infinity
speculation that just outside the city limits
a world of cliff and diameter beyond human ken
lies waiting with an insistent and nocturnal jazz
to step into the delivery and speed with diesels
of amphetamine and renown into unmeasured voids
the future ! cities consisting of a single note
skyscrapers of rampant thought a symposium
of alcohol and elucidation like the trial of Socrates
home-coming and sorrow impossibility of return
mortals for a brief hour alone with shaking hands
hugs and kisses goodbyes that everyone forgets
a rousing drum a skilled bullet a distant war
a jungle where infamy reigns a thousand years or more
helicopters and unsought climes that burn without regret
a pious lingering in the dawn-wet grass to remember
the suffocation and lore of love's mistakes
he and she triangles and pounding temples to wake
another day missed from a calendar made of stone

tomorrow will be the epiphany of all tomorrows !

forward the lamp and ogives of the waning moon

night after night in a single night this one !

dare we toss the map and fling to destiny our fate ?

plunge like oriental planets in all three languages

and bury the soul's febrile pool between the eyes

linger more by seasides with bodies of the Phantom

the you and I them and forever more pine for

the mountain and its hidden metals of deathless passion

watch ! the fields unfurl their heats of corn and memory

the girls who multiplied the incense of identities

and passed into reaches of the Invisible before

our yearning sight the very scope of lipstick and

its variable and violent pronoun the Kiss !

to think we can have it all without knowing why

and in roadside stones and markers replace our name

with vertigo and the indissoluble embrace of death

another rumor of daylight and graduation's knell

no telephone can ever explain the unmitigated loss

of Scheherazade all bliss and longing like opium

adolescents in the clutch of an opposite eternity

lies of mobility and weight the prescience of leaves

to keep silent as we wend our blind-spotting way

into the immortal labyrinth

        "I'm gonna roam this highway

               until the day I die"

08-06-22

THE LESSER HYMN TO VISHNU

"toda palavra tem a sua sombra"

Clarice Lispector

the bee and fish in their swarming ampersands

the lotus that blooms in the naked eye and

hands that sprout from purity of air yearning

to form alternates of marble and sandstone

what is memory but the missing word the formula

for sound when sleep reigns supreme the slender-

waisted girls whose dance in sinuous glass

is meant to madden gods and turn mountains

to simple pools where love's reflection envies

the moon in its great inconstancy and dream

the year and its compound digits of passage !

mirror and number image and counter-image

weight and gravity the scales tip on the side of death

masterful tales weave in and out of the loud noise

in all three languages which means nothing within

the ear's circular plan to destroy the labyrinth

sections of an unwritten alphabet mnemonic

structures built upon a wind that blows away

the hills whose dialects once housed poetry

the plowman and the warrior and the avatar

who shows mercy to beast and rock alike among

the wandering satellites of the black homophone

whose fierce sun obliterates all nine heavens

what ! the wavering chronicles of the Island

gold and mercury in sheaves as light as time

what can ever be accounted for ? is a human life

as valuable as the leaf that sprouts overnight ?

green fuses fission and implosion science and sight

wherever the face turns the direction remains one

and trembling fingers that forage for shadows

in unbidden grasses longing to climb the sky

are but suffixes to a list of unremembered nouns

childhood ! an aggravation of grammar and chalk

does anyone ever come back ? lessons of plight

and romance of war-threats and city planning

astrology writ big on the minotaur's monstrous brow

captive to illusions of transformation and paradise

the body persists in a rumor of being and breath

toxic fires feed the birds the mind designs for flight

it all comes down rushing with planets doomed

from the start with the immense waters and alcohol

of outer space dotted with perplexing minarets

that sparkle like asterisks at chapter's end

you choose ! it was only yesterday around noon

in front of the courthouse when everything happened

bewildering theft of electricity and resonance

you choose ! which kid was the one in the runaway

accident between births ? pray to Vishnu !

ten times recycled in errant deifications

ten times salvation was at hand

you choose !

08-07-22

THE HIGH-SCHOOL YEARBOOK REVISITED

vibrating in the heart's desire the plain that
stretches from grief to its unseen counterpart
as if French poetry mattered or the word-order
in Virgilian hexameter the price of life is breath
sounds mere challenges to silence abrupt caesuras
unexpected hiatus sorrowing ampersands
deafening noise of raffia in the air's incunabula
can words be deified ? the thing beating in
the pulse is more than just blood but a yearning
to circulate beyond the realms of inertia and ennui
to embolden the pronoun to drop its definition
assembling memories before they come to a halt
the drip drip drip at the back of sleep a muted
urgency to reconstruct from the rout of shadows
a single moment in the abundance of light
when the self recognized its other in the maze of love
fields and hills dialects of heat and the winnowing
atmospheres of a summer suspended above
the darkening pool of eternity shouts ! and to
live imperfectly in the gold assonance of youth
two or three seconds in wavering bliss before
the cliff and its accident of unreachable distance
alter the sequence and semantics of time
rushing out of control on amphetamines and
indecision for there is no one who recalls
exactly how to use the keys to prevent speed

and gravity from overwhelming the process

wheels spinning in the Greek fraction of an instant

when metal loses all context and the brilliant

unfixed sun blots out all reminiscence bringing

to a close the future promised in the yearbook

faces elide into photographic densities chiaroscuro

names dribbled in disappearing ink fictions

nothing more and that we ever shared a compartment !

holding hands in a reverie dancing in the dark

listening to the silent grammar of the leaves

in the abandoned confusion of infinity's labyrinth

08-08-22

DROWNED WORLDS

hour of unfinished breath the long countdown

summer at its height a crisis of water and color

who comes first who comes last in the round-dance

grass is hypothesis of myth and memory leaves

contain the origin of speech and heat goes in circles

above the reflecting pool where pronouns merge

with the dark eventuality of its bottomless depths

the invitation said bring a friend and so you did

Narcissus beloved of the goddess of denial and envy

and together you approached the painted rocks

the margins that fluctuate with time and night

together you wasted precious mornings sampling

dew and plucking buttercups and dandelions

why did you think the wine would have no effect ?

between stone and shadow you gained on noon

the famous moment when statues acquire thought

the designs were everywhere the court of justice

and the civil war cannon and the afternoon

parades to the drugstore with you trailing behind

thinking Narcissus to be no more than a child

a secret in the air snatched him by the hair and

pulled him to water's edge and there to devour

himself in the mirrored diapason of light and

oblivion to proclaim his own infinite beauty

and plunged despite your protests and cries

into that watery realm of fame and indignation

Joe ! you shouted Come back ! drowned worlds

epiphanies of endless sky and brooding cloud

theater and nothing more of mortal error

it all happened so fast one day on the snowy slope

the next navigating unknown dance partners across

a nocturnal floor strangers flexed on alcohol

and jazz the swift flight to a planet of cities

emerald alabaster pure junk and drums

how did the world go away ? a dive off

the high board into a water of shouts and

terror the glee of being and being no more !

08-09-22

"LA LITERATURA NO VALE NADA"

Roberto Bolaño

for Indran Amirthanayagam

a course in cloud physics or the destruction of letters

one by one apocryphal omegas or zetas fallen from grace

we suffer from the plenitude of sound and meaning

each shoulder over-burdened with petty human grief

the cathedral that cries out from its knees sorrowing

because water has neither margin nor gender in sleep

the stone the cup the horse consciousness itself

sacrifice the Horn of Africa ! adolescent epigraphy

windows that are placed inside out and cities

like onion skin placed one on top of the other and

put to the torch because someone named Helen !

relentless resonance of hives deep within the ear

labyrinth of language at fault the baseless noise

reassembled and put to the vote and statues taught

to speak think and see ! blinking in the face of

the soldered sun's blank homophone louder than ever

in the seamless advent of light just before dawn

memorization of wave-length and photosynthesis

hypotenuse and isosceles where ant and bee dwell

deities ! summons and warrants ! shipments of

enlarged photos of space before the Big Bang

poetry dissolved by mercury ! poetry in chemo-therapy

nerve and insouciance of girls named Opium and Ecstasy

sacrifice the Horn of Africa ! Sri Lanka bankrupt !

Pakistan on the verge ! Kabul declared insane !
they keep repeating the same old litany about money
banks are holy temples the rich have no feet et cetera
meter and rhyme abolished by rightwing nationalists
Yemen erased from the map ! Abu Dhabi is supreme !
the world is a spinning top gone mad scarcely visible
in the cosmic scheme of things and dreams and
alternate realities transfusion of dialects in the Deccan
slumlords and the House of Windsor and face-down
as a silhouette etched in concrete by the Nagasaki blast
Harry Truman ! all flights have been cancelled
only five billionaires are allowed to remain on ventilators
what has literature to do with anything ? Superman
and Madonna and the fluttering vultures of the IMF
unexamined fictions in the dying twenty-first century
David Bowie and John Lennon understood !
sacrifice the Horn of Africa ! none of the keys works
the doors have all been altered and there are test-tube
babies walking like zombies in the suburbs of São Paulo
human excrement instead of parks and greenery
life after death life after death life after death
what other poem is there ? narcissism and greed
bipolar politicians prime ministers in zoot suits
Nehru's face stamped on Islamabad street signs
Hare Krishna ! electricity psychoanalysis cyclotrons
the future has come and gone in triplicate carbon copy
nowhere is the present tense of any use dot dot dot

Mozart wrote the Bible ! the movie version rated R

Mary Lou is Scheherazade the rest is funkadelic

what has literature to do with anything ?

sacrifice the Horn of Africa ! give it to Bill Gates

shop around Motown synthesis silent Night

08-10-22

NELLA SELVA OSCURA

do we still walk in that wood you and I

phantoms of an unraveled memory as if

to reach the moon fingers touching

insect kingdoms arrayed beside small

inscrutable designs like Chinese asterisks

the distance between two blades of grass

links to a ceremony of vanished dew

imitating poetry of the French impressionists

we gathered adolescence in sheaves of damaged light

envy of words and a language too delicate

for the leaves it inspired the vast panoply

of unseen events that storm the noontime sky

the lawn suddenly grown shorter by a thumb

the sheer improbability of getting home by dusk

you and I lost in that wood of dense error

which path stone or leaf could signal

the recondite dialects in the hills at day's end ?

what was to understand ? insolence of nouns
like bees swarming in the wrong direction
could this be the way out the exit to sunlight ?
furnished with planetary symbols and accidence
we hit upon the city and then other cities
disordered mistaken places of false chronologies
buttressed by myth of height and cloud
as in a theater of statues learning to be
there was an excess of parallel lives
re-encounters with those lost or disappeared
in fields of heat and rumor in a past that
was no less remote than a recent yesterday
months seemed to exist on fingertips and
years were sedentary lessons in a Latin text
great cycles of space encompassed in a single verb !
differences between north and south argued
a measure of silences and yearning if only
the book could be memorized with its pages
of undecipherable scripts and nostalgia
when read aloud individual syllables lacked
any real meaning merely sequences of notes
tones buzzes and humming fraught with tears
it was to grieve ! the soul in flight half
way to its destination simply turned to smoke
in a summer air of faint recollections
distribution of sounds undistilled mélange
of everything that happened since birth
to this still point when without compass

somewhere within this ominous wood

we came face to face with our own eternity

08-12-22

THE IMPONDERABLE WEIGHT OF THE PAST

temple of Minerva salt-encrusted mirage

white on white blank and blanker still

the endless horizon the perpetual void

the sleep at the end of sleep even as we

walk slowly the unmoored shores of rumor

hand in hand slipping away through knots

of atmosphere and distance some unspoken

heart an error in pronoun and usage a fault

to rectify in the following life we saunter

into a daze of mirrors and dust an emptiness

that comes with the long passage of years

voices as if disentangled from the leaves

a hand that yearns to understand its shape

and grasses that lure shadows to their doom

ruin built on ruin motion of stone and echo

remote thoughts only half complete that

issue out of the mythic hills to the west

toward which we tarry slowly slowly with

nothing more than the multi-chambered

dark mansion of recollections shared between

the phantom likenesses of our own selves !
do we then turn to find beside us No one !
the great radio program of unseen doors and
noises that shiver in an eerie phonology has
taken us by surprise into somewhere else
an archaic landscape of urns and ogives
skies plundered for their gold assonance
mutilations ! gods of statues truncated and
sent plunging like ill-fated planets from
the ancestral heavens of etymology
down to the bottomlands and pools
which we skirt in passing wending our way
homeward in the unnamed dusk of fireflies
a screen door slams in perplexity and
always asking what is the half of everything ?
we enter the charade and dance of memory
faded faces eroded names darkened houses
numbered streets and avenues someone always
unexpected who appears in an upper story window
or a book and a column of ants and heat
dizzying spires of summer air the deaths
that surround with their enormous immobility
trees and the souls that have fled through
their branches seeking oblivion and as ever
the playgrounds of echo if only if only
the terrible intangibility of the past
did anything at all ever happen ?

08-13-22

AT THE SOURCE OF THE POEM

dignity honor betrayal satisfaction

seduction agony justice resonance

sheep and doves and clouds far above

white that floods the dreamer's eye

stone gravel roadside tombs equality

the shifting moving dead the verses

none can hear recited solemnly in sleep

trophies mutilated statues rusted cannons

lawns where voices bury their sounds

grass and its unexplained nouns darker

than evening dense and rich polyphony

of silence when everything gathers for

a moment before dispersing in altitudes

far above the sailor's unclaimed corpse

gods are etymologies of immortality

false promises of substance and air

shorelines beckoning hands farewell

cinema of apotheosis among fireflies

leaves screens stairways distances

memory lapsed in the coma of eternity

bee-hives cement foundations Paradise

which is the other which is the self?

rejuvenation state secrets nocturnal abyss

parks cemeteries hills dialects yearning

distinctions memorials speeches rectitude

crematoria myth nymphs absolution

shadow-play fossils language x-rays

pediatric isolation mourning forestry

lakes fogs ditches mountains grief

at the source of the poem

08-14-22

WHAT PHOTOS CANNOT RESTORE

such as it is and when they had ceased falling
the many and nameless into the various abyss
ditches face down in lakes of mire no more
by the moon above guided nor by the voice
of the heavens often heard in sleep the signals
worn on arms as bracelets shining of the goddesses
in raiment pure as waters of the celestial realms
stepping among the mangled and mutilated torsos
the heroes as it were of many a written schoolboy-
verse efforts to purify and the overwhelming thunder
grief a-plenty and rivers surging their putrid banks
earth ! ungiven to mercy the left and right the up
and down and who could count as far as it goes
in the night not recognizing brother or son
in the relentless fray the missiles and flares
asterisks and ampersands soundless syllables
bottle-green eyes of the prophetess on her steps
chain-smoking a single cigarette and ululating

tears and weeping the everlasting sorrow for why ?
can nothing come back ? photos cannot restore
loss of memory capitulation of metal and thought
serving dust and the power of mud insects reign
over the futile plots of ground the fields destroyed
by dialects of greed and lust the agonizing will
to desire what can never be possessed and dreams
suffixed to the illusion of breath the haunted who
abide by the ruins and houses and tents and air
darkened by birds of prey and drone and buzz of
swarms invisible and awful prepared to finish the day
this just one out of many ! lessons unlearned
--of what is beauty the symbol ?

08-15-22

THE DANCE OF WORDS

what fate is sealed by words alone
what sounds in sleeping leaves remind
of lighter times of days of greenery and
shining and surfaces of distance like pools
within which shadows gleam darting like
fish in elegant display reflections of far-off
lightning bolts or gods themselves disguised
as argent clouds or sheaves of mercury sent
through the heavens with messages meant

for mortals of their births and deaths
words alone epithets and roadside markers
directions or errors whichever way the dazed
soul takes confronting sun's emblematic spore
was once more than words alone a design
of breath and mind the play of give and take
here stood the rock and there the tree dividing
you from me small discoveries of noise
increments of time called days and weeks
we grew into syllables and punctuations
pauses between enigmatic accidents that
defined the grammar of memory's errant route
was then the first to fall and others followed
swift in some invisible battle-field where seeds
of ire and envy planted turned to weaponry
metal and rust aggravation and yearning
the body's mysterious intent to understand
the drug of love the puzzling use of pronouns
what mask to wear when chasing fireflies
what person to assume in the school charade
until one day unasked words alone failed
darkness filled the rented room forty floors above
the street that raced with ambulance and charity
fixities of thought turned fluid in that small space
one two and three no other numbers counted
placing the head on its remote dialect of stone
echoes not words winging in the labyrinth of air

bearing all that remained of life's brief song

the dance to hold what one could never know

08-16-22

THE POET ANSWERS A QUESTION

with what clarity of vision did you write
      The Structure of Hell ?

it was Talmudic in spirit and infernal in nature

with either hand on the slipping globe and

the golden assonance of the ear's tempests

deafening even as the lines came and went

with a Dantesque lucidity traveling and descending

from one gyre to the next 'til I came to the still

point known as The Death of Stalin and even there

who could halt the passage of words in their rush

to annihilate their sense and self even as I kept

Looking for Mary Lou in the wasteland of illegal syntax

coming up with nothing but false illusions back alleys

bar-room brawls noon time bouts with Homeric wine

assiduous and collateral damage to the temples

where Diana and Aphrodite hand-wrestled for

a spear of grass for an evening in the Upanishads

for just one Saturday left alone to brood on

the Hapax Legomenon despite the din of noontime

soap operas on the wide screen and the jostling

up and down looking for the moon in the least likely

and hustling and jotting and constantly scribbling

did thus The Tragedy of Momus come to light

in the bracken weir of the work-a-day world

our hero spent in cribbed catalogs classifying

fiction and politics and social unrest in the Mahabharata

elongating wherever possible the ampersand and

its forerunners in tragic citations to lost works

such as Fiat Lux with its troubling references

to fraternal death to loss and miasma and plunging

darkly the planets of aspiration and cosmic disorder

wherever was not possible writings and inscriptions

and longitudes of feeling the one single thread

that running turns ever redder until and to this

hour a day is no longer what it seems and bury

the child and force the knee to retribution and struggle

as the pen might to understand there is never enough ink

never the right syllable always the misplaced vowel or

the fractured consonant on The Blank Page

and so forth amen et cetera a paean and a hymn to

That Goddess incomplete unrolling scrolls litanies

and roadside illegibility highlights that score

the poet's failed efforts to elucidate these brief

moments of enigma and breath before

The Translation to Heaven ...

08-17-22

AS THE WORLD BURNS

to ask what for the coins crowns floral displays

window-dressing life sequences for what ?

look around not even the French poetry book

nor the Buddhist hybrid Sanskrit nor the severance

pay and the docked items from the list of forgeries

the multiple and supreme dead the grasses counted

between their fingers the ashes tossed into the Grand Canyon

today's drought vivid discourse between waters and

the Biblical flood the temptation to levitate to forget

three feet off the surface without wings only a

disposition – it is not to write verses any more

to lop off the branch the golden fruit to mire the self

in destinies of distance and unreckoning like planets

off course mule-teams hauling solar cupolas into darkness

such as it ever was rows of houses numbered and

discarded for sleeping late odd and even tick tick tick

the ear devastated by a soprano angel who cannot remember !

forests of communities burning in the grief of that ear

swallow-tails circling the great Umbrian tomb

in the long solemn evenings without detail of death

and longing and trusses of camphor and castor oil

saliva of the late gods of antiquity turning to smoke

resin and iota and paraphernalia of forgotten rites

sacrifices animal and vegetal and mortals too !

knives blessed by Moloch and the angry divinities of Jerusalem

desiccation of Eden and Palmyra and wherever else

paradise once bloomed Hollywood and Bakersfield !

how is one ever to get home again ? the clematis ivy

with its beautiful red flowers adorning the driveway or

the hollyhocks like painted tissue-paper petals waving

in the nostalgia of a gone memory far from Minnesota

patio and diversion phantoms sipping mint tea and mandrake

when will the next world begin ? here are small spaces

allotted to tiny houses to witchcraft and divination

here are precious stones set in the eye ready to burn

throughout the night when the mind is most apt to increase

and all of the cosmos split unevenly in half divided

between the twins of fever and suspicion

here is virtually everything caught in error of being

tinder prepared to blaze at the tail-end of the universe

and speeches of dying politicians and movie actors

wielding high-powered rifles and elephants running amok

in Times Square where the neon clock registers midnight

on the rim there is a love-song a fading phonology

wistful attribute of stars dead three trillion light years

in passing – to ask for what ?

08-18-22

THE SOUND OF DISTANCE

the sound of distance moving away from itself

syntactic units surrounding blank spaces

of life the definition the tender buds the promises
nothing gained by an afternoon out of time
in the great bibliothèque of Antiquity
elbow to elbow with a phantom nymph a voice
calling forth for one more repetition and silence
isolation of sound bites reel to reel cognition
a finger gone missing in the grasses of renewal
dazed and celebrated Joe staggers from a Yucatan
of bar fights and thought-struggles with stars green
with alcohol and hill dialects the worsening dark
plight of millions stoned and brandishing a mystic
rod a cone a hat a fluttering device that turns
hours around backwards and the very sight !
when and how ? one minute the sidewalk
establishes its constancy and the next the abyss opens
beneath our feet and howls and presentiments of
the denizens of Inferno so proximate and obvious
possess us even as we measure the distance to the Mayo clinic
and the tolling bells of five PM and the abstractions
of French art and imperialist colonization and movies
Joe turned the windy corner by the Kahler Hotel
and simply disappeared and not until decades later
did he resurface in Victoria State Australia ! dead !
yet there we are still listening to the roar of diesels
daydreaming of the far east which is their destination
a Buddha's footprint away ! life begins and ends
a few breaths a walk in the park of paradise a dip

in the pool where eternity snares unwitting souls

picture post-cards of Greek vase paintings Achilles

taking a deep nose dive into Hades ! pronouns

and epithets and dictation and asterisks and ampersands

the whole paraphernalia of the Roman Empire

under Domitian and the high school kids laughing

it off infinitely remote in the snowfalls of yesteryear

Joe ! a footnote to the tremendous time-trap of oblivion

tomorrow – me too

08-19-22

EL MISMO CHICANO SOY YO
para mi hermana Laurita

seen from a distance no memory allows

the scraggle clad kid tagging far behind

oblivious to but not envying the experts

who can manage to hit the ball high into the air

counterclockwise and manage to get a homerun

every time while you simply abide in the sun's

enormous and buzzing rumor of heat and eternity

what is a letter of the alphabet ? what is a wind-chime ?

what are vespers and longing ? who dwells in

the hills just west of the city limits ? what is a dialect ?

is alcohol the answer ? or a map invented by the Popol Vuh ?

where is there to go if not away ? is a girl friend the essence ?

and how do they say that in Toltec ? air with its
hundred and one compartments of sound and music
is great and the efforts to swim against the current
and stand up beside the shadow and declare the House !
how can one live outside the window ? are the plums
over-ripe and the gravel too loud ? how can anything
be accounted for when everyone is secretly laughing ?
the walk home is always longest in the afternoon
and the shouts from the pool and the metronome
that measures the size of the piano lesson and mostly
coming to consciousness ! what is a wet-back ?
and looking in all the shop windows it suddenly
becomes Christmas again and the bitter snows
and if father will sober up for dinner and not shout
all the way down to Laredo and nostalgia for corn-meal
and tortillas and pulque and the aggravation of
learning to pronounce English correctly and forlorn
looking askance hoping no one will notice the item
in the newspaper la Vergüenza ! growing up as other
constantly on the alert for news of normalcy and pronouns
that distinguish between us and them and to always
be the last to be chosen for the team because just because
of your name

08-20-22

THE BEE IN THE ATTIC

instability of air and darkness in the ear

shut out the summer solstice of time and

memory the blank epistle hovering between

the dual silences of a postponed midday

alone the bee lost in the attic buzzing

insomniac and aphasic in the mind's dense

labyrinth of interjection and caesura

is it the same as a Chinese box or a sand drill ?

are there invisible windows that open on gravel

or do the stairs no longer work and the noise

of smoke and prayers between cigarettes

the secrets one has to keep from the fathers

and their electric hammers and the cotton

wadding insulating the world from this space

the droning humming buzzing madness

a month encompassed in a matter of minutes

groping one's way toward the fallacy and

when an imminent thought breaks through

the floating ampersands and distorted flight

what is the identity of the soul in question ?

hands are attributes of a missing reality

the bed shoved into an interstice of July

heat ! insolence and aggravation of the archaic

a rock put into place where the head should be

and fingers and grasses of intuition and

darker still the interposition of light

like a knife aimed at the first of August !

to wake to this incessant ricochet of breath

and expectation of grief to hear someone

sobbing between the yellow soiled sheets

the transpiration of some divinity prior

to the invention of order one by one

the intensities and the directionless flare

zooming and angling for some lost planet

wild honey ! phases of the moon

somewhere out there !

08-21-22

THE PERIL OF EXISTENCE

you never know how close you come

to the Jade Inferno you never know

when a god becomes an ambulance

bearing copies of mortal souls to their fate

kids playing cops 'n robbers too close

to the sun and one goes into convulsions

and no apostrophe or comma can help

was this Priam's valiant son ? did he ?

closer to the Jade Inferno and the god

mocking with his mouth the dreaded siren

chasing through busy city streets when

noon is ripest and most deadly and metal

has no concussion like the bright shine

reflecting the confused loss of cognition

in its sudden beauty of yellow alabaster

or hives turned inside out so the blackness

shows for all to weep not knowing why

was the brother listening ready to take

the chariot and the swerving horses

to the enormous empty road ahead ?

never know when your turn comes

to approach the Jade Inferno with hands

palsied and infirm of foot and yawning

the abyss is right next door where shadows

of kids playing doctor tend the wounded grass

and suddenly a goddess with plaited braids

and a smile that stuns takes the kids one by

one and nothing you can do as laughing

she returns them to the Jade Inferno

08-22-22

THE BEE AND ANT

in the throes of indignation

one god says to another

let's blow it up ! smirks and

smiles and hands like dynamite

the clouds rent apart the skies

torn asunder the notion of time
on the edge of grass the hurt and
suffering to the bone the nylon
hypothesis to continue on with
motors and fractions and school
lessons aimed to kill why forever ?
says to the goddess in repose
her lap smothered with love bites
the fuse is there the flame and
torch the match to light the rest
of space so there's no tomorrow
and chariots they whip up and steeds
blacker than endless night and
verses recited as loud as the sun
chase the dumb mortal to his den
and gives no mercy shows no
taint of breath but surprise taking
pronouns away shifting masks
from face to face and blank statues
talking talking numb as sleep
and history they crumple up like paper
and myth and language both denied
it's afternoon in the glass and
shadows eager to depart with book
and quill and poetry of massacre
here's the clinic and here's the drug !
off they go over the cliff and plunge

like weary planets from the scope

so long ! they had their chance

to cut stone and progress through

narrows of water and memory

enough ! didn't heed the cry nor

ceremonies of vision and hearing

wheels ! sands ! the abyss eternal

had their moment to operate

but only doubled the dangers of

identity and forgot to turn off

the ignition and set the mind

on its distant pyre not listening

to what the leaf designed nor

what the bee and ant sleeping

in the ear had once dreamt

08-22-22

THIRTEEN NUMBER

stood grinning in the doorway Death
mace in hand and only five houses remaining
before thirteen number the highest in the series
and shadowless and the sound of gravel
night-stiff trees by the side yew and cypress
what day in the exterior of time was this ?
turn to me and hold what there is to touch

frailty and illusion and nothing more
take a step without moving the feet and cry out
the self has no embodiment but the mirror
it holds in the left hand and pronouns to eliminate
in the doorway motionless hair unkempt a
blowsy direction of air dense darkening
whatever else is to be written to be scored to be
announced without punctuation and in Spanish
below the belt Death enticing beautiful half and half
the moons of the treble noise ! turn again to me
and say the words that emerge from stone
speak ! once more before thirteen the highest number
and penetrate the other side there where angel
used to stand quivering like the flame of love
no more say I ! white-armed Hera ! transom
and gibbet the holy section of atmosphere
and the world below a dice game and booze
in the doorway half-past noon the evidence
of the grimoire the text upended and throttled
like ignition in the wayfaring mind searching
for the five houses and seventeen windows
the advance of fate and the noose and drill
ambulances and cavities where the brain of water
flows bearing with it the Image and whatever
else is loose in the grammar of memory
to stop and wait while grinning mace in hand Death
takes no step not moving from the ill-advised

alphabet and to the rear something else ominous
thirteen number the furious moment when everything
imitates itself in a history of glass and resonance
in an instant the end will be perpetuated in a repetition
of sound and ampersands !
why me and not you ?

08-23-22

VARIATIONS ON ILIAD VIII, 381

yet even as Hera daughter of Kronos
yoking her gold-harnessed horses
and what to make of the disorder and
early grief the weeping hidden in the eaves
the mists and flood gates opened and
seas unremitting in their terrible noise
even as Hera white-armed and wrathful
designs revenge and humiliation do mortals
sleep unawares and thunders mighty and
evanescent rolling through the ear and
the panoply of metals and chemistry
weaponry and gadgets waiting to sack
the citadel and the ten-fold city with its
layers of streets libraries and clinics
the very heights ! even as in a dream
the unfurling hours dwarfed by steeds

unruly and swart of the sun his dominion
overpowering with a single consonant
the minds of men vague and besotted
with glories illusory and cheap nothing
but ornaments and girls paraded before
glass and smoking lavender cigarettes
the byways and dead-ends of night unholy
squandered good virtues in the name of War
even as Hera exulting cursing ire-filled
plies the nameless avenues in search
of meat and devotion and the warriors
greaves and fillets and fitted with ear-rings
and bracelets and spears sharpened like
vowels in the tongue of the oracle yea !
the warriors painted and set into motion
by the potter's wheel and loud headstrong
plunging stupidly into Stygian waters
thoughtless enmities between gods embroidered
and trussed for a long night's brawl what !
it can no longer be today ! there are no other days
no situations with dates and fixed promontories
peninsulas of gas ! even as Athena sheds her
shining raiment and pleads with the floor
to go into battle dressed only in tears and
sobbing amulets and specific verses unrecalled
the small whistles of memory the children
playing ball on the sands of oblivion tokens

and symbols of sonant gold the plural of death

even as Hera kicks with her proud sandaled foot

the funerary urn spilling the lukewarm ashes

pronouns of the unidentified and forgotten

what does the Cloud-gatherer have to say !

08-24-22

HOW DO WE KNOW WHO WE REALLY ARE ?

if I am humanly possible and I must be

in whatever dictionary or lexicon you look

observe the failing sound the noise from afar

the twain and the triplicate of pure air

talking in someone else's sleep with my

twin's other voice ! echo of unheard echo

stone and rock and gravel underfoot

wheels and pyramids and music of the spheres

a lesson in triangle a fomented quadrant

cities ! maps of their underside and sewage

localization of ego and unfounded rumors

of personality and mask the shattered asterisks

of two days on trial because the sun's homophone

remained rigid in a swiftly mobilizing space

cosmic instructions to destroy ! whenever possible

the disunion and harmony of grasses rising

toward their unspecified evening and target

death ! resemblances to the House and

its avenue of utter sadness and distance

I am that child ! the one enmeshed in memory

of the half-recalled day the arcane possibility

filled with words and associations of myth

chronology of supporting vowels and the consonant

alone in its function of separating silences

I am still here shadow walking the rim

each has a hand to offer none has fingers

to repudiate and the process revolves tacitly

through pages of isolated oblivions

who is to say ? fever and redaction of text

title after title eliminated by the Censor

until we arrive at this small place

judgment and dream impossible to extricate

skin and its song from the ovarian maze

we are born ! and only once before shifting

into the red zones of unnamed planets

unsighted copies of the universe legends

soundless verses to be recited in the afterlife

the drip-drop of dew on the leaf-tip

that alerts the Ear to its own conclusion

08-25-22

THE MYSTERY OF THE FIRST REPETITION

for Solomon Rino

I hear the voice of some goddess or other astray

among the mules of insomnia already darker

than imagined the stalls meandering through

verses indistinguishable from the clauses

that put statues to sleep the broad-rimmed vowel

now long now short of the evanescent text of light

not for a moment linger there half-dead heavy

with rock formation and distance which is nostalgia

resonance of hills perturbed by dialects of imitation

the elongated memory of a former life in italics

how can we capture the grass ? intaglios and brooding

on the half-forgotten name the portion of air that

simply eludes definition clouds and thunder

in the theater that won't go away with diminished

recall of the face of some goddess or other dim

among the illusory metaphors of a silver age epic

warrior and bard and stoned mythographer

who is at the point of no return the library steps

the engraved lions of wind and oblivion about

to take shape and move as mortals in the crowds

and automobiles and talking wings ! consonants

and the decibel that renders understanding futile

note after note of the unstrung harp and clarity

in the sudden monsoon that pours through the brain

Orestes ! asleep at the wheel dodging missiles

the rife and spite of a misused existence and come

to the end wandering in the mudflat outskirts of Troy

or Thebes and the Sphinx speaking in gravel riddles

night-shade the effervescent moment the epiphany

when the mind goes into its first repetition

terrible recollection of the drugstore when time

ceased having duration and glass and perfumes

and the mingled voices of girls eleven or twelve of them

and their hair all locked in a room without doors

or windows and the fast and irremovable page

where everything and nothing is written forever

08-26-22

ENCOUNTER OF ODYSSEUS AND POLYPHEMUS

so much and so many winds tempests the curved

waters signatures of air corrosive debts of light

in vain we struggled to set up the masts and

unfurl the sails in the full sound of the orchestra

drums and ear-rings and shallow-faced kings from

afar watching the sun's glistening hoarse homophone

blackening in the verse's pitched oracle night

approaching even before midday past its hour

surfaces a glint in the Cyclops's immemorial eye

bellowing of cattle and sheep in the midst of cliffs

fury of voices rattles demonic hissing serpentine

and the maze of vowels unthought consequences
of coming to breathe the atmospheres mephitic and
rusting oxides the shields and panoply a warrior's
last hide-bound gear dream-spelled and flirting
with the goddess hidden in her apparel of gesso
and adamantine substance the scripts displayed
in her gaze the lethal promises the salt-girt storms
of sound and devastation of memory books and
quills and inks of spatial dimensions the world
at large pawn in a flawed dice game and more
than anything the slain at the altars and blood
the envelopes of hair the still palpitating hearts
of love ! how to describe the infernal mess flight
and error the enormous rumor of mercy among
the celestials and the writing of this and that
the scores of missing children and their grass
the tremendous distance between thumb and
forefinger isolated and nostalgic afternoons with
nowhere to go holler and disorientation of
volcanic figures painted on cave-walls and who
and what and where is the exit ? Splash ! cities fallen
into churning seas and heat greater than ever in
cycles that last two minutes and messages in glass
fixation and devotion images of salvation and lore
of the dead who are scheduled to return evenings
in the hills of longing far to the west of dewfall
alas and evermore the forlorn sleeping in rock

dreaming texts of infant alphabets drone and hum
the hive ! the perpetual moment of eternity
in the sudden passage from adolescence to aphasia
leaf and montage of silence the ineffable note
were we ever more human ?

08-27-22

IN THE SPIRIT OF THE GREEK ANTHOLOGY

who is the most grieved in our midst ?
fractures of number divided by soul
wending its way from hive to light
winged devotion and scintillating
blind small figurine of eight cycling
on the wheel invisible rotation and
digit a memory of grass and pools
what was only a noun resemblance
to a name a sound rounding air and
wind against the brief cliff of accidence
what waves of transgress and math
leaning against the noise as if to hear
what is to see and what to learn and
where ? looking to the below of time
to fossil and microbe and anemone
sometimes roseate and gossamer pretty
as a painted thought on glazed clay

this who this misty-eyed the long-gone
immemorial of hand and depth his spirit
claims nothing but a silent epitaph
syllables drifting aloft fluted column
of doubt and error to reckon sidewise
reading the evanescent script of breeze
forgetting the shapes of letters and
glyphs storm of ciphers enigmas and
birth-mysteries evolving cocoon of death
to him belong the lost adjectives rumors
the accident of existence the deceit
of identity the sorrowing fogs and
miasma always the tortured foot to
lift and take a step and falter plunging
into the ear's undiscovered seas
listening to the shell where echoes
are born and the lone cry of the gull
and wings and reflections glint and
gold assonance of the last wave
distance of the fleeing soul
shadowy flux of waters
the eternal
Max

08-28-22

KISMET

just as Jupiter fierces the green fields

with pest and famine so the body indulges

death with its hap and dread and we mere

shadows in mortal guise strutting the puny

surface dream and masked in love's illusion

pen and scribble verses of man's decay

the lot of plant and animal alike dead-end

of light and disdain of air the demise of cities

planets that orbit the mind's small ring

and sound crashing in the ear's fragile shell

shapes of noise sights of bottomlands and

depths of water mushrooming to the skies

a Latin meter or the complex oriental vowels

of texts that cannot unravel and mantras and

jeers the gaping face that mirrors ecstasies

and angst before moving on to a lasting sleep

do I know you from somewhere ? the morgue

perhaps or the last rites of an unnamed hero

between leaf and grass the footfall of silence

murmur of insects praying for a final rain

ineluctable speech of demolished statues

quarried from the remains of archaic thought

do I know you from somewhere ? marketplace

in Old Algiers the song like a skein of dew

and mist nostalgia and distance pyramids

that ghosts climb in repetitions of memory

we danced and shut our eyes and lay in

fields spreading far south of the necropolis

we knew each other from somewhere

in the half-conscious trance of adolescence

then moved on to futile spheres of intellect

forgetting the touch of skin the patina

of perspiration emboldened passions bring

the constant longing that comes of birth

the look askance of the heart's first mystery

what was once and now only oblivion's lintel

myth and reverie ampersand and et cetera

of eternity

08-30-22

NIBBANA

"... Mahayana a avut loc exact acum un minut și jumătate"*
                                        Mircea Eliade, Adio!

horizon and hill both involved in heat's

furious infinity a mist a haze trance formations

of rock and leaf distances measured by ants

and the enormous yellow phases of the bee

sun unmitigated in its rampant homophone

blackening registers of mid-day accidents

the girls slain in their grass of tenderness

the boys in the drug of their desire all hands

plunged head-long into death's small pool

sound the carillon ! who can be remembered ?

only the sound and silhouette of passing

between the revolving doors of existence

signatures and mottos cheers for the squad

or a blind-date the heart's oriental regret

faces dissolved in the lye of an imperfect afternoon

a rusted civil war cannon and the 19th century

court-house vacant but for multiplied ghosts

without voice the solitary trek home evenings

when all memory of light has been erased

and behind the shutters depths of the ear

sunk in unfathomable waters of a previous life

what is to wake ? how long ago did the first ?

ages pass in the minute it takes to die

mornings without the sun and messages from

abroad about the Buddha's passing beneath

a solitary tree the immense painting of breath

taken by the early winds of autumn and sorrow

unendurable effect of birth misunderstood

here and here but not there ! allow for nothing

but the long and eerie dialect of echoes that

riddle the siesta of oblivion

  *"The Mahayana took place exactly a minute
and a half ago"

08-31-22

WEARY OF LIFE

cattle raids movie versions of life

Saturday afternoon in the Upanishads

learning to unmask the individual only

to discover the other individual ! Atman !

soul the brevity of breath and light

conscious or unconscious wearing skin

and talking prattling on about what !

sunk in one's own thoughts submerged

in the great carnival of dreams

to wake ! a thousand and twelve Arhats

carved out of teakwood and dispelling

cloud fabric and the ulterior skies that

take flight above the congress of death

similitude and metaphor of language

downtown with the girl-singers

nostalgic for what can never be and

little by little coming to terms with ending

the illusory farce the staged text of

coming to be and going forth into

the glass scheduled for tomorrow

the cadaver on the road that's us !

me and them you and us fickle pronouns

personae and Sanskrit tautology

loud and resonating for years in

the ear's delirious oceanic maze

I hear you ! there's a parade next Monday

and you'll be marching with your tuba
smart in your pseudo-military regalia
chariots of the sun ! blazing blackness !
death is ripe and who isn't hungry ?

09-01-22

A MESSAGE FROM ZEUS

tomorrow when the light makes
new satellites on the mountain-tops
I'll be gone –
    who said that ?
do the gates of heaven shut forever ?
is the sham of breath a lost memory ?
make me happy ! toss me over the cliff
and joyous hearken to the gods one last !
waters that seize sleep by the arms
clouds that rain gravel all night long
impotent rage of Hera ! is day a loss ?
frequent mirrors that delay consciousness
and faces that emerge from quicksilver
hands that bundle mown grasses toiling
in yards and fields where children become
absent hollow reveries and echoes
ricocheting through hills of dialect
the great longing ! enigmas and mysteries !

when did we ever walk this path seeking

the plastic toy that is the key to life ?

send me a message about the dark !

is two the only real number ?

one afternoon when the sun stood still

over the adjacent park we leaped playing

the jigsaw puzzle of mind forever incomplete !

in which window did it all happen ?

remember the time we watched angel

plummet head first out of the sky ?

the moment of the highway crash

when metal received the heavenly specter

sirens and drones buzz and hum

of ambulances and hives the stretchers

bore the Greek kids away from the scene

it was the first painting of death

a picture postcard showing Achilles

bound for the Mansion of Pluto

did we understand ?

tomorrow when the light makes

new satellites on the mountain-tops

I'll be gone –

09-02-22

SEPTEMBER SONG

who is the author of this great chariot

which cannot find direction nor in one place

remain still its solid axles of molten butter

and its wild swart steeds all hoof and muscle

gleaming like cities in motion high in the skies ?

I am the sun-king ! cries from somewhere a

voice a sonant gold syllable a feathery tuft

of memory indistinguishable from the waters

that flow through inconstant mortal dreams

vowels and echoes of rock and cliffs that hang

even as they walk across the liquid roofs

beneath which sleep the dead of yore the fuming

disregard for realities and gods the myths

that cling like curtains to the obsessed mind

who created this north and distant south

these wayward wests opposed to the mountainous

easts where they say is born the latest day ?

the fringes of air the purplish iridescent thought

that we too we will assume birth-right and totem

agonies the flux of breath and darkness roaming

through small paradises of drug and pronoun

charades ! the antique luster of glass gleaming

as an idea on the long avenue that leads

from high-school graduation to the cremation

ground in the Deccan spooks and phantoms

myriads of us clustering like fireflies against

a screen door the lattice-work of consonants
language and futility ! the same dense wind
that brings the sea's ornamental surfaces
to the moment of cognition and aphasia
brothers ! don't fight ! the world's bubble
is not there at all in your playing fields and
maps for it is all foretold and extinguished
in the march upcountry to the Volcano
leap ! partake of the weed that renders madness
the lucidity to see through the cycles of birth
and reckon how much is left to experience
who is the lunatic who painted these histories ?
nothing to recall everything to forget !

09-03-22

GRIEF IS IN THE CLOUDS

and mountains when they talk
it is with the silence of the ages
only in dreams can we hear them
stone and cliff of adamant distance
nothing of what they say ever comes back
and meteor and asterisk alike sound
in the night-skies their mournful siren
bearing still another soul into the vacuum
astounded we feign worship and imitate

prayer-wheels revolving the agitated mind

around a copy of the archaic syllable

interred in the ear like labyrinthine gravel

wake ! what's to remember of the light ?

one by one our steps circulate in the sands

and are erased in the small measure

it takes for the body to forget itself

hills of western nostalgias ! grasses

that come rushing to embrace the dark

silhouettes and pronouns dissolving

in the storm of leaves by the eastern gate

grief is in the clouds lowing like cattle

ruminants of a former cosmos faint

and ruddy like the dusts of the Iliad

what is there to know ? an escape valve

is nowhere in sight nor doorknobs

nor window sashes only the pallid

resemblance of the goddess in glass

come evening in the houses of memory

09-04-22

IPHIGENIA AT AULIS

no more of the day's ruins a lesson

in Greek fable rock and choir of birds

sighted north by north-east over waters

to set sail there in freshly caulked boats
the narrows to define by dream-spell
oriental luxuries the waste of memories
heights to ascend the shining of nouns
that have never been spoken for things
and attributes hidden from mortal ken
do the gods devise such stratagems ?
yesterday was supposed to have been
a celebration of breath and loud !
eager to move forward the mind and
its patois holidays underside thoughts
patterns of rain and storm the vertigo
of life each and every moment unsure
as to foot and wing directions to take
full throttle distance anguish and burden
shoulders weighted by cathedrals of care
heat of the sun ! Mycenaean puppet-theater
airwave frequencies jet-stream flows
disease the constant factor in any death
lesions in the body politic Attic debate
over syllabic decay the waters rising
too fast ports deluged the Trojan Horse !
there we were playing at odds on the shore
waiting for the right moment to set sail
mast and oars in place men lined up
according to vowel and consonant of choice
waves lapping surge and foam language

so many nuances hills distances eddies

a hand a forked tongue a vision to deny

haze and meltdown of summer afternoons

wasps in attack formation trees lying down

leaf and grass and sand which is the most ?

the names we were given to what avail ?

would three o'clock school bell ever ring ?

threats of horizon and unnamed planets

heaving carelessly into view in daylight

the trick is to die on time ! Mother !

09-05-22

DARKNESS AND LEAVES DISCOURSING

for Miriam Tarcov

the clear lake then and inane sleep

emptying its horn of dreams and no

more longed to regain earth the fleeing

shadows that once embodied pronouns

was nowhere but silence and trees bent

near altars and embers still warm and

memories great and pellucid to the skies

what was to question of the waning light ?

did some animal still dwell in the mind's

fugitive desire to comprehend ? what !

discerned inert the figures by the roadside

victims of some enigmatic accident or rule
inventing language and systems of sound
to convey impotence of thought and grief
were births before and after to blame ?
whether to make a weapon of the hand
or in its fantastic shape to imagine ?
unquestioning at first we walked the sad
path home daily to a surfeit of mystery
the one who came first was the one who
came last in the series of vocables and
syllabic descant and in the winds violence
and troubling hemlines of oblivion night
and juxtaposed planets traversing unknown
spaces towards some demise and still
no drug that could preserve the motionless
proclaiming poetry in the mouths of kids
whose afternoon was spent in scripts
and alphabets the lore to reconstruct
the myth and the waters edging around
the day's bright phenomenon of noise
the spectacle of ear and resonating eyes
what was to be repeated ? over and over
the path that leads inwards as always to
darkness and leaves discoursing with houses
umbratile and vacant on the margins
where cities surrender their phantoms
loud and archaic to the immense distance

that persists between echoes of longing
the hills where the sun buries its steeds
mourning the inability to revive them
for one more round of creation

09-06-22

EL SUEÑO DE LOS GEMELOS

when evenings lose all recall
I dreamed I was born an identical twin
great sport it was for one to be as two
from the Pillars of Hercules to
        the Pyramids of Teotihuacan
clamor and weeping on the long pathways !
idioms of a reversed night and song
lyrics of a broken string and waters
jettisoned to make land appear farther still
a park and a tower and the muezzin's
mournful cry at dawn's distant rally
which of the two was the One ?
mysteries and enigmas and playing fields
how did everything pass in half a second ?
yesterday was a version of the hemisphere
a dwindling photograph of infants
nuzzling in Mexican chiaroscuro
each was what the other wanted to be

appearances and pronouns exchanged

as freely as hands in search of shape

permanence ! alternate eyes and feet

walking the rim of space back and forth

teeter-totter and flying swing into the dark

wings ! question marks and affidavits

the summons to witness an Accident

I dreamed great snows in an apple orchard

and streets with noise and glass a-gleam

strangers stopped to ask did we know why ?

language divided us into paired dialects

phonology of despair and isometrics

we assumed the cavities of windows

to personify immense longing and its hills

too soon one of us died among the clouds

mirrors returned nothing of the passing

I dreamed I was bereft of my other half

and cried out on pathways of dusty disaccord

one was never two ! two could only dream !

09-07-22

THE BATTLE PLAN

for Indran Amirthanayagam

how can all four Vedas be contained in one man ?

and what is the dharma and karma good or bad ?

can the fates of constellations and planets known
or unknown have anything to do with our birthright ?
on the left let the air open up its portals to the light
unseen mountains and horses and the division between
heard and unheard the vast munitions of the seas
with their electric fish and opaque virtues darkening
on the right let the winds settle in rock and cliff
let the descendants of the hills partake of speech
making sounds and noise that bedevil the ear
I am as mighty as the blade of grass !
gurus and seers and hierophants and barefoot monks
mendicants holier than the gods who wield thunder
and the tridents that bifurcate the wild oceans
what is the west ? here and here are the dialects
and binomial fractions and the split atom and fuels
that bear messages to the afterworld because of victory !
cattle rustling and theft of crowns and gold-leaf
bank notes burnt in secret glassware and jewelry
decrepit paper worthless numbers zero plus zero !
world is an illusion of gravel and the heights
no one is greater than the last breath taken before
sleep the grand participation of night and the south
where warriors futile as ants gather making incense
aggravation of the senses nominating queens and
inventing motors and tires that revolve like the skies
what is more important ? on all sides let elephant
and tortoise do battle with the unmanned chariots

invisible birds phantoms of the soul and mind

when noon strikes with molten brass it will be eternity !

who can interpret the leaf ? ivy clusters around

the written word which none but the blind can read

I am deaf and live on cigarettes ! prophets and angels

spurious avengers of the decimated deities of time

epitome of history in a few grains of sand

no more ! outflanked by altars and sacred pyres

earth turns like crumpled tinsel in the vacuum

vowels that have outlived their pronunciation

and the long senseless burning of the uneven consonants

once uttered by the oracle in order to survive :

what are the benefits of power ?

how can all four Vedas be contained in one man ?

09-08-22

MORTALITY

poets and soothsayers vagabonds both

pulling sounds out of the gathering air

declare words and noises truth and

assign meaning to the whizzing arrow

as it passes through ears of stone and grief

what ? are humans not given immortality ?

instead their lives are a matter of punctuation

and syncope an essay of breath the intake

and out of analysis and futile speculation
here was a marker that read yesterday
disregarded by the road as it went lost
in hills where shorn of thought archaic gods
laze by brush and stumps and loud declaim
the sentence of eternity to passing clouds
what lot of fitful gravel and errant grass
is ours ? feet that stray in dark passages
minds given to the rent of unpainted skies
windows that look in on themselves as night
unfolds its tent of extravagant stellar doubt
and children as ever the bounty of deities
on the hunt for ever more perfect specimens
and sophists ? questioned by the judges
what can they say but go south !
where the dead in their immense fields
of sunless afternoons evoke nostalgia
for a time that never was and trees and
houses untenanted where evenings stake
infinities of wind and shapeless mountains
brooding in a mythic west of golden vowels
there is but one breath given to the soul
and alphabets of `dream and heights
the unraveling movie known as memory
and restless bodies shifting in theaters
where screens flood with fireflies and loss
hands plunge into masses of perfumed hair

and kisses exchanged by yearning mouths
passionate acts of devotion and amnesia
by playwrights and plagiarists alike
who fumble with unfinished texts and
search in vain among darkening leaves
for the syllable that concludes mortality

09-09-22

IN THE BLINK OF AN EYE

how fleeting the eternity of our childhood was !
so much learned in a single day the sun and his
horses the plow and the steering wheel and language
all the parts of the noun the syllables of make-believe
why did we think mind would last forever ?
who was the first to reckon the moon was finite
that its phases were nothing but alternate shades
that if you went too far south you would disappear
in what they called the Elysian Fields—clouds !
did we ever know how to number the stars and
lying there of a summer night become infinite ?
we traded maps we guessed which was north and
which was west the mountains and the rivers and
places that never existed except in Egyptian tombs
hierophant and augur who taught us how to scribble
and lawns of constant reverie and the wild grasses

darkening with each touch of your missing finger !

X Y and Z portents of the future in a lost July

hailstones and metal carapaces of descending angels

a book and then a thousand tomes devoured in an hour

we learned to forget which pyramid belonged to whom

sand and leaves the innumerable mistakes of light

sound and symbol and sleep the everlasting took

you away from the continent of breath and time

and left me here pondering the eternal moment

when you turned the corner to wave goodbye

09-10-22

MI VIDA

why'd that Greek kid have to die so young ?

and to hear sister tell about the day Dad died

still painting and fully dressed they said he

wouldn't make it to Christmas and dead before

midnight just like Max who would have known

gone before the last day of February was complete

lives and moments and argent lined brows where

clouds meditate upon the ruins of a former sky

deaths a-plenty winnowed by the scythe and autumns

that stand still while summers pass into their shell

barely a memory of locusts in high song and heat

that turns minds red with passion and dying

was it Achilles the first to go painted upside

down on a forgotten urn and the words for Hades

misspelled backwards in the broken cosmic glass

and worst fate of all Joe in his newspaper boy attire

riding that rusty bike up and down the hill of Fame

shouting for all to hear I'm the real Boy ! Aiyee !

comic book lives all in italics and gossip columns

that recite the lies of immortality photographs

and parades down Main Street atmospheres like July

in its splendid drowning and trees that testify to

the soul's swift passage from nothing to nothing

how many others I watched fade from the canvas

name and body diseased by the phonology of time

who could blame the angels from turning aside

as they plunged burning from the wreck of Paradise

metal and paper cigarettes and stairways that stop

half way up to nowhere and sitting before the camera

whose eye like the bird of prey devours in silence

shapeless names the size of air ! above all Mary Lou!

shorn of speech and mind witless ciphers jotted down

in a rainfall of alphabets awash in seas of oblivion

incunabula of the very gone rock and fast evenings

that bear grass corpses into a faint empyrean

silhouettes of ash and unfinished exclamation marks !

asterisks and insects flying blindly into the Lamp

everyone a missing pronoun a skin gone wrong

effigies in shop windows looking to surprise a Friend

no one can look back the mountain has taken over

the west with its fake empires and endless queens

nothing but a syllable suppressed by silent leaves

my dead ! what is to embrace but the Wind !

my lonely dead left to drift into the silver lake

of night

09-11-22

AIR

air filled with the hidden ornaments of desire

jewelry of souls passing from the firmament

in how many directions does air go to completion ?

winds decked with tribulation and sorrowing

linger the breezes among the blind leaves of night

suffer the thirty three gods reckless mortal ambition

wending madly through air's impossible tunnels

air five hundred floors up from the crematoria

sifted with half-dreams of birth and experience

lofty turrets of nothing ! air the multiple of itself

genderless and infinite noun of silent noise

delinquent cloud rafters theater of lightning and

violent summer thunders abode of the deities who

have invented the torrent of syllables and sound

language the matrix of air and cognition ethereal

insubstantial the mothering air of confusion and

doubt meteoric suffixes of light spangling heights
no hand can reach and left to laze among grasses
air mingles echo and aphasia in the maze of gravel
that lines the unseen pathways to the heavens
air ! music's cemetery the dying promise of gravity
air ! distance and revolution of space and time
disorganized and uncataloged airy volumes
an inch in any way up or down north or south
air is the eternity intuited by children lying
on their backs watching nocturnal constellations
born of air and the vast nothingness that precedes
and follows mind's instantaneous photograph
that captures air in all its improbable shapes
air ! if only we could touch its beautiful mystery
of secret infinities and ourselves become immortal

09-12-22

CANCER

which of the many are the few who
without understanding perceive ?
strophes like arrows sharpened on stone
in all directions flung the vowels scattered
like raindrops on a cloudless day the hymn
to the immortals the spears of combat
the chariot wheels caught in muddy ruts

the catastrophe of the moment—who survives

to tell of the knife that cuts the soul to the quick?

what is breath in the onslaught of consonants?

being? grasses lay down their flimsy heads

and pray for another dewfall the verses

that dun the ears with retreat and ceremony

syllable after syllable puzzling noises caught

between asterisks and aphasia the entire

conflagration of mind unassuaged by prayer-wheels

meditation trust in some superior force or

even meaning itself in the tremendous corollaries

of sound and nothingness and the children

who thought to live forever on lawns of distance

and sleep their eternity is no more than a leaf

prey to worms and drought and the whole sequence

of heavens obliterated in the inconstancy of reality

who is there to recite the famous litanies?

the opened book only reveals a continent of fault lines

words misused and inoperative and tales

senselessly retold to screens of fireflies

edges of space and time in flames

error and rumor of birth and consciousness

the armies of night draw up their steeds and

take careless aim at the unseen target

invisible birds fleeing into the Unknown

09-13-22

THREE IN THE AFTERNOON

came flying out of the library fiery steeds
horses black and bright as the sun ablaze
the kids stood back almost nonchalant prepared
to hear the tumult and rout of warriors
on the marble steps and the skies to rip in half
and clouds the size of distance turning purple dark
to rain meteors and punctuations of pure fire
the world ! the cosmos spilled from its axis and
in harsh daylight doomed planets come plunging
and books all thirty three trillion of them smoking
and the chargers heedless of direction sped straight
to the clinic and made noise of hoof and brass
on the newly paved streets of shadowless glass
the reams and quires of thought as if nothing
in the face of this invincible evidence of eternity
in the following seconds the crashing of sculptures
and massive unseen forests and architecture
quarried from archaic philosophies and oceans
burnt ! and unconcerned the kids proceeded
to their trysts and drug-store mooning in love
with Helen and Beatrice and Dido and whomever
else the windows reflected back from infinity
three in the afternoon and everything that
could ever happen concluded ! lists of kings
dynasties of mountain and sand rivers divulging
banks of epithets and languages and cliffs high

as the heavens from which cars aflame go diving
how much in so little time destroyed ! wreck and ruin
syllable after syllable of nonsense and rhetoric
cities by the thousands with their intricate maps
reduced to instantaneous ash and the geographies
and outlines of continents and blackened isotopes
what else ? and the kids exchange phone numbers
and promise to be there when the ringing starts
and voices of unseen gods vow to be forever and ever
the end-all of mind and catastrophe alike waiting
for the Saturday night dance and the fireflies

09-14-22

HERMETIC

"Una noche conocí al Diablo ...
    y supe que me iba a morir"
        Roberto Bolaño

and how and to what end this day
the again and the unrepeatable together
does the sun withhold any of its steeds
from racing to the mountain ? there is dark
the shadowy afterworld of thought and loss
whoever plunges the hand from its shape
wandering as a bat's voice in the midst of night
scraping branches against the void the leaf

marked for silence and its fled vowels far

from the light in memory's battles on fields

of clay and sand the swinging and invisible

weapon descending without gravity from heights

known only to Hermes conductor of the dead

and purveyor of language and of us by number

counts the days until their end never knowing

which and the reason why we forge nevertheless

into unpeopled distances of sleep the unnerving

chrysalis of stone and depth wondering if

to wake is better and the wounds resounding

in the ear where trees invoke the death of noise

we struggle but that is only a word and the airs

and intensities of the Wheel the unknown and

rounding still another corner only to encounter

the abyss the notice of decay and amnesia

mind's subtle parries into the unthinkable

like useless toys left to dust in the attic

and from a sudden view summers surge up

from the rim of time and birth for a moment only

and return then to the deep and unfolding bottom

it has been a revolving instant taking with it

the atmospheres and constellations of perception

the unimaginable if only one could hold it

before dissolving forever into the ethers

09-15-22

WAR GAMES

dropped their invincible bows shattered by
the sun's threatening and dark silence come midday
the rout between classroom and infinite bewilderment
the mountain nowhere as near as first thought and
arrows making a canopy like night over the chiseled
domains and urban thoroughfares and who was
the first to go and followed by minions like ants
in the wrong direction the piercing indicative
of the battle-shell the waves endorsing a counter sheen
the day's imbalance and the furious glass of time
into a thousand pieces broken do they stop then
waiting for annihilation or does memory assuage
the following critical moments when street and lawn
and the small blazes behind windows and the fingers
lifted wet into the oncoming airs and shivering clouds
the distances all then more remote and noon's subtle
demarcation between breath and the inane fraction
when eternity begins and the motors all around humming
like invisible wasp hordes the histories and directories
the printed word itself a blur of ink on the ledger
doorways gape open and the hurtling libraries
vacant of their knowledge go plunging into a painted hell
this demonstration of the gods' super-powers thunderous
and phonetic in their decay the alarms and sirens
the ambulances to no avail the crematoria going full
blast the countless and we do remember them ! sent

with their unencumbered souls into the smoking void

an illustration from the hymnal or a device no one

knows how to turn off the legend of life and its school

dappled afternoons chattering and jabbering mindlessly

the Greeks and Persians ! or from unseen steppe-lands

Zarathustra speaking in flames and the orient aside

of languages lacking grammar and sentences fulfilling

sibylline predictions oceans in length unforeseeable

the vast transmogrification from childhood to adultery

unknowing texts and inferences of grass and gravel

the unpaved way to the mind's alternate egress

death ! the improbable recitation of birth-dates

nouns and pronouns proclivities toward insanity

the inclination to deny the moment ! when there is

no other moment senseless and brighter than ever

the irreversible instant when everything happens

and the generations of oblivion and forgetting

09-16-22

ODE TO GARCÍA LORCA

what ! a year goes so fast the sun has not yet set !
playing fields of clover and dandelions the swarms
that flood the air yellowing distances of bees and
hidden in the ear the tree of life ! who can say ?
tomorrow cannot be ! the hand forgets its shape

and feet that circle sleep with no design falter
the cliff stands nearby and seas of raging silence
was once a child and his toys and the maze of
unthought plans to traverse the constellations
with a plastic ship and land on moons afar red
with phases and atmospheres where gods die
a day alone is too much and its hours the sands
that rush through the shapely-glass and voices
near and far that beckon enticing with words
none can unravel the syllable and descant of fate
is this not Saturday ? and yesterday and its lawns ?
the grasses of dark and evening's silhouettes
and Spain alone ! walls and citrus groves and
shadowy music of splashing alphabets of echo
bright once the flute and resonant the lute that
sleeping fingers ply and García Lorca ! a face
a death repeated in furious glossolalia a stone
beside the eternal vowel now buried near Rabat
a minute ! never too long to hold between the lips
seconds that rush between continents of gravel
Sacred Heart ! the middle name evoking Rome
and phantoms of empire the knees that bend
so subtly before giving way to night's infinity

09-17-22

LAS VIDAS DELS TROBADORS

Molt me sui fortz d'un chant meraveillatz
opposed to now the inconstancy of space
dynamics of sound through one ear to the next
following sequences tragic and desolating
how can one survive knowing so much death ?
outside where sun stirs in patches and loud
the distance of its wheels noisy bric-a-brac
come to set in the dark western seas a nerve
remains the flux of detail the small grasses
on the hill slope and anemone and dandelion
and especially blue morning glory and the seed
of oblivion interred in the false patina of beauty
falling outside the quotation marks a narrative
of oxygen and trust unsettling news that always
arrives at the wrong time the hour of abiding
twilight windows crossed out and walls more
than ever silent with untold truths a divide
between what has been and what never was
school and what is the reverse of life ? Latin
diction covered with gold-dust semi-animate
beings half hidden in the corners or rafters and
the extent of grassy knoll and hill-sweep away
from the margins of thought inclinations to doubt
the next existence the folly and ridicule of this one
between armors and feathery pride the essence
of it all reduced to a thumbprint on a blotter

sitting through an opaque cinema chiaroscuro
horse and rider blurred in a camera angle that
excludes breath or the right to knowledge a long
siege of heat and afternoons without recall waiting
for the rains for the bridge to fail for the attack
of the myrmidons the great round citadels of
ocher and ebony and within the dalliance of
courtiers and mistresses of state highness of
mirror and draughts the fierce and empty howl
where ? is there nothing left but the remote Hour
the impervious language of distance and gravity
failing planets plunging like iridescent plumes
into the waters of – texts and the unraveling
scripts of sand and mud the cant of monarchs
buried to the waist in human mire the immense
and resounding echo that fills the ear with
syllables of gravel the ever enigmatic that
occurs just before sleep takes over forever
Et aysi trobares de sa obra

09-18-22

ACHILLES ADDRESSES ATHENA

cried from his wrath-laden heart Achilles
birth is a death-sentence ! I am the enemy of poetry
brazen-faced Athena dare to raise a spear

against the Father ? years as I child I spent
by the foam-girt sea and to this day not known
nor suffered joy to mortals the moment of infinity
ear to stone and fist in the immaculate position
to sleep ! to sleep ? sands the size of stars and distance
the envy of smaller beings midges gnats myrmidons
what chariot wheel can know this rut ? worms
that isolate the heart and devour their teeming selves
darkness ! leaves that flutter in agony of evenings
unparalleled but never to return and in hexameters
rivaling the opalescent heights like mists that
mountains bear in fierce solitude rock and stone
the grasses that wave waiting for my head to fall
a pyre of human passions a flame encircling
ten full years of doubt and strife redolent summers
pine resin and myrrh perfumes from Sidon and Tyre
myriads of women of unpronounceable beauty
nothing stays ! there are vowels left wafting
in the ear and trees stout evergreens deathless souls
arching and aching in the unblown winds ! why ?
feet as levers that yearn to ply stairwells and smoke
dignities in the dust and only yearning !
which is the word that cannot be discerned ?
mind is a futile grammar of tenses and weddings
there is no place called home no pig-faced men
bewitched by Circe nor islands of the sun illegal
posits of earth strained consonants hills of dialect

and treason the testimony of gods longing to die !
me ! a threat to puny and craven warriors stealthy
with opinion and logic waiting for the moment
when the spear-tip enjoins them to eternity
alone ! man's dismal lot sirens and euphoria
me ! come nightfall and the moon's crescent oblivion
flickering with memories like fireflies in the screen
and loss and endeavor and the final noise sent
like splintered lightning through the constellations
me ? you have only the scorn of refused languages
and in your eyes dozens of cities razed to the ground
implore to have my shadow back

09-19-22

TWO SONNETS : THE VANISHED MOMENT

for James Littles

is it darker than usual ? my heart the groves
and fields the summers and losses like locusts
in ravaged furrows bewildered we spent our youth
hailstones and drought scourges of chronologies
without history mythographers of the unfinished
minute unplanned loves faltering and rising against
the sun's majestic and black homophone the fates
scribbled on leaves or inserted unexpectedly in books
the steps and chiseled walks leading nowhere but up

unseen and diminished the future each had devised
a wreck on the highway scattered angels half dead
from drug overdose jazz and melancholy Sunday
afternoons doused in cheap red wine and marijuana
inches from hell ! where did they all go ?

horses of the sun ! even the horizons are vanished
the technology of distance the furious and fuming
disregard of the gods in their own quarrels over
how to wear human skin what dross to refuse how
to speak without stammering each and every edge
to sound a miracle relapsed into the void white and
red blood cells chromosomes isotopes the whole detritus
of knowledge and thought a simple dram of madness
Spanish and unequivocal in its nocturnal wilderness
the stars ! named and unnamed like pronouns glittering
for the moment only masks and personae stage-play
nonsense and noise littering the ear's futile demand
for silence and clouds more beautiful than anything
turning bright orange flushed with the end of time

09-20-22

THE FINISHING TOUCH OF LIGHT

breaking news that from dust and flames
a choice either a half-life or no life at all
sounded the martial instruments the clangor
and rhymes of warfare the plans strewn over
the ashen plains mountains that refused to
limit and horizons passed from view the moon
solitary refugee in the shaken firmament alight
with asterisks and plunging planetary hairlines
nonsense and erudition in the shining steel that
cuts both ways and the lion's mane ascribed
to heroes and the shattered greaves and the thumb
and index of awful measure the distance between
this breath and the next and galloping steeds
that haul the weary sun from this pole to that
and bards and minstrels jousting with words
that play on men's minds the promise of reason
and default of truth the everlasting shape of air
the bristling totem beast of sleep the armor
the stone where the severed head finds repose
great and slight the envy of the gods watching
the chess match of the dueling cousins whom
Krishna dwindles with his famous song and plaint
temples smitten with a single bolt and thunder
and theaters of clouds the fascicules of noise
that render the ear senseless and death at last
beautiful as the celestial nymphs come to dance

before the chattering shadows of bedecked

warriors in full regalia of jewelry ear-rings

a thousand bracelets spear-heads of pure diamond

for what ! radios fall silent as leaves at evening

no voice beckons adolescents from their drug

earth ruined by unpredicted tempests rains

and quakes alike the finishing touch of light

09-21-22

THE ENCOUNTER BETWEEN JESUS AND JOHN THE BAPTIST

mirrors ! embodiment of the soul !

look-alikes transgressing the waters of life

you is me and I am That

at first I thought you were a Mexican

now I see you are quite probably the Messiah

dress me up in your love !

white raiment on white raiment brighter

than the claustrophobic sun

yours are the decapitated hands

the flower that dwells within the stone

the sulfur in your eyes

your gaze that blames all mankind !

you are the woman inside the Man

yours is the hair that burns without burning

there are signs in the sky like unknown Letters

you are the empty room all houses envy !

there is no language that distinguishes us

I am the Alpha and you are the Omega

there are deserts instead of cities

and Cities no greater than a grain of sand

I have crossed a thousand existences

just to meet you on this river bank

and the multitudes that have drowned here

the voices querulous and indistinct

the far-way and the longing for Spain

the cruelty of the Persian satrap

what of it ?

I cannot sleep for thinking of You

and you with your locusts and wild honey

a song in the fingertips

memory of grass !

if you put your ear to the rock

you will hear the diesels hauling Jerusalem

to its place in the Kabala

Moses was wrong ! there is no movie theater

there are no colors no numbers no infinities

just the eternal oblivion of a day in childhood

this is not the place for speech

there is no salvation only silence

let darkness take over

09-21-22

CATCH A FALLING STAR

shall we paint the air with breaths

the first and last and when cinema

becomes obsolete and radiography can

no longer capture the Buddha's remaining thought

does the universe have sense revolving on its axis

of invisible fire ? whence came we here

to this place of desolation and distance what woe

what lachrymose divestment of mind what utter

revolutions of birth and re-birth the dying

who cannot be assuaged the wounded who within

us stalk and stutter and memories always incomplete

longing for hills and the dialects of the lost

who have gone before us on highways of perdition

do the dewy stars lack all conscience leaving

us to notions of flight and anguish wingless

tottering on cliff's edge rotating in grasses

evening accumulates in its effort to deny sleep its virtue ?

to die ! to die then of being unable to die daily

the afternoons and libraries and tolling bells

the indistinguishable rites of literature and desecration

totem lies ineffable but beautiful and pronouns

exchanged with partners of the dance to become other

sideswiped by chariots of the sun by vehicles manacled

to gods for whom light years are a flick of the match-stick

games of chance dice and lottery and counterfeit money

to purchase back what lives ? Nirvana and darkness

the spear-head and tumulus of a foreign battle

oceans and droughts endless famine on the moon !

salvation that comes in the morning mail

in envelopes filled with human hair and the aging

and toothless dominance of History retold

dismantled and rewritten in illegible mirror-scripts

a tomb and the head of Orpheus still singing !

waters of mercy ! the arcane and removed vowel

still lingers in the unborn wind a sorrowing echo

interred in the ear's irreversible labyrinth of noise

tomorrow ! which of us will still be talking

syllable by syllable to the unearthed brother ?

nine times Lucifer dismissed the burning asterisks

nine times the skies retreated from their hexameters

09-22-22

TEOTIHUACÁN TALKING BLUES

beware the furious borders of light !

there is no awakening there is no endlessness

in every inch of air a body is buried

Five Suns ! a hundred ways of shining

and yet all is darkness the envy of Seville !

sky ? what remains are blood-soaked clouds

roaming vagrant toward the west of the Gospels

a voice greater than the effigy of Time

intones nostalgia of ghazals and jarchas

remote and minute legends of minarets

distances only the immortals can comprehend
even as the conquistador with his mules
claims the dust and iodine of history as his own
Sunsets ! miracles which cannot exist
when all is night the unfathomable inch that
gives birth to the alternate cosmos of memory
Noons ! brightest spots of eternity that occur
every twenty or so years and the last known
meridian was the long summer of 1953 !
advent of the Hieroglyph serpent and hummingbird
eons of unknown scripts unraveling from
the tops of the pyramids of Sun-and-Moon
filling the ears with a sonic honey labyrinth
of the worm and jaguar Mesoamerican myth
cutting through lush verdure and mountains
skulls talking about sugar and nativities
chthonic and wounded deities chattering
with the borrowed teeth of language
about What ! the activity of the Knuckle !
Mariposa de Guadalupe ! wingless and adored
by stone and gravel thoughtless flights
into the dream-spell of Joseph Anthony Argüelles !
embodiments of the traveling vowel and lipstick
movies and craniums and motor accidents
alcohol on the runway ! when was the reverie ?
lawns and snippings from archaic photographs
twins ! the revolver and the rusted blade
the bottle of mescal pool-hall wizards

the South Broadway of the cornfields

Holy Maize ! motels where severed heads rest

Malinche ! translations to Inferno and molten seas

incarnadine waters of the deathless sewer system

that runs underneath all metaphysics

Once ! birth gives way to grammar and isolation

what else is there but profound silence

integration of number and disease

long trek upcountry in creaking armor

muskets and thunderbolts decimating La Raza

victory of the Most Catholic King-and-Queen

in the year of Nothing plus Nothing

Remember ? we were there climbing up and down

the irretrievable and holy steps / countdown

to the final Noon of Infinity

09-23-22

LET'S PRETEND

how many Saturday mornings ? each lesser

than the one before and the chorus of the dead

the magnificent but phantom horses the books

leveled to the ground without detail words

and the sorcerers who produced language

for hours an end listening rapt to the adventures

of the syllable and its wrath the uncommon vowels

the protagonists among consonants the holy and

the lightning brought down to smite and teach

a lesson sitting around the glow and harboring

thoughts at times unclear and longings for other

days for a number less frequent than seven for

an empire that cannot be conceived in forests and

tangles somewhere to the north of pronominal

feuds the masks and glitter of make-believe even

as noon approaches and the armor in the shops

dangling behind painted glass and the ships

of imagination buoyed on the motionless water

a fraction of time circular in notation and vague

the past which is distance and voices of heralds

mute and black sent from the vast solar homophone

rutilating in the firmament bringing light and

smoke and stairways and adolescence the freight

of ideas and learning by rote the symbols of

breath and stone the mortar that holds sounds

as they reach for air the unforgivable and music

Trojans and Argives listen to me in my Doubt !

the planets are no longer in session and newspaper

accounts of the Sabbath are riddled with false

etymologies and spelling errors the famous rumor

of birth and the remote hills of its promise now

only the numinous mistake of life the small dialects

of grass and leaf the falling sand and the rains

09-24-22

"GO BACK AGAIN TO WINDY ILIUM"

the great golden vowel fallen into the dark waters

when hopeless and lifting their brass-tipped spears

held still firm and night all encompassing with

its futile syllabary of stars and asterisks plunging

this way and that like man's senseless fate and Lo

the goddess in large dusky raiment approached

but promised nothing only stood and looked as if

glaring smitten by some bitter remorse or failing

heaven-wards she went spending no time dissolving

memory and speech alike and dumbfounded the heroes

slept in a wasteland of museums and distances How!

to wake members of some half-forgotten verse and

astray the mind recalling words for horse or mire

searched the vast and formless shoreline for a trace

a clue a signal of their dim humanity hair and shoulders

pelts askew and the waist laid bare to the oncoming tumult

consonant and oracle diminished by the day's new flare

the mountains almost speaking a menace of rock and

cliff the violent torment of the seas coming up to the knees

why! to beg the missing gods as if in a stage-play and

dire portents in the woods the color red emblazoned

for a moment in the ivy's entangled alphabet and nothing

assuaged by the morning breeze and the embers here

and there doused sifting through the ashes for a name

a face to address and mourn the peak of anguish loud

in the faltering Hour and from nowhere a rushing noise

a riot of symbols half-moons copies of the pre-dawn sky
grasses elemental and overwhelming where the dead
in their awful assemblage of hearings and circuit courts
lay mysteriously absent from the powerful solar hiatus
noon with its lack of precedent and statuary and lawns
the sound and terror of the next moment which never
comes

09-25-22

ZOOT SUIT

para Armando Rendon

skies lurching on chariots gone astray
cloud-work and hoof the empyrean stamped
with the ire of the constellations fates and
destinies trash and marijuana smoke listing
in mid-air noontimes in front of the halls
of Justice impunity and disregard for natural
laws the ocean on the brink of drowning !
infatuation and mirror-image passing shadows
girls and boys jamming on the dark fringes
catapult and vicissitude of passions the lesser
images turn into hieroglyphs of Aztec noise
zeal and impatience of fractured vowels
Spanish tom-toms and spit in the drugged head
communion wafers on the Street and hipsters

jargon of serpent and zopilote pillaging
the sacred Toltec stone wedged between hives
buzz and warp hum of trolley cars stuck
on the third rail that divides Los Angeles into
forensic hemispheres of adultery and stardom
promised gods manifest at special hours
somewhere between Boyle Heights and Watts
bright yellow sulfur and creased pants like
underworld silhouettes on parade shimmering
shoe polish and Mariolatry on painted tins
thunderous element of indecision and pride
mind in its terrible self-deceit and glass
shattering the myriad reflections of asterisk
talking planets vestiges of oracle and myth
who will recover the sound ? ancient augury
of syllables disheveled and mocking in the ear
rock and rutilating sierras on high the passage
between births littered with incomplete thoughts
masks and pronouns like winged insects vainly
struggling with the Flame ! Quetzalcoatl !
riots on the curbstones of Alvarado Street
sneering and more archaic yet Pachucos
sinister as gargoyles passing through el Centro
shoplifting in Sears and Roebuck brill cream
combs prophylactics tension and electricity
dressed to Kill ! as they say in East LA
where the three-headed demon demonstrates

what it is to be Mexican alcohol and flash

singing Nadie comprende lo que sufro yo

La perfidia de tu amor

09-26-22

SANCTUS SANCTUS SANCTUS !!!

even as darkness and the rugged shoreline nigh

where drawing their keeled ships and clouds

gathered the distant quarrels of the gods into

a dusky sphere none could interpret and the skies

yellowing then menacingly heavy purplish

lacking all glow do the souls of men then fail

and all things lose importance the book of the fire

and the texts of prophesy and natural wonders

and the knees quaking and shoulders over-burdened

sorrows and memories of once radiance the hills

yonder where they say the Lamp's swart steeds sleep

all is a wondrous error and the cities with broad

paved thoroughfares and the stables and palaces

and places where washer-women go in the mornings

the stubble and rock of the unplowed fields alert

to the least of insects and the chattel and kine and

words for disaster that pound the ears at midnight

the full cup ! spilled the deep-red wine at the table

and the guests dim with dissolution and rank with

envy lusting and half-dead already and from birth

it was ever so and the kneeling before idols of

divergent shapes and the roaring and incense in

the temple where the oracle reigns and to misunderstand

and quote from false syllabaries and notations

that the prize is at hand and war the futile bargain

will settle the worlds into terrible fractions the past

a faint rumor and the perfumes and unguents and

shops where glassware and tarnished silver tempt

what was ever true ? lingering beside the Corpse

the paid mourners thrive on grief and nowhere

to be found the correct pronunciation and scripts

employed for counting and subtraction and what

hour will it end and when will the ships drawn

up for night and sleep sink ? even as vowels fade

and the color red once the pride of kings no longer

clings to printed cloth and gossip from China claims

silk and the commerce of undergarments and

the unholy becomes Holy ! Sanctus ! earth tilts

slowly imperceptibly off its axis and science regards

the cosmos as explicable ! death in a matter of days

will come to all even to the elusive planets that

plunge in the telescope's powerful eye and drains

from the west the final ray of the unspoken sun

for Jack Foley

09-27-22

THE VEDIC INJUNCTION

by night even as wane the fires the small sparks
stars to the earthly eye asterisks of sound and broken
laws of grammar the ability to articulate to speak
across the sea's broad bent back waves of misfortune
watching the multiplied fleets gather like storms
and sink one by one into the swirling liquid mass
just so the sleeping ear takes in the noise of language
that holds memory fast in its syllables and again play
from childhood games and rout the hills to climb
against the sun's terrific decline hoof and spiral of air
contexts of cloud gleaming with distant lightning
a whole chapter devoted to the disarray of vowels and
resurrection of the soul howling remoteness of the vast
where consonants conspire with each other and from
quarries deep in myth do gods come forth to break
the seasons with their grudges and quarrels twins
and sisters and flighty parents with winged feet who
ascend invisibly from mind into other attributes
of intelligence and amnesia thus parting constellations
whole beakers of immortality in a second spent drunk
at long banquets of recollection and ire the upended
furniture the walls come to dust the ruin of atmospheres
long treks of thought into the maze of ideas and waters
how ! wherever the grasses of evening reach to that
still-point called noon when statues learn to utter
mercies and profanities at the levels of consciousness

the reticulation of hive and ant-heap into dialects
chasms of misunderstanding the lengthy attempts
at poetry of unwinding meter and accent into verse
memorized and obliterated simultaneously and fortune
the illegible palm reading of mankind forced mountains
collapsing tides and the many shapes of rain pouring
down on the cities – to breathe again in the open as
children on their lawns of babble and chalk a riot
loud of forbidden laughter and the goddess herself
a wreck looking askance into the glass of alteration
be other ! if one could but remember that moment
when person and mask laid aside the whole being arose
from the sleep of ageless rock formation to assume
in the speech of leaves a distinct yet senseless morphology
half-life of eternity ! Thou art That !

09-28-22

ODE TO THE GODDESS

the gods are false ! poetry proves nothing !
painted words on rushing winds mere dreams
the flash and poison of memories the distances
between thumb and index a history of tissues
and excrescences of mind the thought-pattern
which is a labyrinth and the teratology of madness
whiplash and shipwreck tales of an absent night

echolalia and syllabary of blind seers seated on
rocks jutting out of sea-turmoil and cries far
and wide of souls in purgatorial sleep remote
in the western hills where daughters of the sun
weep and mourn in the coming dark loves
that were meant to be and what goddess stepping
out of raiment pure but with deadly aim exists ?
winding sheets and leaves chattering fitfully
in the endless Hour she wraps the secret of mortality
around her fist and gives anguish to the color red
what is the Republic ? what is oath and promise ?
airs that swirl darkening in the bedlam of experience
what was this but a dying child and schoolyards
resonant with hieroglyphic noise and joys ?
too little have we encompassed in our philosophies
a sound that comes roaring for an instant in the ear
and asterisks that define the universe and prattle
of marble and acanthus leaf and statues bidden
to talk when clock strikes noon and courtyards
and chattel and the rivers that bend and sway
what grief and agony and to call it life and glass
that reflects nothing back and hands that design
maps of sand and feet stepping on oil-slicks and
gravel the looming wheel the disasters of Light !
did a deity ever manifest in a traffic accident ?
machines and digits and numbers without sense
storms and rains and trees that pray for death !
is there a need to pronounce correctly what

the Buddha said or to settle debts with time ?

the goddess to whom we turn for repetition

what is she but the embrace of sweet Oblivion ?

09-29-22

A SCENE FROM MEMORY (CLAIRE BIRNBAUM)

Listen,

liquidated "frissons

d'amour" in an unlighted sky, dawn cracks the envelope of

liquor and barbiturates hoodoo downers and peyotl jargon,

as if the world seen from a rooftop were "real"! jazz omicron

tilted in a felt clasp dancing cheek to cheek with

death's swarming girlfriend(s), darling "you send me",

darkened theater thoughts before psychiatric swirl

fuzz membrane issues solo for recording device and Greek verb

forms, later on the gastroenterologist will have his say,

as will the black photographer on his way back to Denmark,

can this be music startling as it is juxtaposed to language

the ineffable doubts the pyramidal scales of sound

forward when really means "back" a few years to Mayowood

nights a softening whim between the myriad asterisks and

Selene the heart-throb moon a chance before dying

how many years does it take to count on one hand

the remaining and stare facing the shivering metal

the nocturnal accident the wheels burning rubber in the ear

to wake if possible text in hand, the long lexicon bound

in azure with cloud lining and argent theories

about the beginnings of most anything, the way she

beckoned primping her beehive hairdo like a Roman empress

ever the flitting behind mirrors a firefly of a girl,

she, not even the photograph remains tucked in between

the covers of the Provençal dictionary processing the spring break

fieldtrip to points orient the smoking embers of flight

from the pogroms and rainstorms of Eastern Europe

the war years the sinister stiletto and silhouette stamped

on the crumbling masonry of ideology and dread, buzz,

Talmudic abbreviations of breath the late sun rising

from his loft looking for his steeds and only the floral

display between mudflats the sky lifting its syntax

beyond and waylaid the romance the etymologies of noise

and stairwells where light is the enemy and weren't

those the days before suspicion became paramount and

the glass-works and steel mills that erased the horizon

the lake turned silver with dead fish and the acting,

mostly it was youth and the highlighted hexameter verses

of Carthage and storm tossed fleets straying forever

lost despite the grammar and full blown irises on the ledge

the Classics Department and the siege work of dust

the Necropolis just south of 63rd Street with the overhead

monorail speeding to Inferno! how can anything ever be the same?

again, doomed, mortuaries of ineffable beauty, a hand without

hesitation and the shapes of air

I RECALL A SUMMER DAY BY THE SWIMMING POOL CONVERSING WITH AN UNKNOWN MUSE ABOUT

la lune, mensonge de vie,

Italian lessons beside the summer pool, unreflecting or

of the future what's to know, gathering around the darker

skirts of the Persephone-types to wit Mary Lou, etc.

how much more writing there is,

French and abacus and sophisms

with a secret omega, delved into the Cretan back file to immerse

the by now polyglot in a longing to, compose the

perfect response to all that has been read, a walking library?

grammatical interludes between episodes of pseudo

Byronic, a flamenco side to the other, shapes

without hands to form them a fantastic, a Mexican actually

silver masks and pyramidal constructs leading to and from

planetary houses and the greater mysteries, the rains

tropical siestas the, not the least the abysmal Lutheran cavity,

hives and subterranean intersections of syntax and

depthless water, how would it work out,

the women, the obsessions, Mother, walking on some

soft night-earth head in dream and sleep in glove,

fades and reveries and, references to the "mountain",

where is now, Now, the past has come to eat its own vomit,

voluptuous annotations and intoxication and the

mysterious, subterranean angel

suffused with hieroglyphs the outer creases of night

spackled faintly with gilt ornament, overdrive and headache,

concussion and snare drum in a whirl

the book that will be written, plateaus of,

dusty vistas of an imagined Latin origin

replete with conga and mambo jive, jungle rot intertwined,

a few inches to the left and the entire Sanskrit dictionary

reprinted like an army of elephants trumpeting

taking with them in their caroming the whole cliff of

intricate basalt memory, listen again, innocent revulsion,

staccato rhythm gone to seed of an absent Hour,

plowed the constellations in search of the single Asterisk

bearing the secret of birth and death in its flash

instantaneous and irreproducible – Life!

spectacular advent of metal and angels in flight

where are the question marks the commas and

grieving exclamations ! I am solitude the somber

remains of the Twin, thumbing a ride

on the Carretera Panamericana south, always south

past the Toltec consonant clusters deep

into the archaic rock formation of Space,

flower-design of recollected speech-acts

statuary and justice ricocheting off the sun's

massive homophone pitch black the vowel of Oblivion,

long gone yearning head turned to stone

dreams : winged messenger composed of air

and atmospheres and grasses darkening

between the silence of the leaves

la lune, mensonge de vie,

10-01-22

WHAT MEANS LIFE ?

brings us no whit nearer to the --- what shadowy longings

cast upon the watery surface dragonflies flitting

invisible winged things alight disappear

have the advantage of existing only in the imagination

release of tension Artemis

to what epic first wine dark sea culmination

of cinematic and perfectly scanned metric quantity

rhetoric's blackened thumb-filmed agony

ours finally and the only one really

matters red kimono desperation against the wall

to hyphenate reality in thus wise

to second guess the rules of abandonment to alter

grammar regulations cycling bits of sound

a shore dimly perceived the map's conjecture

Nymphs ! cast anchor in the blind seething waters

lotus fronds perfumed askance and eyes

that dwell on the innate object of affectation

do I know you from somewhere ?

too late the day's last hour liquidated in oranges

trundled reds silhouettes of syllabic azure

the skies redundant with memory and now

settling into hills where dialects are spawned

litigation and civil-war cannons rusting on the brink

to have lived there ! did Kronos give us the gift of bravery ?

what remains but the sifted dust powders once incarnadine

mirrors with no backsides and the lowing

in sleep of animals no one has ever seen

a dream ! a porphyry lined cloth a belt made of sinew

she comes forth radiant in garments of distance

one two three ! Bang !

whispers and intaglios the mourners file by

bearing an inaudible corpse to the Museum

where scattered asunder the jewels of fate

speeches mummified by the process of rock and stone

hands littered with gravel and semiosis

the production of meaning and amidst the cloud-woof

the span of eons copies of the cosmos at birth

grieve Ye ! puzzles and oracles and the remote ear

of the leaf darkening in the sun's bewildering echo

10-02-22

OCTOBER ELEGY

from what place do we take illusion and doubt

to us gifts of the craven gods the sport of light

and death breath rescinded and altars smashed

a thousand Troys in a single day ! maps unfold

deliberating the paths to mountain and seas alike

men with turret-helmets wearing long bear-skins

ancestors ! now but flitting shades bats gibbering

in Pluto's umbratile palace whence no one returns

suspicion the bane of clarity and greed for just one

more of anything and the child mourned inside the man
for whom the shop-window's glister and toys was all
winters come and go and summers fleet as the firefly
whose instant of bright is eternity and months that
lapse in the palm of a hand and language itself
dross of sound and multiple noise of meaning and
deceit and what are the parameters of a single day ?
with mobility and gravity canceled the planets
simply plunge into a black hole of forgotten silence
today is cremation of the gods ! one by one names
and attributes turn to ash pronouns lose similarity
metaphor and parataxis cognition and perception
poetry itself the hollow essences of verbs of motion
dropped final vowels the messages borne by Thoth
to chattering half-wit deities mere resemblances
to dialects buried in collective unconscious which
is nothing but gravel rotating beneath invisible wheels
we are children no more ! sight and hearing interferences
of pure mind and the sudden appearance of bodhisattvas
at the scene of a multiple vehicle pile-up on the freeway
nothing connects ! right-thinking is loss and the words
the dead remember before passing into cosmic bliss
are but shreds of the unending monosyllable of sleep
depthless waters ! explanations are pointless banter
trees ! your leaves alone harbor the dark mysteries !
trees ! your leaves alone harbor the dark mysteries !

10-03-22

CHORUS (MARY LOU)

you called me once

you called me twice

you never called again

it's been a long long time

buds spring open noisily

blossoms languidly disclose

death is no secret but your voice !

I have forgotten what it sounds like

what you used to say and why

the rooms are bare and empty

the phone no longer rings

it took three large volumes

but Rome has finally fallen

the second floor is shut

the windows glazed over

and the lawns forever frosted

gravel fills the big hiatus

death is no secret now

the notices keep on coming

this one and that one too

have joined the immortal choir

yet I seem to have been left behind

you called me once

you called me twice

you never called again

it's been a long long time

I know which street leads to you

I know the entrance to the school

the walkway to the library

and to the drugstore too

what use are they to me

your voice I cannot recollect

was it plaintive and whispering

or peremptory and loud ?

what does it matter now

the fields bereft of corn and

the long highway going south

where the dead are said to play

is plated over with oblivion

songs and radios silent

pom-poms and graduation threats

the mingled Friday nights

crowded with boys and girls

faceless entities fading colors

shouts no ear can retrieve

automobiles and football scores

endless tedium of words

promises we tried to keep

languages that buzz and hum

the dialect of tambourines

the soliloquy of survival

such and such that never was

we sat on the terraced hill

and gazed into the future

a hospital and anesthesia

hands that never wed

you called me once

you called me twice

you never called again

it's been a long long time

10-03-22

SCRAPS

(i)

what's the news _default rewired
table normal no list activated   the dead
in their enormous and unknown southland
paramount and without sanctions and night
the great ships the poetry of evanescence
billowing in torments agues and suppositions
language to no avail the customary debt
overruled by the hundred statues who claim their noon
lapse and mortuary of desire and overflow
of kids prattling and raving about colors
and the cloths to wear and skin and its diseases
tropics of eyes and stray islands the oracle promised
to no one and set foot on the disappearing plain
aghast as gods come and go in the plethora of wind

and what's to make of the tripod and the ant-heap ?
promiscuous absence of Aphrodite so it says
in the manual to fix the breakdown in motor
revival askance the double-joined soul spooling
its anterior threads the red is the most it can be
high resolution of light and diameter fixed
for a moment only before aching for dawn
and the swart steeds that plummet bringing
down the awful chariot ablaze with the day's surfeit
a versification of the atmospheres where shines
the remote palace of the deities built on sound alone
at what decibels does thunder act ? theaters
where youth enacts its aspirations for immortality
had not love interrupted and the seasons
out of order the rush of hues and noise of hills
dialects and transportation the detours to heaven
ancient rock smoldering in the histories
a debacle the speech acts ascribed to the Statistician
in the agora they are refueling the mounts and
setting forth to ply the walls and munition-dumps
trusting in war and the leagues of petty city-states
each with a tongue of its own and laws and recensions
life in the hind quarters of the Text a riddle of
punctuation and aphasia the twelfth disorder of the mind
myth of syntax the blowsy afternoons in memory
greening and evening the hospital of the intellect
what is the cure for the grasses ? slopes and rivers

unmapped sequences of sand the endless idiom
only the dead can understand the highways and broad
asphalt ribbons bearing away motels and signboards
a catch in the throat tears and confessions
the park suddenly deserted and the police van
roaming in the dark searching the bushes for a flare
chance is the remaining spoke of the wheel
as it flies out of control across the blackened sky

(ii)

grief is the one behind the stepladder
two is what happens before birth – anomie and regression
typically sorrow in East European a dialect
remorse and three the spindrift as you fall asleep
praying to never wake again the thread and license
which is memory on its crash course to number
relief that all names cannot be remembered
or the shape of every leaf memorized in the catechism
a hand is to replace the snow as it catches on the weathervane
tomorrow that is a syllable four removes from air
what is meant by gospel truth is no more than bread
or the table it rests on and the resident knife
it comes to naught the daily effort to forget
the remains of words slowly diminish the color red
as it circles the mind which is madness the immobility
of thought rendered preterit and clouds aching
to become seas and the depths of darkness

the origin of pronouns separation and debility

does anyone ever mean ? a mask is a person caught

in the act of shoplifting for disregard the overture

and cache of unheard notes which are gods

in descent behind the western hills of myth the spent

and irregular verbs listed in the appendix to the Bible

it is because divorce and penitence are at high noon

the eye that avoids contact with vision and the ear

forever lost in its silent labyrinth and the Minotaur

of noise and specialty lamps and division of sound

into paragraphs of amnesia and stammering

you will come to rue the day the brow of speech

talking and fumbling for syllables and the reaction

of light to breath antiquities of scrap metal unearthed

in the quadrant where buildings imitate worlds

of vast archaic forms numbness and pedestal

oratory in its Greek void going on and on about the ships

and the black reveries of spears as they find their mark

postcards showing the evolution of Achilles hermetic

and isolated in the shivering homophone of Beauty

such as it is death is the issue at hand

veils and fluttering monograms wrists loaded

with a thousand bracelets of mercury pure and illusory

we step aside and watch the chasm open preparing

us for a kind of immortality in the next instant

10-04-22

THE TENUOUS DREAM OF LIFE

"La route est longue, et je suis vieux"

    Flaubert, La Tentation de St Antoine

I've got my brother on backwards today
another scrape with the law—honest officer
we're identical but that doesn't stop the metal
or the car from shining long drawn out dreams
confused identities dharma karma et cetera
one eye gone bad take out the other ? Jesus said
on the mount and according to the hills over there
dun colored in their dialect of convergence and decay
the west was not won it was another episode
of aggravation and cinematic mendacity and
stepping aside to let sleep have its traffic and
how the other came to be and the grasses mown
late in the afternoon wearing the same Mexican shirt
with both arms inside out the fugal disposition
of birth time and dying entire libraries worthy
of the name and studied the ore deposits the stage-
coach robberies the magnificent divine horses
plunging roan and palomino off the existential cliff
to name a few the distances weary and rock and
shade and the rivers running to the side nameless
and sidereal and trees mysterious entities a goddess
between them and eternity just shimmering
on her invisible skin a song a hair-piece a comb
scandalized as they say in Greek her nuisance of sound
a staccato in the ear a fiery portion of heaven and

call it love dumbfounded in ethereal silence

stepping back to better observe the clause and

its penitence so much otherness in the least detail

punctuation setting apart the asterisk from its blaze

and of a night the celestial backside cluttered

with a maze of constellations and error the fiction

of memory piecing together and upside down the pants

the shoelaces the different colored socks and

upstairs someone else instead of us shifting boxes

looking for the keys cursing the day was ever

and the father figure reeking of bad alcohol and

cheap hair pomade owning the stairs and the secret

of flight and ingenuity if only we could share

his Spanish and his fuming Toltec anger and surprise

gravel is the opportunity to give rumor to infinity

wheels and interminable drives down the southern track

and mountains most of all the divergent size of the hour

when dusk sheds its purple advantages and together

absolved of mercy the death-wish embraces us

whatever clothes we have on whatever direction

our moony loneliness is taking us toward some sunset

beyond the map we were so carefully drawing on the floor

the house and the avenue the entire thing happening

so fast that before we knew it the clinic was done

the accident of breath the cold x-ray machine holding

the body against its own recollection and Bang !

10-05-22

WITHOUT WARNING

for Miriam Tarcov

delighting in the memory of sound the trellis of

noises on earth hum and buzz of insect swarms

and the sun's emblazoned monogram and scepter

and the unrecovered poems the rock and thistle

of dreams errant and toilsome the path to travel

by noon too weary to proceed and the sea but

a silvery glint in the distance between carapaces

of fog and cloud and what of the cities once supreme

on their separate plates of organized metal and

the remote roar of their traffic between web and

inconstancy the chiming bells the tolling to mourn

forever the irretrievable losses waged in the battle

between breath and destiny how was it justified

the grasses bent in the ceremony of sorrow felt

in the marrow and never to be healed the wound

dealt by sheer accidence the highway and its sudden

escarpment the hand from the heavens reaching

down to pluck the unsuspecting from their speed

the revolving and unraveling threads of the Parcae

the imminence of the color red and the lessons

in blank paragraphs to be memorized but never

learnt day after day the duration of light unatoned

and the voices of liberated souls the profound

accents the vowels slowly escaping like gas and

hearing itself the relic of a lost cognition half

a lunar rotation away or fiction of the constellations

alphabets of asterisk and despond forever fleeting

into the absences of space and let the head fall

heavy on its immortal stone and sleep

10-06-22

TAT TVAM ASI

living on borrowed time !

as many books as have been written

there are that many more to read

and who has the will to do it ?

living on borrowed time !

months go backwards and days !

what are they but minute excrescences

vanishing salt on the waves

insects gone sightless in evening grasses

and the harrowing Greek

who stands at the top of the stairs !

scribbling empty thoughts of a vacant mind

space and more space outside of space !

what is gravel but mulch of the stars ?

today is not a holiday of numbers

but the reckoning of one less cipher

despond and depth of memory

gathering dust in bedrooms

and antechambers closets and
chests laden with sleeping under things
dreams that circulate every twenty years
of unwed brides and war-threats
everywhere one turns the steep ravine
the tumultuous breakers of the seas
colors that blend and become irate
clouds that hasten the death of distance
what is this but collision of the fates ?
subtractions from the mire of mind
what is to endure but another endless summer
with brief eternities of forgotten words
dormers where history regards its mangled corpse
science is useless ! philosophy a worn isotope
books ! vessels of megalomania
constant rearranging of vowel and consonant
recollections of matters gone wrong
of attitudes and heroes painted on museum palms
back and forth of bicker and quote
platitudes of assertion and right thinking
a Buddha posted on the dead-end street
and seasons that fold into his cupped hands
with sad resonance of fallen leaves
living on borrowed time and longing
centuries dilapidated and unrecognizable
fall from the litter of dead novae
reconciliation of southern hills

where the dead photograph each other

amid dialects of riot and scorn

loci of misinterpretation forever !

psychology of syllables pasted

to the ends of thoughts and

oblivion and aphasia rotating

soundlessly in the attic of cognition

who is who in this pronominal chaos ?

"tat tvam asi"

10-07-22

BRIEF BUT INFINITE

gathering their garments and weeping full loud

in the midst of the clangor of death and spear rattling

the chariots come round the steeds of pure perspiration

do the gods then best score the game of doom and chance

drowned the self in remorse and watched as burning

high the razed palaces the mountains themselves a-glitter

with the infernal blaze of the penultimate day and the rush

of hot winds scorching the mouths and eyes of onlookers

the steep boulevards come crashing the fleet sleek metals

bought at such a price steering off course and veering

straight into the suburbs of plenty the abundant parks

the small deer startled in their own reflections as even

the drinking pools turn to flame and the chastened beasts

nowhere to go alert to the least turn of mind –
there you have it the sound of infinity doubled in its text
grammar and meaning exploited by the letter and the school-
master in his dun colored attire startled at the vision he has
and imploring the kids to stay just a few minutes more
before the bell and the dash out the door down the steps
out into the eternal afternoon of statuary and grass
how ! minute insects drawling their fervid chant in fields
where stray lovers go to die and trees on the verge of
memory and appealing with branches and stricken leaves
to the heavens if another world is possible if the map
strewn across a quadrant of sky could be redrawn
and antiquity the immemorial verse of glade and shadow
relieved that a drop of water can claim so much and the eye
turned back on its shape takes in the mirrored realities
passing in a trice between birth and death the kids falling
in love and disregarding the warnings the monitors of
the gods treachery and beguiling charms the drugs and
soporific songs the dial turned all the way up for a favorite
music and that was the time ! ear to the turf to capture the
very noise of distance the shields and griefs and mounting
rust the attributes of heroism and cowardice regal epithets
dust in conglomerated glory and clouds in their constantly
changing alphabets script of the heavens and here and there
loosened from their human fabric the souls of the others !
all in the afterschool reverie and pastoral the memorized
lines of lark ascending and the rays of the sun heightened

in the brief but infinite stretch of words glossed in their prime

a springtime late in arriving a painting addressed to the air

so much emotion in the brush of vowels and the cadences

before falling back into the enormous sleep of stone

10-08-22

TO WRITE A POEM

how often does springtime come

before you realize there is a fatal day ?

when are adjectives appropriate

and what use are metaphors if hand

precedes foot and head follows stone ?

nothing is ever learned correctly always

a misplaced vowel and a wing broken

at the heft a ship sinking into the horizon

when was rock the better of grass or

colors of wind are legends you can never

undertake a swift demise of air a sure

and prolonged illness of the undefined

trouble when the statue begins to move

the stakes are placed ahead of loss and

each god invoked is the last to be known

the mysteries are in the underbrush where

the dead struggle to recall language and

its pitfalls the error of birth the rumor

of immortality poised to exceed sound
how is the expression of grief ? who is
the one ? plenty of time to sleep afterwards
the notion of height before the fall and
switching light for breath what's to recall ?
seen rounding the bend the beloved of
summer's forgotten fields and birds
that rhyme with memory and drugs
too strong for syntax to unravel distance
from the knots of discord and nostalgia
to write a poem ? use ink and shadow
fingers lost in evening's unseen lawns
or the simple hieroglyph that stands for
the mirror's brief infinity caught while
memorizing the face on the reverse of glass
great auguries pitch and sulfur Inferno !
between this moment and the next hiatus
everything that's ever happened ! mind
revolving in its labyrinth of noise and
space shifting from east to west where
death resides with its riddled consonants

10-09-22

ORPHIC !

the first time was the last as ever

no record of the other time when

nor the fixity of space and its

illustrated pages of lost fire and

noise endless reiterations of eye

and ear taking in pronouns more

distant than yesterday's summer

the mind-field and gloss of air

tremendous for what is absent

revolving centimeters of thought

a thumb an iris a drumming hand

sections of eight innumerable and

soon forgotten like the basement

with its magazines and smoke

illicit pictures going from lamp

to darkness between the knees

gong and filter of reveries deep

into the hour's missing face

how ? grief the inexplicable at

day's end the puzzled alphabet

trance and sound of repetition

as if anything could be made new

again and sort out the remains

between gravel and sand-bank

rivers of night eddying secretly

toward world's inconstant edge

what ? inwards turn behind glass
where unravel dreams and spools
mind as ever inadequate to
match sorrow's unending tide
is it to contort defying the visible ?
comes a point in time when nothing
can be retrieved or altered the thing
stays the same persisting painfully
until the stars back off from sleeping
forever and the following daylight
reveals wreck and ruin of rock
archaic formations of language
remote and melancholy Orphic !
no ear retains what leaves whisper
come sunset in the western hills
darker still the silent grasses
of shadowless memory

10-10-22

THE IMMOBILITY OF THE SPHERES

what did we know ? there was grass and the sun
and streets with houses full of strangers
to play was a way to pass the day or learn
by going to the library and reading everything
about submarines and ancient woods and

animals that talked but could never speak
what was to know ? the future was just
the next day idling on the lawn or going
to someone else's hours and on our knees
playing board games or drawing battle scenes
did anything ever change ? one day was new
but so was the following and going downtown
with mom to buy clothes and look in shop windows
and wait for next big holiday was that to know ?
learn to smoke cigarettes and comb your hair
in the mirror and use the phone to call girls
by name and play instruments imperfectly
preludes but not fugues and the drugstore
and the big brass bell from on high at five
every afternoon and suddenly there was grammar
and foreign words and perfume and incense
and mostly alcohol and cars and speeding to
towns by the big river and what else to know
was a year gone by then many many more
of time the roulettes and wind-up clock and
swimming and summers in eternity and trees
baleful or mysterious at the end of the street
hills where they spoke dialect and odors and
stifling rooms atmospheres and suspicions
to know was the big question growing up and
dividing the ways of being wearing suits and ties
and dancing awkwardly and becoming romantic

with orchestras in the ear and longing and fear

of separation in photographs of melancholy space

of cities and lakes and overhead trains and signals

and enigmatic lyrics called the blues and violence

unexpected tumult of language and cash and having

to work which is responsibility and the spheres

way up there predicting who would go first or last

death that is being greater than the grasses or

the stars and the crashing on rooftops like broken

angels and laughing it off as if there were no errors

just the long unimpeded highway through mountains

and geography and weddings that didn't make it

who would have known children would get sick or

die suddenly in the night was that what it meant ?

today is just a rumor the rest is memory in all

its wrecks and collisions and burials and ashes

what could we have known ? life's diseases

beautiful edges to glass a silence beyond silence

and the immobility of the spheres

10-10-22

ACHILLES SPEAKS FROM THE HEART

then must I speak fully from my heart

there was never a day so baleful such as this

nor do clouds make way for the bright rays

and the mind remains confounded as to which

is the right way and which are the phrases

most fitting to display man's character in troubles

and no praise have I for those who hold back

or reiterate the counsels of yore no longer tested

and do I raise my hands do I implore the gods

those evanescent shadows ? no more confide

in them than one would in the mirror's reflection

faces and pronouns and winds of aggravation

the grasses on the knoll and the setting sun

among the groves where trees darkening strive

for true immortality and the rains and buffets

of this countless day these deaths that swarm

around our heedless acts these minions and

myrmidons when will this ever cease no more

than the pounding waves on coral shores nor

the airs that blow through our mortal ears

infinities of sleep and the unkenned worlds outside

our puny space and the glories ! futile libations

spit and wrath the useless acts of a lazy afternoon

summers are gone ! cruel seasons are what's left

and you stand around bandying fancy verse or

consuming cheap alcohol and pretend that driving

chariots over the cliff is a prideful end ! folly and

errant noise the residue of our lives on this false

terrain a history of rumors and half-finished statuary

look to the caryatids mounted on Diana's temple !

they feign would yield to some dumb hero's pleasure
it is to eternity their sealed mouths speak not the talk
of regeneration and the soul's endless desire for flight
prison-house of the body arms that flail and rusted
armor the spears that whistle through the night
mock battles spurious reasons to claim and possess
what goddess has ever been owned ? yet you poetize
and ply with syllabic rants of beauty and vain promises
words ! from my heart I pour out this bitterness
to have been born and increase archaic script
with the measures of sterling youth and come to this !
raze the courtyards undo the looms storm the stairs
all is smoke and glass and slight of hand – breath
is to yearn for and the enigma
how else are we to die ?

10-11-22

TEXTS / CHASMS

to end and I have said this once before
is it possible the universe has no beginning ?
game's over nothing left to play sun's gone
over the hills song-birds left in the chill
where is there to go ? lost words missing
pauses a hiatus between syllables and rumor
as always on the left winging in spirals into

the dark by Hades' gates where toilsome men
prattle on about the soul and its dividends
is this the so-called right thinking ? history
in all its baleful shreds and rags has taught
us nothing other than its own base circularity
a thing of the past ! Hermano ! that's you
ashen given to lofty speeches talking into nights
without end brides ensnared in your jazz
prophesies and warnings about time-keeping
yet here we are decades into the Tombstone
inviolable rights of man escutcheon and greaves
the islands are sinking glaciers imponderable
measures of eternity dissolving infernally
how did you escape Dante's ladder ? only to
return as a fragment of memory a fading photo
a child on a lawn inescapably yellow and listen !
the car wheels on midnight gravel and grass
hidden in whispers and irreversible windows
looking out to the famous roadway East
diesel and error and labyrinthine secrets
unmapped topographies of mind and breath
how far was the reach ? came crashing like
unexpected angels on a spinning roulette wheel
highway accidents and jigsaw puzzles the shape
of water and the brooding skull grinning back
across eons of radio-messages
how did we divide our selves ? the person and

the mask the pronoun and the sealed envelope

profligate times in the pool-hall of the gods

you and me you and me snarling likenesses

to a pair of kids on the outskirts of life

the town wasn't big enough the stage too small

we shared the lawnmower and the mailbox

playing with the finger and its compass

waiting always waiting for the surprise Map

entry to the mansions of great Oblivion

lachrymose dungeons ! texts ! chasms !

10-12-22

WHAT IS BRIEFER THAN OUR UNCOUNTED DAY

spent the winters allotted now question springtime
trees in their abeyance of infinity rooted in depths
too profound for memory what diminished beings
in comparison we are with our languages of platitude
and contrivance no meter no matter what makes sense ?
death in the nerve the sleeping and unslept the waking
to defeats as inscribed by the bards helmet and trunk
greaves and the sorrowing that comes with putting on
armor and ahoy to set sail on phantom fleets to islands
of baleful enterprise and legend the swift detail of fate
arriving as love's insane quoit or the debacle of sties
and palaces of mud and erosion of pollution in the air

stench of history decibels of radio voices too distant to
apprehend and the distances of fields and the mountains
to overcome and the lesser singularities of outer-space
mysterious as the rings worn on the beloved's fingers which
are but symbols of mourning and absence for who are we ?
despond and betrayal wherever we turn our gaze and to linger
by the high-school entrance waiting for the steps to develop
into pyramids and the kids descending wearing feathers
and tattoos and the zing and bite of spears in the wan light
the afterlife ! that's what we are witnessing the evolution
of death the minstrelsy of pronoun and devotional hymns
listen ! the rapture and penance of cherubim half present
in the dreamtime of our brief and illusory existences
did we ever keep the promise to meet again in the drugstore
to moon over impending passions eye to eye with the stranger ?
to extricate identity from the revolving mirror break the glass !

10-13-22

AN ODE TO CLAIRE BIRNBAUM

to the wilds we trusted to unsequestered thoughts
many a sleepless night watching the starry void
pale its refulgence transferred to fickle memory
wasn't that a day ! the time we stared in amaze
as angels plummeted like planets out of orbit
right into the oncoming metal and blare and sheen
of noon's trumpet flaring daze and moments of

great unconscious as if to saddle a lifetime in those
brief and few reckless moments of youthful accidence
wheels and asphalt and burning minds imploring
the cities of the east for an extra hour and theater
and sagacity blown to the winds coming up to our
knees the unmitigated waters of unkenned orients
mountains and mouths of fiery wisdom if only and
that was the clause and retribution and the letters
gained by a few moments of study reciting conjugations
and irregularities of sound vowel and caliber and
searching for the right and just and plowing under
the divinities whom we sought in vain not recognizing
how they walked amongst us or mingled in taverns
the riot of alcohol and lubrication jostling to vie
for victory with the color red and distances even
more puzzling than the footnotes to the Text enigmas
and rotundities of sleep windowed in repetitions
and copies of everything we wanted to know and
it wasn't quite the same and the Bride fulsome bright
with her mysterious and evanescent body in what month
out of time ? how it all crashed with the burning seraphim
rushing out of control from their kabbalah and glass
and flashes of regret and the flute and harpsichord
of an afternoon in repose before the breakdown waiting
for the Late Movie to begin its redundancies of action
and silence all over again and without tickets and
the endgame of death that youthful aspiration

10-14-22

PRETENSE OF LITERATURE

"Literatura e teratologie"

Mircea Cărtărescu

tears of dust ! how often do we go back

without ever getting back ? hearts of furnace

and spite the sulfur of memory and the dead

whom we follow down the unmapped trace

how often ? to have ever written out of error

and windows that looked out on blank spheres

monumental rumors of the cosmos ! star struck

planets spent in the energy of a single moment

girls with wild hair or braids and pins and combs

passing through the mirror's cyclopean eye

surge of the hour with its revolving zodiacs

animals and spires and loosened tracts of

wood and maze the virtual descent of mind

a book in hand a promise to read every letter

sphinx of doubt and tension the embrace of

intellect and desire and ever the world as seen

through a fractured lens and cliffs that howl

and winds that buoy the failing light and

whatever else frail recollections bring to bear

on tragedy's battered stage the laments and

griefs the armor left to rust beside the word

that stands for mother in some unknown tongue

did we not suppose tomorrow was the lesser half

that life was but the remains of an undeciphered

script sound and noise and fingered beads
the grasses that run backwards through space
asterisks and exclamation marks that litter
the heavens with pretense of literature and
always the sunless instant when the reverse of
breath and thought shatter in the glass a poem !
heavy with its smooth stone the head ! and all
else is the unfulfilled silence of the leaves

10-15-22

THE DISMEMBERMENT OF TIME

"Se July Cesar, Rolant et Roy Artus"
what has come to pass was beyond belief
today is no more possible than yesterday
great conflagrations in the left eye alone
where in tumult and disgrace archaic gods
tumble aflame and bellowing like cattle
hit the metal surface of the reverse of time
planets enraged and triangles like bees
flaring and swarming in an enormous Zed
what more is there but illusion of hands ?
time present and time past ! what if sands
and the irate waves of the preterit seas
what if zoology and the invertebrate skills
of the mollusk and on parade the statues

of a fictitious civil war and noon that stays
and won't go away withering lawns with deceit
and the kids frozen in attitudes of love-play
and hate learning to drive motorized metals
and cliffs too what if ! a letter symbolizes what ?
it is to write in mirror script and dream only
when awake and deny sleep its continent of Mu
all the possibilities of what could have been
are Now in a trice between thumb and index
foreplay of philosophy and glass resonant
as the mountains that escort poets to Hell
what am I to anybody but an integer of
birth and death a statistic in the montage
of air-flight and submarine-clouds a wheel
made of melting butter and skies of theater
did I ever ask for cognition for fortitude
and memory ? asterisks and bells of thought
clanging on battlefields made up of lies
whistling arrows and truants of stage-fright
what is the cathedral of shoulders but grief ?
am I to look askance when thunder mobilizes
all its vowels just to shatter the Sybil's endgame ?
boom boom and Bang ! cosmic utterances in echoing
repetition of the origins that have no source
loud ! free for nothing that lasts the breath that
always forsakes its beholder and the semblance
of the soul in the shape of the color red vanishing

as ever into the plethora of silenced voices which

are the adolescent stars of nocturnal yearning and

what is the number that follows infinity ? but what ?

children ! you are the masks of death ! innocence

the forms of water and the transformations of

sound known as language vessel of misdirection

are we in Yucatan today ? and Brother ? a rout

of consonants and the sobbing of hieroglyphs

mastodons of Oblivion ! yesterday is an accident

of diesel engines in the window that looks east

what little remains of noise and the holy trance

of leaves and grass the solemn rush of evening

take it away !

10-16-22

CARCASS OF LIGHT

walking through your own corpse

the day before tomorrow eclipse of air

what does it matter if it's Monday or Thursday ?

glass is resonant and vengeful and

there are reflections everywhere as many as are

the accidents of men and refracted waters

and mountains that split in two every Friday

and fires that rage to be known from

within the bowels of rock and pastoral

interludes before afternoon is out and

shadows drawn even nearer and spools

and threads unwound that are mortal fates

what does it mean to be young ?

to yoke a pair of dazzling white horses

to a chariot riding into a maelstrom of dust and blood

with Krishna at your side how can it go wrong ?

but it does for you are a corpse from birth

a skeleton of glowing magnesium

twin to an identical corpse raving with hair

and prophecies and pyramids of black thought

eleven cities and twelve ships

and chattel and booty plundered from hexameters

drawn out through eons of memory

but what is the flickering star-light of the cosmos ?

destroyed nightly reawakened by chance

in the wake of spatial seas in turmoil

cliffs and ravines where the carcass of light stirs

half a remnant of the age of Gold

the other half the doom-spell of eternity

nothing lasts forever not even the infinite number

that determines the end of time

today is already next week and darkness

is in every leaf and running through grass

and fingers of isolate cognition

searching everywhere for the switch

that turns on the light

10-17-22

CIRCE'S BANQUET

pigments of the zodiac the mysteries of each moment

who can count more fruit than flowers ?

the secret number that follows death is stone

life in proportion to the grass of memory

even as it ebbs into the mountain's lack of gravity

share the bread spill the wine embrace the phantoms

who have come to dine wraiths still jangling

jewelry rings and bracelets ear-rings upside down

and greaves and fringes and fading hues of cloth

hours ! how many remain on the abacus and

how few still belong to night when bewilderment

is rife among the planets and morning has no due

to sip wine by the hearth of gods witless and

without a clue as to breath and the firmament

that it guides and we are soon worn careless

of the sounds words make of the absence of guests

haunted only by the rattle of a remote machine

something that measures but does not regulate

a force is whittled down to thumb-size

mention of asterisks stripped to the bone like fire

is there such a thing as action ? does the finger braid

its own shadow in the puzzle of a lengthened afternoon ?

what comes and goes ? the ambulance of time on Tuesdays

bearing frailty in its body of metaphor and silence

to a home composed of distance and ruddy dust

clouds ! warp and stain of infinity in texts of mutilated air the suggestion of transmittal or incorporation or

of justice in the spire that discriminates between space

and the great foreign dreams that surround space

we are beasts by Circe's wand commanded !

crumbs and stale lard of the banquet that regaled us

ghosts sopped by rain and torment on the voyage

to the outer banks and mists and fogs of opportunity

the failed human heart has ever missed

I am Ulysses ! a voice from the opposite ear proclaims

the small pyrotechnics of thought go scattered

and fall hush evanescent in the unending dark

10-18-22

WEDNESDAY NIRVANA

"kiccham maccānam jīvitam"

if this isn't Wednesday what is !

what in the cycle of centuries is this Wednesday

coming and going lateral and bilateral

what no eye endowed with sight can see !

great spaces informed by cathedrals suspended

by consonant clusters and vertigo and

the tiny niches prepared in the Dewey Decimal System

for the most recent dead uncataloged & all but

forgotten in the alphabetization of lunar cycles

the densities and the mirages ! one hour is no

different than the next one hour is uncountable
Wednesdays are a forgery an unreality of number
this afternoon will be memory dedicated
to the crematoria of the gods whose secret
is infinity and what follows infinity if not another
market day in the hill towns of Umbria
underwater salvation ! dilvuial origins of sound
temptations to reorganize sleep and its resonances
suburbs of forsaken entities ! aspirin and clouds
that misinform the nature of the sky and
to recall what a terrible thing ! who are the supernal beings
circulating in the upper zones of the fiery ramparts
in search of the obsidian pyramids of 1953 ?
we are but inches in the infernal distance of time
thumbs turned backward in the displaced lawns
mowers and histories of the eventuality of today
it was only yesterday when it wasn't Wednesday
glass and totem fingers gracing the air with figure-eights
and Joe lying there exactly as predicted by
the seers who teach that all moderation is excess
calendars without Wednesdays ! Wotan's day
excised from the numerology of oblivion
we are not necessarily here today but afloat
somewhere in the rings of a great Crab Nebula
first person dual future indicative in the grammar
which is the entry to the language of the gods
one by one counting backwards to the hand that holds

and the rest is incineration and the peace

that accompanies the longest day ever record in zoology

the fierce ! the yearning to remain constant

to be irreversible in the eternal flux

when Wednesdays no longer matter

and Tuesdays dominate the spectrum of madness

Bedlam of chariots and Speed governed

by the diesel windows of memory

"difficult is the life of mortals"

10-19-22

COMPARATIVE PHILOLOGY

for Solomon Rino

sex with the goddess whose backside

is the coffin of memory what could be

more contemptible and in isolation ?

years hence and the used car lots and

the burning sidewalks of Los Angeles

and the literature of fiction and truancy

running ! what did we learn the day

we went to the peep show ? afternoons

are legendary and eternal and the wife

of deceit and pre-empted psychosis

drilling her kitchen with backlashes

of suicide and divorce the heights !

counting the steps to the Lucretian text
origins of physics and atomic theory
to the cyclotron just before Viet Nam
"going to Chicago sorry but I can't take you"
soon it will be the movie theater showing
re-runs of despair and the torn concert
and vertigo speaking an early Italian
wearing crimson wigs and platform shoes and
selected works of Aristotle in blue buckram
libraries of incense and totem beasts carved
from teakwood and iron in the dining commons
grasses running red by mid-day and plaster
of Paris nudes illustrating decline of Rome
bad poets and motorcycle figures zoom-zoom
roaring below the 63rd street Elevated tracks
and jazz when all hours are a pre-dawn cycle
Charlie Parker ! how it all languished with
rumor and the Nelson Riddle Orchestra
aching to know and mourning and grief
in seedy bars reeking of ancient Greek loss
sitting in a nose-dive reciting mantras that
fit the back of a postage stamp on amphetamines
roof-top hallucination of the future
greeting Alba and her twisted lover the Sun
and all that comes afterwards in an instant
the rush of accident the cacophony of silence
hospitals and provinces wider than galaxies

mountains to traverse and death's sweet riddle
just an hour ago !
"sorry but I can't take you"

10-19-22

THE PROSPECT OF ETERNITY

para Armando Rendón

who but the Sacker-of-Cities stood at the mind's
doorway shadowy and great as if risen from
some troubled ocean all about him the wet and
moreover his glistening buckler his eyes agleam
all swart his hair and shaking ever so slightly
is this how it is to wake again in this life somehow
as if renewed and the birds in the skies caroling
and mysterious trees casting lots and roaming
the phantoms of memory the unmeasured without
guile the plodding and erroneous the students of
envy and ire the fomenters of metal and flame still
seeking some kind of reality a world-shape a stage
to keep making the same error the rumors of love
and the chrysalis where hidden the heart beats
with yearning to be alive again this moment if
not the next and come crashing the redundancies
and resonance of distant cities of playing fields
and court-houses with their rusted civil wars

and the collapsed judgments and litigations

to be moving still among these vague constructs

and suppose this too is illusion a dream a trance

with units of light and sulfur and western hills where

dialects become subjective and hands exchange outlines

fingers of grass and ears where leaves sprout to listen

to the untranslatable message of the gods all the

what-ifs ! absorbed by the light the substance of thought

dissolves in quicksilver reflections the struggle to

understand and achieve a footstep in the yard and

observe the houses all around their windows lit

with an alien familiarity the voices of bread and

softened ginger and warmth of secret hearths a

childhood laid bare ! yes is a hello too big and aprons

checkered cloths red and white and the stars high

and formidable refuse to shut down for the factories

and noon constant and eternal to lay the stone in

its place at last shivering and old and what else ?

10-20-22

THE RECOGNITIONS

what ignites desire's flame and marks the brow

with apostasy and seeks the outer sky beyond repair

sorrows and the wick of grief the body disdains

burning with the mind's blown taper its remains

the ashen groves the fullest depth of rock and

hills too far to span and dialects that score the ear

with assonance of futile gold and memory

which country is this of thirty three thousand gods ?

between temple and tavern no distinctions exist

rioting by day and rioting harder yet by night

which deity inhabits the unruly body and which

is the one that entices the heart uselessly ?

ghazals and coblas and music of epitaphs echo

in vales that don't exist the plaintive threnody

the sirens' song of desperate reverie and what !

nonchalance of being despite histories and myths

no One is ever two and the third is only mourning

I am gone to heaven's doorstep pining my life away

what was once glimpsed in fields of everlasting heat

was also lost in dreams of so many former births

today is eon of anguish awake after a sleep

that lasted six hundred years and new to this place

to these books and reprimands bewildering

I prowl streets where metals reign painted and loud

knocking at windows and listening to captive birds

with script and symbols puzzling to the eye I turn

the gaze inward to pyramids of immolation

death 's provinces extend beyond waters of anguish

fastness of clouds and vowels of faulty worth

why take a step up or down the smoking ladder

why submit to whiplash and honeyed balms

words are but inarticulate grasping sounds

noise and rumor of salvation the song of skin !

to the south I turn awaiting the imminent day

when Sun with his molten steeds will cease to travel

and I and I and I stammering and stumbling

loss of wits full of transgressions vanity of mind

pronoun and mask the paraphernalia of personality

whatever else characterizes the body by name

scrolling down the relentless path I too cease

aiming for direction forced to ponder the enigma

once I was this that and the other with a brother

whose identity was quite the same as mine

recognitions in grass and evening's remote flames

fingers we intertwined drawing from the mountains

a last syllable and breath the mystery that we were

10-21-22

UKRAINE

not even numbering as sand or dust that flies
in hot summer winds nor the peninsulas afar
nor cities such as Egyptian Thebes with its hundred gates
accept as many gifts gold inlaid women and throngs
of linen-bound slaves and to enter heaven accompanied
by Selene the moon herself shall I accept this mortality
but inter the head in its stone and wish for peace

or nothing else and constantly to fly weapons

thickening the air as hosts of green bottle-flies

these threats these garbled noises sputtering like foam

from the mouths of rhetors and senators but listen

to the augurs to the oracles consulted at the back

of the groves or on the small floating islands that

at hand is nigh the end when brothers consumed

with hatred plot against brothers and cousins and

uncles vie with cheating dice to claim the realms

as their own and exile in deep woods for up to thirteen years

those who would share the earth with equanimity

all is upended upside down left and right confused

nation states divided into bickering clans and populations

starved with drought and famine the rivers run dry

the course of the mountains misdirected and theaters

filled with those who can afford hundred-dollar tickets

splendors ! maze and contortion of mind sleepless

agonizing over market shares and falling stock markets

the price of anything is too high food cannot be exported

and glaciers menace the seas with their melted detritus

at hand and no less than three days away the split atom

ready to assay its measured distances of flame and

hell which is not a written essay but the yawning abyss

beneath which the souls of our feet already burn

what more is there to say ?

10-22-22

A HYMN TO APHRODITE !

nor in the arms of Aphrodite embraced a life
would me deceive and tarry longer night-spell
what is this light received but suspicion and
lengthened mountains that western into seas
crashing still the ear with promises of sleep
did she but keep me immortal and in marble
skin prevail and nevermore the seasons sense
the failing months and years uncounted like
the painted word and swords of epic name
me bard supreme would trade in earnest
this other time for the life I was bequeathed
can I her flushed cheeks or fluttering eyelids
and roaming across the map of her desires
describe any better the passionate moment
the eternal agony of her unpossessed and unable
to keep such to these molds and outlines of art
the fiction of detail and circumstance romance
on the revolving door her studded distances a
refrain from an unremembered melody hair
aphasia and apostasy that flung aside mount
to plugged in clouds scores of angels and
snakes the epitome of love as it were could
I but disentangle the soul from its mortal knot
or sleep dissemble and the ears hissing nor
the values of statuary on the prowl engines
heated by just the thought and waking in

another language forced by vowels that cling
and mooring waters dangers ply the second
a photograph reveals the encumbered plight
rows of agony and faces half-shorn of light
a foot gone wrong two fingers on display and miles
of grass fleeing south from fields of summer heat
a month repeated for its resonance unnumbered days
the fixed noon of eventide and marble sweating
for all the sun that's left to climb its unfinished
task like schoolboys truanted from grammar's
oblique infinitives rooftops and cigarettes and
hidden courtesies beguiling the girls whose
evidence is the long comb and lipstick's trace
that mirrored returns a melancholy memory
dancing on porches in mid-air the nocturnal
asterisks braided into auburn locks that smolder
flickering just as eyes that deny their sockets
aiming eastward to the orient's dawning sounds
and how to retract the shadow's love-potion
pinpointing noise and its reversed syllabary
only hierophants understand O Aphrodite !
your dense and deafened soliloquies implore
the heavens for one unjust tack and frailty
platonic as remorse to hold and be held by
that imposter Zeus ! and as for me lesser
being left to drift in your antipodes shipwreck
of disorganized consonants a speck to wander

recalling that enchanted instant in your white
arms Alas the death that awaits and longing

10-23-22

A HYMN TO PERSEPHONE

a national emergency ! the temple of high math in flames !
Sacred Heart ! every summer you come and go
every summer you disappear like a moth in smoke
your bracelets of ringing gold your earrings of assonance
purer than mountain springs where horses deign to die
fields of immortal dust ! harvests of glistening heat !
wherever your foot sets its beguiling print a small noise
emerges a voice of unimaginable distances a feeble
vowel crying in the eaves of fame such tenderness
no skin can bear nor song of the vast unawares a sound
lessened by its own cloud-fantasy strains to thunder
in your ears the dread and somnolent voyage south
into the underground where father Pluto sways trying
to remember mortality and its speeding colored metals
and especially sky so far above resembling a painted sea
forgotten by mariners and the dead who plow the waters
that none will ever sail and Yes ! your transience and
oversight each time you come back through the glass
to ovations of leaves and caryatids molded by deceit
once Greek you have become Etruscan evanescent

in hues of tombs and mirrors where combs spend hours
time itself is startled by your constant leave-takings
you are immortal absence ! a disease called Memory
eats away at your inner self and what ! mothers mourning
the fists of sorrow and cathedrals in search of shoulders
or like an ancient Spanish verse half Hebrew half Arabic
you metamorphose into a temple relic a forged number
a unity in dissolution moving from furrow to furrow
a shadow desperate to have its repeated body back
a resonance slowly smothered by mothering earth
10-24-22

GLORIOUS ACHILLES

possessed by demons scorched by fate's burning temple
turning in the vivid verse of archaic tongues the heroes
lamentable and supreme agonize over thought-patterns
twisting vowels to fit their needs hurling heedlessly
spears and darts into the plentiful sky where painted
gods fluctuate between immortality and absence and
settle no one's debts in the constant melee of language
and the heroes warriors in adolescent guise loud and
symbolic in their aggression and mock humility
I know them ! look ! Achilles first of all jarring and
wild with ego slamming fists into cushioned walls
wailing in his sleep about his lost and enigmatic youth
ankles spurred to flight hands independent of arms

bracelets and ear-rings like an oriental princess
struts on soft Persian tapestries greater than the King
of Kings ! what is the dust of ten-fold Ilium the heights
and hundred sons of Priam and all the grammar of
untranslatable idioms up in a flurry of consonants
like midges or wasps swarming the human condition
does Achilles bet on an extra week ? months pass in
the instant the sun rises and sets backwards and flutes
and marble agonize over future shapes and rivers
underneath carry away the mysterious unfinished lines
of hexameter in Mycenean sub-script iota and sigma
how many suburbs will mourn ? across great oceans
of unconquered waters where phantom fleets drown
repeatedly the sun's violent resonance is but an echo
slight and dissolving in the chimerical western hills
dialects proclaim short-lived Achilles is all but dead
half-sounds and midget variations of noise cymbals
and sistra and furtive Egyptian songs drill his ear
with enmity of the galaxies even as immense horses
drum earth's frail surface and wailing of sirens
ambulances lurching ceaselessly around the circle
the goal-posts of sleep and the cheers of girls
a hundred and twelve of them dressed like queens
and the foot that stirs ancient dread and death
at the tip of the scales how many stones does it weigh ?
Achilles ! your riddled fame hoarse with recitation
the leaf that grieves the spent distance of time

10-24-22

THE ACHRONOLOGICAL HISTORY OF THE GODS

as with all things cosmic there is no beginning

and left to our puny rusty selves delving in quaint fable

the mastery of a single myth ! cross-wise looking

over the faint residues of light the empyrean yawns

broad-faced as the sea at irregular hours

a puzzle we are born with and number the books

and set them in rotation and wonder at the contents

what is elevated we assume must be a god moving

among many gods though we are merely looking through

a glass and it is ten in the morning of time and grasses

run to the unformed waters and darkness of hills

all things are performed for the sake of repetition

the magic is in the loss of order unbordered and miniscule

though the eye is great it can take in nothing

of what went on before when there was only chaos

and the trimming of color and the impurposive sound

of space generating itself and for this we are given language

which is a motley aphasia punctuating memory

with a necessary amnesia and all follow the threads

of sleep into the immense quarry where divinities

are hewn and massive temples governed by caryatids

and the thought-blossoms of hands looking for shapes

the cloud-weft and theater of noise and lit horizons

waking we are no better than animals gifted with remorse

and the task of cataloging and enumerating the invisible !

when there are no origins it is only blind intuition

listening to the sea-swell and cries of distant birds
that a poem is born a recitation of deaths and speech-acts
anomalies of recollection and distortion the walls !
cliffs and sundered rock and the gravel underfoot
which are the expression of grief and the small role of ink
and dissolution of navies and mountains ! the gods in each
of the interstices lurking with baffled eyes at our
endless cycles of birth-and-death revolutions of mind
what is to them that we sorrow ? knowledge !
foresight and aggravation on the shores of experience
interred the best of us turn to sand and foam
the boats caulked and with blustery linen sails set forth
again and again and each time from far above
the hemline of intelligence the gods review the lists
and set fire to cities and misdirect fleets and havoc
tempests of life ! little by little the world's dimensions
shrink with the tumultuous inventions of progress
and yet there is no technology that can account for the gods
whose chronology is an abyss of inversion and madness
and what are we but the mirror of that abyss ?

10-25-22

THE GREAT ENIGMA

with great sadness I announce the birth of light

for we only gain in order to lose

from which mountain does the sun rise ?

and among which dialects is it buried in ritual ?

by her lip and rings by her unkempt tresses

does the goddess stepping lightly over the waves

grace her presence in the morning breezes

rose-scented yet infirm as salt she disappears

a hand is no greater than what it can shape

and the eaves are alert with the small Latin of birds

who has eyes ? who has ears ? is there a book ?

space littered with hieroglyphic disasters that

only astrologers can read and the lists of clouds

whose names are the abracadabra of oblivion

so many refutations and repetitions

air and the fragrances of dawn and grass and shadow

to these we are born and the mingled sound of leaves

and reflecting waters and shivering assonances

of metals hidden in the eyelid of one sleeping forever !

how can we get around it ? who was the last to see her ?

cavorting with winds and memories of stone

nameless and ever elusive dressed in thought alone

how ? mysterious levitation of earths and spheres

between which her phantom being dances in and out

there are porches filled with fireflies

and pools that emerge from the distances of night

with fishes whose electric eyes probe the depths of consciousness
before we know it we are dead ! we never were !
brother with his torn trouser-legs and striped t-shirt
is the image of the sun as it collides with time
together we are pedaling backwards through fields
and oblique horizons of heat and resonance
it is alive ! chasing butterflies with human minds
we lapse into the eternity of a stop-watch
the goddess is a firefly ! the goddess is a butterfly !
everything vanishes sooner or later
in his torn trousers running down to catch what ?

10-26-22

A PAGE FROM THE ILIAD

to abandon the fleet leaving all to the sands
time's shifting measure of incorruptibility
home ! will we ever get there ? nostalgia of
windows of lamps lit forever in anticipation
of voices interred in feather-pillows to disguise
sobbing and grief and the vanishing outlines
of bodies that used to sleep between verses
how is the great beyond to be obtained ?
looking around all is a scrap heap littered
pages of lost books almanacs portents of
final winters and planets out of alignment

with the invisible axle of the cosmos and
silently crashing in the ear the enormous
and unending histories of when we lived
on earth piracies of technique ovations and
home-comings when the annual queen rotated
her language and semblances of absent gods
the future ! came and went in shop-windows
advertising vacations on the sun with longing
whatever the outcome of today's battle whether
we storm the Trojan heights or simply sit idle
by our one-wheeled chariots feeling celestial as
all adolescents do when school's out and gone
to libraries of dust and drugs and ringing brass
chimes of eternity and whole or in halves hearts
are promised for the brief but infinite night
of the dance with girls ephemeral as fireflies
it all vanishes ! watch the boats listing on the shore
and from some vacuous but glittering cloud above
the gods laugh at our dumb sport feigned warriors
Saturday-night heroes of the Dance token names
assigned to shields and forsaken mothers whose
poetry of intense separation and dread with ear
to the glass waiting for the reports to come in
and to light the pyres come Wednesday morning

10-26-22

THIS ARCHAIC MOMENT

for Marilla

what was the best we had done ?

what was the striving and struggle for ?

of all the flowers we had plucked

which was the one that lasted more than a day ?

verses memorized and recited to darkened halls

princes of fire ! how many faces will you recognize

in the swift passage from this to the next world ?

depths ! whoever has ears to listen and

folded hands head bent downwards for the plunge

while far above the holy integument of sky

a change of skins occurs a transfer of breath

a renewal of spirit inevitable and yet unknown

for what did we play so hard to gain ?

metal and shining and speed the glistening day !

grammar cannot account for all the accidents

for all the missteps for the wayward glances

that caused entire histories to deviate and earths

smoldering in the glass of greed and the waters !

who can remember everything ?

the betrothed in her fragrant veil and trembling

how many repetitions of the wedding day

before she understands ? ancient legends of stone

abutments of rock and heights poetry !

come running the grasses underfoot and

the tender isolation of the remote sun and

the dews on each spear-tip and death to come !
how many details did we try to grasp in the evolving
scroll and pantomime of life ? enough assonance
to fill the vacant ear of time ! sometimes jewelry
and other times sultry rags and decay and evermore
losses and longing in the fleeting window-pane
where have they all gone ?
is it only you and I who remain ?

10-27-22

THE UNWRITTEN POEM

there is less to say now
and fewer words to express what remains
seers who created phonetic rules
to be memorized a thousand times over
blind bards in whose ears rushed the memories
of troubling and ancient wars that still go on
crashing spears and sinking navies
courtiers in silk sleeves imitating and re-creating
such epics as were cast before in stone
isolation of the world from its origins !
what is there ? light / breath / death
numbering on the one hand the principles
and on the other the defects
and setting forth repeatedly on the voyage

steering between vowel and consonant
searching for the perfect metaphor
to bed each night with a lost syllable
love and its reruns ! dreams that it will all
happen again only in reverse and better
lose the soul to a hiatus ! dash around the corner
for the secret assignation and ride trains
high above the streets and riddle the skies
with a question that can never be asked
each new day that breaks is one less
in the uncountable abacus of infinity
wrap the mind around its own longing
pierce the skin just once with song
fireflies of dazed immortalities !
come to the point of no return
so many have dropped off the edge of the world
even the sirens are muted
concrete and drought and madness
the masters who have elevated technology
obviously have not stopped to read the silence
heaven ! infernal supposition of the dial
and the button and the slow green flame
that consumes everything

10-27-22

THE DREAM WITHIN THE DREAM

in this dream all is sorrowing and darkness
faces half-erased or eaten by some tragic canker
and weeping over much the still fresh wounds
and doubts and suspicions and the fray of
consciousness with itself to elude the inevitable
moment when the lamp is extinguished and nations
that have been at play no longer have a place
on the map for all is discord and the room tilts
this way and that though language has nothing to
do with the moment and mummers searching for hands
lost in the recent yesterday of winter and desires
quelled by the indifference of the gods and no voice
loud enough to surpass the noise and reach the skies
a verse truncated in its center where most vowels
converge and the small memory of schoolyards
and music subsiding and who is so deaf that death's
terrific syllables do not resound in the brain-pan ?
one is not to boast of understanding nor unspoken
wrath and the chariots assembled outside restless
by the plum tree and the messenger found lifeless
by his swart steed still pawing earth that holds
to its bosom the greatest of warriors written in
hexameters a passage of no return and wailing
yes and the inconsequential repetition of names
sounding like weary brass in the stagnant air--
such is news of the long sleep of unparalleled breaths
lives consumed by a drop of hate and dialects

and defiles and cliffs and the unbearable volley
of echoes rehearsing in the empty house a sadness
of betrayal and despair the bodies lined up
invisible on the gravel and haunted hooting of
owls as if assenting to the ruinous mountain of night
who among the children will be first ? the given
soul the innocent shell shattered on the roadway
the signals were never read aright and copies
of words nothing more than intimations
of sound and swarms of pages and thoughts
left to flutter in vague atmospheres of illusion
how many long unremembered afternoons ?

10-28-22

SATURDAY : ELEGY

confusion now preeminent the longings
and cannot master memory nor the fluted columns
the caryatids blind to the futures that have failed
chariot and wheel thumb and index the sun on all
sheds less luster the endings are nigh the walls
razed to the ground cities and more cities as
if naught had ever been in their place and the dust
in heaps and storms the rain clouds ceaselessly
lowering threats and municipal graveyards where
names pile up and the detritus of echoes the once

beautiful in reflected glass passing from view and
myth and story half-told the toil of voice and sound
when was a Saturday ever more Saturday ?
cathedrals buried in shoulders burdened with doubt
a singular accident a phase of suspended anxiety
emolument and graft of the gods emblems of speed
and despair painted metals in the shape of emotions
fixities of thought circulating in stone and the ear
deaf as ever to the imploding gravel of midnight
will mother get home tonight ? who is crying ?
is it enough to have been born ? each day a new siege
belt and hammer tongs that handle flames a cage
filled with fireflies that are simply yearning
off with the switch ! the movie version is too late
as long as the street seems to be it never gets downtown
we are left kicking leaves against curbstones
translations of color copies of noise distances !
hills on the move in the shadowy western dome
and highways ! the restaurants are all in Greek
vehicles and pedals and the sadness of routine
where is the right note ? a book with unnumbered pages
situations where each word is its own universe remote
and unsettling drift of space away from its center
and on and on the dross of weeks without days
and years that suddenly cumulate into an apogee
is it enough to have been born ?

10-29-22

NIHIL EX NIHILO GIGNI POTEST

not me anymore not the one I used to be

not the goggle-eyed fluke stoned in the subway

rain-wet with a volume of Greek myth

in each coat pocket lying there within earshot

of the washer women not that one anymore

would-be poet too young to understand the passage

and its tempestuous waters naufrage delinquent

of words and thought pre-Socratic and archaic

double-tongued from birth twin-eyed scant

of mind traveling the inner track semi-quaver

in Lucretian hexameter declaring blind-sighted

NIHIL EX NIHILO GIGNI POTEST

six decades to the minute embedded in Tuscan

dialect ca. 1210 CE inventing memory from

the start and which way to end it on what

roadway map long discarded cardiac maze

dot dot dot of infernal hiatus the longings and

subterfuge confessions in latent hotel suites

celebrated Bodas de Sangre with secreto de amor

now a dizzy mist below Golden Gate Bridge

deaths along the way the worst kind cruel

losses of brother and son and inscriptions in

early Brahmi on copper plate trying to but

not adhering to Buddhist precepts about

what-it-all-means not that one growing up

10-29-22

SCHOOL DAYS

"fratri contraria Phoebe ibit"

                Lucan Pharsalia, I, 77

chaos return and no stops to shorelines as
earth's hairpin curve routes unmasked deaths
tolls and levies hands the minds of discord and
disarray why is futility uppermost and the skies
numinous portents ricocheting heat and blazes
smoking futures done in the prospect dimmed
cities limited to recesses and violence impending
battles wars of subterfuge and suspicion in verse
row after row of school kids rehearsing ears
filled with hum of the distant fields buzzing swarms
and the pinnacles tottering with memorized stanzas
bruiting rumors of Cyclops and dangerous isles
bring it home and pencil in red the fractions that
make no sense no matter how they add up and glass
and the footwork of the dance petty sidestepping
the cup filled with apparent honey mead of the gods
athwart chariots and buckets plunging this way
and that irregularity of line the algebraic notion
but these unaccounted deaths these highway incidents
language of the spheres ! were the perplex only
whole and intelligible the grammar an illustration
pasted to the back of a notebook spiral-bound
and worn from use cribbing and jostling after
the bell has rung long as the eye in its circularity

of vision letters and squiggles looking to the left
a horizon of error and Phoebe her round features
molded quarters of luminosity contrary to her
brother aslant in myth prepared to chase and
devour human kind as it were and the planets
orbiting the self-same noon hour by the courthouse
the civil war cannon the trodden grass and weeds
anvil of time ! we have come to be less than before
the myriads that spilled over the morning fray
now a reduced lot tattered and dog-eared with
fewer thoughts the vacancy on the moon the even
more remote mountain of night hidden behind
hours of mathematical learning the small and
uneven brace of ciphers called Pythagorean and
the promise of rebirth in an orient just starting
to become as light among the silenced leaves

10-30-22

HOW TO READ A POEM

not in italics but invoking goddesses
for a start Isis in her world of silt and organdy
clashing sistra loud in the inner ear where
pages turn of eons past and those to come
imminence of light folded into a triple darkness
to discern between each cosmos the letters

sacred and profane the will to overcome
hiatus and hesitation and form words on the lips
and let the punctuation care for itself in celestial
ruminations known as silence and caesura
chaos and augury and if the left eye stutters
it is a visual aphasia confounding sound for color
and the debacle of seas tossed in a thimble
tumbling waters of noise syllabic utterances
recoil and resonance the right-leaning grammar
awkward between its elephants of arcane stone
efforts to glean from the positions of glyphs
the miniature pharaohs upended on slabs of air
underground fossils protruding wings of the dead
who went before in solemn procession degrees
of sleep and trance rehearsing for the audition
sibylline orientations at the pedestal of thunder
other goddesses to perform in great lunations lasting
hundreds of epochs in the midst of kamikaze stars
violence and retribution ! what all words mean
in the singularity of language--the tom-tom of death !
rhythmic hands excised from their noun-phrase
statuesque and billowing an unanchored Venus
haunting with her chimerical bodice and waist
magazines of photographs mounted in a kaleidoscope
which represents the Tetragrammaton and its
fatal error transgressions of atomic theory writ
large on the back of a postage stamp a puzzle

to invert and abuse staring upside down into a glass
held like a rumor of the western hills where dialects
arise from the ghostly memory of literature Yes
how many ? which is the opposite side ? why ?
eaten to the quick by fireflies the mounted bard
of the sierras waving his sombrero of poetics
recites in gestures of pure echolalia the Work
illegible and staccato hexameters ready to burn
arma virumque cano

10-31-22

CANTO D'ORFEO

how many ears does it take sounding brass
quires that ring in the world's empty skies
a head a lone as stone that floats nowhere
a loss and a longing the bridal day so distant
when was it ever so loud that none could hear ?
no leaf to count no blade of grass to yield
a poem no greater than its last line singing
no wilted palm no fashion of painted clay
symbols and syllables to design a tongue
a sibylline whisper in disjointed sleep am I ?
which is the hand that braids and which the
one that in consternation prays for its shadow
lengths of rope and roads of dubious intent

a library open only afternoons and trees too

holy to approach and yet the lyre that zings

the strings and thumbs the index of sacred noise

linens draped over a recent corpse and

wails and laments the rock set in the way

and waters remove themselves from their shape

and hasten knees to mortal demise in dust

decibels of horn and pipe deploy the air

how mistaken the mask I wear the foil I ply

pronouns scattered to the clouds and shouts

beyond human ken so far way while the heart

that loved ceases its tambourine and gods

once noted for their indifference weep aloud !

is it a shoulder I left behind when glancing

back to make sure and all went crashing

a pitiful remnant of her mortal image in

a pool as deep as the unheard Note and there

a face reflects on what it was last Sunday

before death's simple toy stopped spinning

and all the silence had gone from joy

only the creaking wain of the stars

could still be heard slowly moving

through the deaf marble of infinity

11-01-22

TWO POEMS FOR DÍA DE LOS MUERTOS

(i)

JOE : THE TWELFTH EPIPHANY

twelve times you've circled without landing

the spheres of integral invisibility

sombrero and wild peyote mustache

guessing the time of the next death wasn't

far behind the last and watching re-runs

of Moulin Rouge and The Third Man

up there on your Zavuyan flying wafer

it's way past dawn and the streets of Tenochtitlan

are awash with human incidence especially

Calle Tula one short block of infancy

puzzled with speechless twins facing

a future of syllabic resonance and disaster

tiny death squads purchased at the five and dime

and fly-swatters and DDT and aching lawns

and fields of unharvested heat the duplicity

of the gods who had promised a share of immortality

too quick you dropped out ! how could you ?

left to my own devices I had to incorporate you

molding my words this way and that to fit

your charismatic Aztec mask and yet

it just doesn't work silver plate ego and

prophesies of years that will never be

flying saucers and Mayan glyphs and a counter-reality

climbing the smoking ladder to rooftops

relabeled Paraíso or No-Man's-Land

most everything is behind glass now or
scuttled away in Granny's attic where a model plane
made of balsa and distance zooms fitfully
destroying passages of sleep and a painting of gravity
so like you to claim you invented the stop-watch !
come away ! it's not far from here to Mappa Mundi
you and me sprawled the length of a summer
lost in our imaginary cities buried in the dandelions
we had to pick in the sweat of an accidental life
you and me had to pick from a clover-leaf intersection
between this existence and the next
epiphany ! epiphany after epiphany
twelve times startled by your absence
when just a minute ago in a single afternoon
whiz bang zoom we discovered everything together
come away ! time for our favorite radio show !
time to learn to drink and dance and riot
in the intense blues of our lost youth
what have the gods against us ?
twelve times the polar star has ignited
and gone into self-destruct
and you ?

(ii)
AND ONE MORE FOR MAX

poetry reading at Chumley's in the West Village
you sat patiently through it with your favorite drink
a Shirley Temple sheer innocence !

and the time we took a cab to get our box of
The Invention of Spain what revelry !
and just weeks later you took the spin headfirst
into a picture postcard Hades waking from which
would be a brief day of shattered light and aphasia
forty years it would take you to complete the voyage
discovery of what makes things buzz and the arcana
and repeated visits to pharmacopeia and intensive care
how many fingers make a single number ?
incubations of thought with memory of kites
hurtling their paper promises high above Prospect Park
or the cognition assigned to ant and bee and the flights
of the once comatose hummingbird
parallel lives how many of them did you live ?
to re-learn everything about the world
how it moves and shifts and how night takes over
most of the daylight hours and the shaking solar spheres
and the sudden appearances and losses of the moon
levitation and the theory of breath up there
among the clouds where logic and reason die
your secrets and dreams had the speed of glass
shadows that leaped up and down on painted walks
and the tiny corners where the mouse God Apollo reigns
week after week month after month forty years !
how did the gift of light play such tricks ?
one day all resonance and bright and the next
an eon weaving in and out of cosmic mysteries
and the supernal enigma of creation and disappearance

your sole mission was to enlighten us

with some fragment of your unfathomable being

a single moment carved out of the random darkness

we call the universe

11-02-22

PURE MIND

for Carl Dolnick, 1938-2022

not if all the Teutonic Knights crashing through ice

nor the literal speech of street signs and addresses

amounting to 5000 North Mozart and summers

by the lake of learning with its cyclotrons and

elusive Classics Departments governed by Lucretius

expounding on atomic theory and the small steam engines

of scientific chronologies if all this prevailed

who would stand to benefit ? to wake speechless !

what defines mind if not the ability to parse verbs

to distinguish hues in the spectrum to perceive through

a great lens the totality of the deaths in the cosmos

witless red dwarfs sprawling crab nebulae patent fictions

harrowing incident of museum and isogloss

effort of memory to maintain order as if the names

of months the enumeration of the years the lesser

decibels that days perform in the rapid succession

of heedless time and to paint the whole conglomerate

of matter anti-matter rust and the Buddhist predicament
where is the center ? and if the son's passing
precedes the father's ? mourning and suffering and
the diminished meaning of articulated sounds
it is wailing in the back brain ! a cinema montage
in chiaroscuro and recited in a silent form of Russian
Cyrillic characters flashed on the defective screen of vision
youth on its invented horses that go racing toward
the point where time and space joined dissolve
and if there is no middle stage no withering limits
only a radio dial playing a thousand percussive instruments
and the overlay of madness to drum up the right equation
that will settle the problem of birth once and for all
pure mind ! nothing is resolved by language
grammar and syntax and the syllogism of monotheism
outer space with its burning ramparts and the heart !
in the end in the end in the bitter end what ?
the nights we spent thrashing out Einstein and Heisenberg
in Jimmy's Bar on 55th street the crucible of existence
and the jazz and expanding chords of physics
the veritable lucidity of lunacy itself a joy !
pure mind ! you were the teacher the Magister Ludi
pure mind ! Nirvana and Black Hole
in the end in the end in the bitter end what ?

11-03-22

EPISTEMOLOGY

for Will Alexander

large gaps in history even larger gaps in philosophy
nothing is ever known about anything but partially
the Cosmos is moored to atavistic error and rumors of light
depth and gravity abound despite the multiple deaths
and the variety and scope of those deaths and what
else is there to account for the shortening of memory
and of the texts which are nothing but lapses in script
and rumor recitations drilled in the left ear waning
and waxing of noise from afar and distances that
can only be measured as increments of madness
the isolating and resurfacing of sound as functions
of mathematics and morphological particles that fail
to coordinate speech-acts in the erroneous relativity
of syntax and dancing in and about the circular
devastations known as cities and modules of thought
engineered to drive fire by desire and the sheer lunacy
of waking dressing and superseding the self with ambition
known to no one the ego within dies and the eye is left
to wander in the vacuities while splendid mimes and
puppet-plays act out the span of man's brief career
in breath and dread and seasons come and go and news
arrives in fits and starts about still another demise
and the mirror reveals shamelessly the end of a man
to understand what ? how does sleep ? and why ?
a Buddha-type in the used car lot assures that prices

keep pace with wages and that to fathom equations
that bring the wheel to bear on gravel or to perceive
that outside the skin a different persona occurs an accident
of being a simplex of horizontal disorientation why not ?
syntagma and rules generative grammar and myth
gods and goddesses of the nether world ! there is no X
without Y ! the square root of politics is evil
the descent of the species into a new painted Inferno
and the flames which are more than real and planets
plunging from the hair-line of the universe fiery
and unequivocal signs that all is a random parabola
a sensation of the nerve and the mechanics of knee and
shoulder with its tremendous cathedrals of grief
knowledge is a slow shift in the parameters of illogic
clouds of childhood and grasses of innocence and streets
alphabetized for their capacity for longing and hills
where dialects rise and fall and the nostalgia
of leaves whispering to one another
simply whispering to one another
and nothing more

11-04-22

THE OLD ARCADIA

come crashing down the ancient woods the solace
of unknowing in their midst the mind's blind
soliloquy of yearning for days past the wan light
now a shivering gleam in the back brain a far off
flicker of the once vigorous and reading the length
of ancient verses the tributes to sound and anomie
the territory of the gods come Saturday morning
issues of breadth and hue sky streaked with resonance
of archaic summers of small tongues and birds and leaves
the learning that was a catapult and to cities undesigned
by haughty river beds or cliffs echoing with tempests
sea-wrack and remote of islands all but forgotten
with caves and enchantresses full of song the gorgeous
concord of voices from out of nowhere slowly stepping
across the invisible demarcation between mortal and
immortal was there a shop window with a clue were
there signals barely noticed a fluttering hand a smile
from shadows a promise as it were of divinity ?
where was the house ? who were they ? a hundred
is no real number the huntress and her bare shoulder
taking keen aim at the human heart the wound and
the cry and the hounds baying at the unseen moon
hills and ravines brambles and thorny words
what a myth ! aching to uncover the message
beneath the rock and the dusty path to nowhere
to remember ! the sounds ! rills of crystal streams

passage through the Mountain dolorous intent
to understand ! lonesome day's end head brought
to a still point like stone and to sleep there unknown
the dismembered mind and the vast stellar map
dissolving

11-05-22

THE LAMENT OF THETIS

such as thou art Achilles I raised you
and dwelt on the fringes of water ruling
over many people and still the day would
not be put off for the fates to have their while
playing as unruly children in the sandboxes
of memory to overcome and quell man's desires
nor would a spear be stayed nor the circumference
of the sky encompassed by the imperfect eye how
longing and loss are the retribution of our lot
neither success nor failure the margins of chance
how could I ? and the ships banging their sails
in tempests while the fierce orange sun has his way
chasing the distant hills to their dark temper
and how is it to speak ? where is the house ?
language is but a small article a ruse to think
we can manage our ploy and cast nets to invisible
oceans to keep the roaring waters at bay if only

prayer and ritual offerings and the tithes

of our summer fields Oh is yearning more

than ever to have back those few uncounted days

much can I say but how ? glass and reflection

noise of the multiple instruments the accord

and harmony and the marriages of script

and sound the brides like vowels lingering

in midair the heaviness of time ! change is futile

the earth goes on wasting and the heights where

gods tease with precious crowns and poetry

most of all recited in the echoing halls where

waxen images of the heroes and mistresses

languish in the heat of anxiety and repetition

what remains of the writing ? landscapes drawn

on the back of the hand and fingers lost in grass

and the havoc and joy of the instant when light

sheds its last and the fuse goes off and the cosmos

much was there to consider and the leaves

darkening in their whispers and dying

cannot escape and bury the head in its stone

listening as ever for the stars

11-06-22

'TIS OF THEE

country's in a bad way and what do we do about it
besides fretting over the origins of the cosmos
was it a bounce or a bang ? museums stay open
half-days and noon hours are consecrated to
statues killed in the last civil strife saluting rust
and corroded marble and the pleats and seams
of the carcinoma sky and opulence of the thimble
damnation of the thread blindness of the needle
how many ways ? distinctions between right and
left eyes the solution a vat of lye and stunted palms
planted in the lobbies of power to symbolize what ?
the language of devotion and strife writ big on the brow
of Zeus Capitoline and his thousand paramours
a legendary end is coming an apocalypse in Russian
and texts folded and unfolded and crippled with acid
who can read anything aright ? house crashes on house
highway and riverbed conjoin in a voluminous incoherent
syntax revolving out of the blackened sun's disease
enormous craters of air burning for no reason and
senator and congresswoman talk and keep talking
in filibuster to keep logic at bay and the simple truth
is there is no truth to be believed and supermarkets
hold the secret in the lies of canned music and immigrants
illegal and analphabetic from the base of the Pyramids
keep arriving at five thousand a minute swelling
the hoosegows of Dallas and Fort Worth beyond capacity

killers on the loose stalkers in nylon face-masks
and worst of all illusionists using Spanish as a disguise
are turning the Commonwealth of Virginia into
a fiefdom of Mexico ! the White House belongs
to the Virgen de Guadalupe and Benito Juarez
September 16th is declared the new National Holiday
cancelling the 4th of July and et cetera and to the death
Patriots ! marijuana heroin and crack cocaine free !
country's gone to rot the dread fright and flu and
commerce and free trade and be damned the world's
a closed border such as it is a tamped derailed fright car
diesels hauling the Rocky Mountains from their roots
rock stone dead memories of plantation childhood
in sepia tint Hollywood and the paraphernalia and boasting
the gimmicks and dialects of used car lot ambulances
intensive care units in all forty nine states west of
the Union and who can count or care to the number
of accidents fatal or otherwise on election Day ?

11-06-22

THE FORCE THAT FINISHING DEFINES

the first moment was the last
nothing in between but the swift passage of breath
adornments of sun and moon and all the asterisks
mind fields of plenty emptied in a second

though you mapped a thousand great cities
and owned half the treasures of the sky
the disappearing eternal moment you could not possess
though hands and signals beckoned near and far
and clouds stood still to let a single thought pass
you could do nothing to still the quaking stutter
of the tongue that yearned to define the whole of time
what was space but the absence of all memory ?
the grasses that whetted your appetite for play
the hills where buried dialects lay smoldering for
the hour when they could be heard loud and meaningless
and the escarpments of distance and the diachronic seas
that rushed your ears with promises of infinity
all for naught the small and petty histories of France
the vast and ancient seasons of remote Cathay
the afternoons of twenty summers but the span
of a stray firefly – what can be accounted for ?
the invisible realms and the consorts and pretenders
to thrones of concupiscence and lust the beauties
of a painting you resolved to finish the following day
mandalas and hierarchies of existence ! Buddhas !
chrome-plate visions and button-down collars
it all vanished the minute you turned to look back !
too late the speeding metal and alcohol that came crashing
in the rear-view mirror shattering the world's kaleidoscope
with its myriad jewels and revolving universes
miniatures of repetition and fading echolalia

hospitals of envy and ennui ! sutures and hemlines

the flounced skirts of an unnamed girlfriend lost

in the fogs and timbers of an uncounted night

all gone ! leaf and root and dew the half-life

of eternity the all too brief shift of light

no eye will ever see

11-07-22

NOVEMBER ELEGY

what wisps of nostalgia these rains a cover

for the losses past the grievous tumults

and waters that drown the heart what smoke

of mountains and waning noise sorrowing

in the ear's empty cathedrals we trusted fate

we crossed the rivers and counted the leaves

we paused at the ruins and gazed into a past

of forsaken doctrines and vanities of sound

echoes of an unwritten poetry dactyls and

spondees weighing less than their vowels

hovering in a distance of vacant horizons

where houses topple on fractured stone and

statuary yearning for another heated noon

fields and seasons and lengthened afternoons

when love's possibilities were numberless

anonymous letters wrapped in rouge and drugs

five-fold promises to never and breakdown

on the road east and phantom hills and surges

the constant let-down of infinity packaged

in marriage vows and law courts and appeals

to own photographs and recorded songs and

pure memories of dancing with oriental fireflies

legends of life ! x-ray and infusion in the veins

struggles to maintain order in the body and

swooning on the marble floor of decades spent

to wake to a today of improbable reunions

the mind on its unstoppable career to madness

picture postcards of Achilles and the Furies

painted breezes dappled overtones of thought

remembrances that resonate in gravel and

repetition of windows darkened forever more

come home ? impossibilities and sutures newly

engraved markers by the roadside and deaths

too many to enumerate and the always lone

catalog of reveries as the head falls into its

stone of dreams--

11-08-22

Vyāsaḥ, AUTHOR OF THE MAHABHARATA

today I feel like antiquity itself

jubilations and joys over life's petty triumphs

but a shallow echo in my oceanic ear

eight-fold the number of horses and elephants

hauling bejeweled chariots across the western horizons

into the great evanescence

Sanskrit ! mountains where thirty-three thousand gods

devise the haunting traps of language

rules multiplying scripts that evolve into endless

schemes of poetry and devotion

sedition of jungles unwary deaths in the defiles

snake and tortoise caught in mid-air by a chimera

birds of omen and disgrace and altars where fires

born of the proper syllables consume human desires

how was I ? footsteps that trace an anterior sky

manifold faces and mouths and honey spun

into words that only baffle the philologist

what am I this day but the remnant of shadow

twin of a mathematical construct envoy

of other worlds come to settle questions

that have yet to be asked

in the entire realm of memory which itself

is an obscure inscription of clouds and light

shimmering like a band around the forehead

what am I but the archaic resonance of stone

glyph and symbol of drifting leaves

secrets and whispers of fireflies and hummingbirds
was I ever more than a husk of letters and noise ?
who would not have his childhood back ?
hospitals of longing and children born and turned
into enigmatic resemblances and windows of awe
and dereliction left to wander in invisible cities
learning and unlearning fragments
of what the Buddha preached
it is the end I face the tumult of silence
and rock the grasses that swarmed when I knelt
to listen but heard only the insignificance
and somewhere in the vast and infinite lawn
of oblivion will bury my numerous antiquities
with the rishis and mendicants of matted locks
those who have survived life long enough
to endure one more day in the Mystery

11-09-22

THE UNSPELLED MYSTERY

what did we gain by being born ?
someone wrote a message on the wall
and the airs filled with delusion and delight
former births ! avatars and deities without form
the entire cosmos a soap-bubble of vanities
exploding asterisks and wordless epic poetry

there we were dream-shaped evanescent
at play with hills of greenery and dialects
that speak like trees and birds to the clouds
that passing overhead contained secrets greater yet
who could discern ? we went through ritual acts
growing stronger and yet so unknowing
the world came and went between our sessions
in sand and gravel and the tumult of invisible wheels
and motors and reckoning of theft and art
who was who in this act of masonry and thought ?
buildings and cities erected overnight and pipes
and drums a parade of summer holidays and
uniformed intelligence and books half-read and
tossed into the ditch and masks of ignorance
and divorce puzzled over cups of Chinese teas
the scribbling at the bottom of each cup
the soothsayer's whispered ears and game of chance
sticks thrown one way and dice that spelled defeat
what did we gain by growing up in a rout ?
alphabets and fourth dimension diagrams
whole months spent climbing pyramids of Sun and Moon
punctuations in Mexican and dust storms of the mind
space-travel ! legends of Masters-of-Whodunnit
triptychs of Beauty born from foam and spray
and photographs that remind of death and
absence and the inevitable day when it all combined
to end without renewal and hands that tortured grass

and soil and bones interred and the lost flame

that bore with it the everlasting Soul

what did we gain by being born ?

chisel and hammer syllable by syllable erosion

of all we ever learned to understand

cognition ! fleeting glimpse of universal light

... that only the darkened leaves recall

11-20-22

ENCOUNTERING IVÁN ARGÜELLES
John M. Bennett

I first found Iván Argüelles' poetry in a small press magazine in Los Angeles at the Beyond Baroque bookstore in the late 1960's. I was in LA working on my PhD in Latin American poetry at UCLA, and the bookstore was then about 2 blocks from my apartment. I am a poet primarily, and had found in the poetry from Latin America something of what I had been looking for and not found in contemporary Anglophone poetry. Ivan's work at that time struck me as the only truly authentic poetry of surrealist flavor I had ever seen in English. Over the years, I have followed his evolving work, written about it, published much of it in books and chapbooks through Luna Bisonte Prods, and have felt a companionship with him as a poet, a real bard, writing, as I also wrote, completely outside the narrow and predictable strictures of what he once called "white poetry", so dominant in the United States. I have also had the pleasure of collaborating with him on many projects, including publications in journals, chapbooks, and as a book, *Chac Prostibulario* (Pavement Saw Press, 2001), a unique long multilingual surrealist/experimentalist poem written back-and-forth over email.

Here is one form of collaboration I call a Hack, which uses a process of intimate condensation and de-reading, in this case of the first poem in Vol. One, and title poem, of this wonderfully rich book *The Unfinished Breath*.

Coatlatl

A ruined sidewalk's
naked glass inches ,
noon returns in rain fiction

Work ignition clatters in
yr diction ceremony ,
deindexing all yr minds :

Their bullets paralyzed
in trash sweating at
la cordillera's base

Its gravel wheeling
thru yr ocelotl skins
twinned asleep as number

Counted back toward
nothing at the waist

Poetry books by Iván Argüelles
published by
Luna Bisonte Prods:

THE UNFINISHED BREATH, Vol. One & Two [2023]

THE TRANSLATION TO HEAVEN & Related Poems [2022]

IMMOBILITY - - Poetry [2022]

FIELD HOLLERS (with Solomon Rino) [2021]

TAMAZUNCHALE [2021]

THE SHAPE OF AIR FRAGMENTS [2021]

DIARIO DI UN OTTOGENARIO [2020]

TWILIGHT CANTOS [2019]

CIEN SONETOS [2018]

LAGARTO DE MI CORAZÓN [2018]

FRAGMENTS FROM A GONE WORLD [2017]

LA INTERRUPCIÓN CONVERSACIONAL [2016]

ORPHIC CANTOS [2015]

D U O P O E M A T A :
ILION—A TRANSCRIPTION
& ALTERTUMSWISSENSCHAFT [2015]

FIAT LUX [2014]

A DAY IN THE SUN [2012]

ULTERIOR VISIONS [2011]

Available at:

https://www.lulu.com/spotlight/lunabisonteprods

www.ingramcontent.com/pod-product-compliance
Lightning Source LLC
Chambersburg PA
CBHW072038160426
43197CB00014B/2544